0

THE COMPLETE HANDBOOK OF BULBS

THE COMPLETE HANDBOOK OF BULBS

H.G.WITHAM FOGG

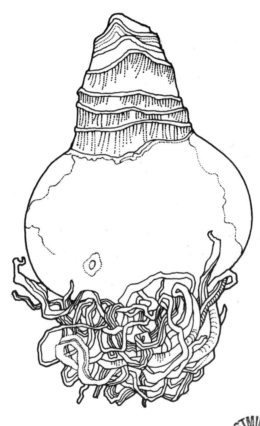

WARD LOCK LIMITED·LONDON

635·944

CONTENTS

INTRODUCTION

Bulbs are the most diverse and in many ways the most amazing of all groups of plants. They can vary in almost every conceivable way: the bulb itself can be as tiny as a mere couple of millimetres in diameter, or an enormous affair a foot or more tall and ten inches in diameter. The leaf can vary from minute, round and long-stalked to fern-like and in many genera strap shaped, sometimes as much as four feet long. The manner in which the leaves and flowers are presented can vary equally: in some plants all the leaves are produced at ground leavel from a central crown while the flower stem shoots up from the ground a couple of inches away: in others, a leafy stem is developed on the top of which a flower or flower truss is produced.

Most varieties will flower year after year but there are one or two oddities that may grow for six or eight years, producing huge leaves at ground level before deciding to flower, at which time they will throw up an eight-foot stem, crowned with a three-foot spike of flowers, each of which may be nearly a foot long and so strongly scented you can smell them three gardens away: after which it will promptly die.

The object of this book is quite simply to give you all the information you need to grow successfully any member of this most diverse of all groups of plants.

Tulipa eichleri with brilliant scarlet flowers is one of the earliest species to bloom

Chapter 1

THE NATURE AND DIVERSITY OF BULBS

What gardeners call bulbs, and botanists call geophytes, are in fact highly sophisticated storage organs. Although a bulb is popularly presumed to be nothing more than a rather swollen lump of root, it is in fact a whole plant complete and perfect in itself in every detail— but in embryo and in miniature. It is very like those miniature paper flowers that one used to be able to obtain from Christmas crackers, which, when dropped into a glass of water, would expand and blossom in a manner that seems almost miraculous to most children.

An onion is a typical bulb (though there are not many other varieties that will make you cry when you cut them in half!). If you cut an onion bulb vertically through the centre, you can see exactly how a bulb is constructed. At the bottom, there is a solid lens-shaped structure which is known as the base-plate. This is the plant's main food-storage organ, and it is from this that both the roots below and the leaves and flowers above will spring. In most varieties the roots are deciduous and die off at the end of each season's growth. There are one or two exceptions, however, where the roots are perennial, and these plants obviously require more care in transplanting. At the centre of the bulb is a tiny stalk with a flower spike: this is surrounded by tiny scales: once the bulb starts into growth, the flower spike will shoot upwards and the scales will expand into leaves. All the scales of a bulb are in fact modified leaves and serve, to some extent, as storage organs during periods of dormancy. The other scales have become modified to such an extent that they will never form leaves, and their

function is merely to protect the more important living part of the bulb contained within them. Once growth begins, the actual bulbous part of the bulb shrinks as the flower stalk and leaves emerge until the moment in time at which the maximum area of the bulbous plant is above

A lily bulb showing the rooting system and the typically exposed scales of the bulb

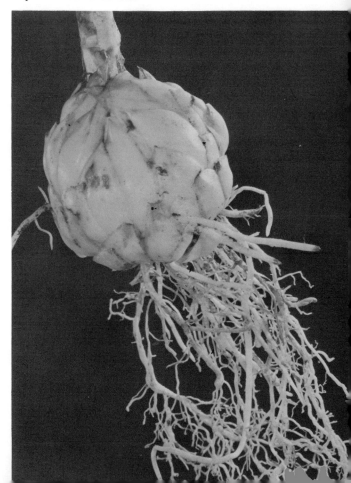

ground: at that point, the bulb is at its smallest. From there on, the above-ground portion of the bulb is feeding back nutrients into the subterranean part to build it up for its next dormant period. The cycle is a continuous one so that the actual scales of which next year's bulb will be composed will be completely different from those of this year's bulb.

Bulbs themselves are sub-divided into two types: there are those which are known as 'tunicated', and those which are termed 'imbricated'. A tulip is a typical tunicated bulb, the tunic consisting of a usually dark-brown or black—rarely white—skin. A lily is a typical imbricated bulb, the scales being naked and not protected by any form of tunic.

Although the title of this book suggests that it is only about bulbs, it does, like most books on bulbs, embrace corms, tubers and rhizomes. These all differ from bulbs in ways which need to be understood if the plants are to be properly cultivated.

A corm is an altogether more solid structure than a bulb. It consists almost entirely of the swollen, fleshy base of the previous year's stem. As with a bulb, there is a substantial base plate from which both roots and top growth will emerge. The bud, however, is tiny in comparison with that of a bulb. Whereas bulbs renew themselves annually, and usually in the same place, corms die at the end of each year's growth. However, the nutrients created by each year's growth are used to form an entirely new corm which replaces the original corm, usually either beside or above the old corm. The gladiolus is a typical corm. There are a few exceptions such as cyclamen, begonias and gloxinias where the corm does not die annually but goes on increasing in size until it becomes moribund. Corms of this type can only be increased by seed or by division of the corm, each divided segment having its own growing point: blind segments will never form a growing point.

Tubers are something different again. Though they are underground storage organs like bulbs and corms, they are not technically modified bulbs but rather modified stems with buds on them. Unlike bulbs and corms, they do not have a basal plate and they have no tunic. All they do is store up nutrients from one season's growth ready for the next season's growth.

Tuberous-rooted plants are different yet again. These are modified roots, not modified stems, but they serve the same function as tubers.

Rhizomes are essentially similar to tuberous-roots, but are generally treated as though they were corms.

In spite of these complexities, the cultivation of bulbs is essentially relatively easy and the basic principles are dealt with in the following chapter.

Chapter 2

SOIL AND PLANTING

Few spring flowers are more welcome for garden display and for cutting than those grown from bulbs planted in the autumn. Gardening with bulbs is easy. Most will come up without any coaxing or skill in culture.

The purposes bulbs can fulfil are as varied as they are. Not only will they furnish beds of formal designs, but can be planned in clumps in every part of the garden including the rock garden, the wild or woodland area, in window boxes or in tubs on terraces or verandas.

Provided you obtain your bulbs from a reliable source and they are planted early enough in ordinary good ground, they will flower in their first year. Once established they multiply year after year, while some, especially the smaller-growing kinds, will seed themselves freely.

All the well-known spring flowering bulbs will thrive in town, suburb or country, and most will flourish in sunshine or partial shade. Care in selection will ensure colour from bulbs planted in autumn, from January to June, while others planted in early spring will be showing from June onwards. Yet others (see the alphabetical list on p.   ) can be planted in late summer to produce colour from September to February.

Although beds and borders can be planted solely with bulbs, many colourful planting schemes can be worked out using spring flowering plants such as *Arabis*, *Aubrieta*, double daisies, forget-me-nots, *Polyanthus*, primroses and fragrant wallflowers. While some borders may be replanted seasonally with fresh, later-flowering subjects, the majority of beds and borders will provide continuous displays of various bulbs without completely clearing and replanting. Many bulbs look quite at home, and flower annually, when grown among herbaceous plants and shrubs. Planted in small clumps or in recesses in mixed borders, bulbs bring colour where otherwise it would be lacking. If you are keen on making garden colour schemes, tulips will give the greatest scope, particularly the species and the tall 'Darwins', which range from black and white, to orange, red, pink, lavender, salmon and yellow.

Whenever possible, the site selected for planting should be open and sunny and have been well cultivated and manured for a previous crop. Never plant on freshy manured land; the ideal soil for bulbs is one which is plentifully supplied with humus material. Alternatively, the soil may be improved by working in leaf mould or peat, adding bone meal at the rate of 2 oz. to the square yard before the bulbs are planted. Slow in action, bone meal provides nourishment, gradually and as required, over a long period.

For best effect plant bulbs in groups, even of three or four, rather than in straight lines. A group of 20 or more will provide a really marvellous show. Depth of planting is most important and many cases of 'blindness' can be traced to bulbs being too near the surface. Except when stated, at least 4 ins of soil should cover the bulbs. The lighter the soil the deeper the planting. Varieties of small size need not be buried deeper than 2 ins. In heavy soil, additional silver sand around the bulbs will be beneficial, and will discourage any tendency towards basal rot. Bulbs will not endure in places where water lodges round the roots for long. While the site must be well drained, regular moisture is needed.

Handle bulbs carefully. Treated otherwise, either at lifting or planting times, they are liable to be bruised or damaged, making it easy for disease or pests to enter. Before replanting, rub off the old dried and broken bulb tunics and withered roots, but do not break away any offsets which are firmly attached to the bulb and which may also be enclosed in the outer skin. Roots of lilies should be thickish and juicy and, unless damaged, should be retained.

Good bulbs will be heavy for their size, firm, plump and free from bruises and scars. The outer skins, except for tulips of which the skin sometimes becomes brittle and peels, will be intact. Some varieties of hyacinth have split skins; this is typical and, although it detracts from their appearance, should not affect flowering capacity. A grey film is sometimes found on hyacinths. This is usually caused by dampness, but has no effect on flowering and can easily be wiped off with a cloth.

When referred to by size this indicates their circumference and is a useful guide when comparing bulbs of the same or a similar variety, but not when making comparisons of entirely different varieties or subjects, since some are naturally smaller-growing than others. While it usually pays to buy large bulbs, smaller bedding hyacinths are more suitable for outdoor planting than the larger exhibition size.

It is useful to be clear about the descriptions of narcissus and daffodil bulbs offered in catalogues. A mother bulb is one composed of a number of old and young portions. It will normally produce a good quantity of blooms and can often be divided, if this is very carefully done. A double-nosed bulb has two and often three flowering 'noses' enclosed in one outer skin. A round bulb has no offsets and is a most suitable planting size. Wall-sided bulbs or 'flats'

A group of bulbs and corms showing just how much they can vary in size and form

are those from which the offsets have been taken away, leaving the sides flat. Chips are the samll offsets which frequently become detached from the bulb at lifting or planting time, and will not flower in their first season. Under good conditions, rounds become double nosed and chips mother bulbs in the following season.

The dwarf narcissus species, as well as hybrids, are ideally suited to the rock garden where their blooms are in keeping with the size and character of other dwarf rock garden plants. Miniatures are also excellent for window boxes, tubs, urns, for planting along a terrace or patio or at the foot of garden steps.

Narcissi and trumpet daffodils make excellent, long-lasting cut flowers and it is worth having a cutting bed of these in some part of the garden if you have room. They thrive in any deeply moved, well-drained soil. Stagnant water is injurious to them but they do not mind moist soil. Narcissi, unlike most tulips, flower better if the bulbs are left undisturbed in the ground, especially as they are not subject to the devastating disease tulip fire. The clumps may be divided—once the leaves have died down—after 3 or 4 years. When doing this it is best to replant bulbs immediately, for preference not later than the ends of August.

Chapter 3

A DIVERSITY OF USES

FLOWERS ALL THE YEAR ROUND

Bulbs are often thought of as spring-flowering subjects, but in the garden the New Year begins not in January but in the autumn. To provide bulbous flowers in the garden all the year round, you should plan on three planting seasons, autumn, spring and summer.

The first planting, from early August onwards, consists of subjects that are quick-growing. Some, such as autumn-flowering crocuses, will be in flower a few weeks after planting. These will thrive in any good soil. Plant the corms 3 or 4 ins deep from July onwards. Some useful species are:

C. longiflorus, C. pulchellus, C. salzmanni, C. sativus, C. speciosus, and *C. zonatus.*

Colchicum, *C. agrippinum, C. autumnale, C. autumnale 'Major'* (often listed as *C. byzantinum*), and *C. speciosum.*

Crinum × powellii.

Amaryllis belladonna The bulbs should be left undisturbed as long as possible.

Nerine bowdeni.

Sternbergia lutea.

Galanthus olgae-reginae.

Cyclamen europaeum, C. neapolitanum.

Zephyranthes candida, Z. robusta.

BULBS IN THE HOME

The cultivation of bulbs in ornamental bowls of fibre or pots of soil in the living room is an interesting and absorbing pastime. By growing a variety of subjects and starting them at intervals, a prolonged display of most beautiful and often scented flowers can be obtained from November onwards when flowers are expensive to buy in the shops.

One of the first essentials to success with bulbs indoors is continual interest; once planted, the bowls or pots must not be neglected although the attention needed is minimal. In the few weeks after planting there is practically nothing to do apart from ensuring that the fibre or soil does not dry out.

Stored within each bulb (provided it is bought from reliable bulb suppliers) is sufficient food to sustain it until it has finished flowering, which means that it will thrive and bloom well without any artificial feeding. Its chief requirement is moisture, but until a good strong root system has developed the receptacles should be watered sparingly. A bowl of sodden fibre in which there are few roots will soon become a nasty smelling sump, leading to the decay of the bulbs or at best to irregular development with a disappointing flowering display.

If bulbs are to be grown in fibre, drainage holes are unnecessary in the bowls being used. Although there are many different types of bowls available for bulb growing, ranging from the simple earthenware pottery to expensive china and plastic containers, the choice need not be limited to these, for vases of various types can be used including those made of bronze and copper, soup tureens, vegetable dishes, old baking or cake tins, in fact, anything deep enough to hold sufficient fibre for the type of bulbs being grown. The economic value of the containers will certainly not affect the growing-power of the bulbs.

Apart from the pleasure of seeing the growth develop indoors, the early flowers produced seem to advance the spring days and shorten the winter. Full credit must be given to the bulb experts who, by patient, consistent work and experiments, have developed bulbs that will flower well ahead of their natural season. Because of special techniques of treatment carried out by specialists, gorgeous displays of indoor flowers are now possible from November onwards, earlier still if you decide to grow sternbergias, autumn crocuses and other quick-maturing subjects in pots or bowls.

Before suggesting species and varieties for indoor culture there are several important points to keep in mind in order to make success doubly sure. The first is to plant only one variety of any kind of bulb in each container. If several sorts are planted there is almost certain to be variation in height as well as a difference in flowering time. If this varies by only two or three days it will spoil the effect and prevent the development of a bold and uniform display.

Next, the bowls and pots must be kept in a cool and not too dry a place during the time the bulbs are making their roots. Unless the bowls are glazed they are best placed outdoors in a sheltered place, on a hard base and covered with a 6-in layer of peat, leaf-mould or weathered ashes. This layer should be covered with a sheet of corrugated iron or asbestos to prevent it from blowing about. If you use glazed bowls they can have paper placed round them before being plunged, or they can be put in a shed or outhouse and kept covered with black polythene, cardboard or inverted pots or boxes.

Bulb fibre mixture should be used for all containers without drainage holes. It consists chiefly of good quality, dust free peat moss, with the addition of crushed oyster or other shell, and charcoal. These help to keep the peat from becoming sour which could be most harmful at the time the flower buds begin to develop. If the peat is a little lumpy when purchased, break it down well.

The fibre mixture bought from garden suppliers is often dry. If so, it must be damped thoroughly until it is moist all through, but not so wet that water can be squeezed out. It pays to buy the right sort of fibre, for if the ingredients are of poor quality it may become sour just when the flower spikes begin to open.

When planting bulbs, half fill the bowl with fibre made moderately firm. Do not add any fertilizer. Place the bulbs upright and, in the case of hyacinths and daffodils, leave the nose showing above the surface. Some subjects including freesias, lachenalias and the small growing gladioli such as *G. namus* 'Spitfire' and 'Blushing Bride' are best buried $\frac{1}{2}$-in deep. Press the fibre firmly around the bulbs so that no air spaces are left, but do not make it too hard, otherwise when roots begin to form, particularly in the case of hyacinths, the bulbs will be forced up and out of position.

While the bulbs are in the plunge bed or a cool dark place in a room or outhouse, they should not be entirely neglected, for the fibre must not be allowed to dry out while the root system is developing. Therefore, look at the

Narcissus 'Cragford' bears as many as six pheasants eye type flowers to each stem

bowls occasionally and apply water as necessary.

In the case of bulbs plunged outdoors, some protection should be provided against rats or mice; the latter in particular seem partial to crocus corms. After the bulbs have been planted for 7 or 8 weeks the bowls should be full of firm, white roots and, once an inch of top growth has developed, the bulbs should be brought into dull light and kept there for a few days. If moved straight into full light the tips of the leaves are liable to become discoloured.

A temperature of 40 to 50° F. is quite sufficient for a couple of weeks after which they can have more heat, but remember too much heat too early may prevent normal development and the bulbs will become blind. Steady growth should be the aim and, if you want hyacinths to flower at Christmas, you should plant the bulbs at the end of August or very early in September.

If bulbs are being planted in pots it is essential to use a good soil mixture. John Innes potting compost No. 2 is often used but it is quite easy to make up a suitable rooting medium such as 4 parts fibrous loam, 1 part shredded peat and $\frac{1}{2}$ part of coarse silver sand with a little decayed and sifted horse manure or, say, a couple of double handfuls of hop manure to each bushel of mixture. Make sure that you do not use any of these manures when growing bulbs in bowls. Remember, too, that pots need a plate or saucer under them when taken indoors or damage may be done to furniture when you water.

Half pots or pans are useful for subjects which do not make a lot of roots. Bulbs can be started in them and then, when the flower buds show, the whole can be transferred intact into a decorative bowl or other container, when perhaps other subjects have finished their show. If new pots, pans or absorbent bowls are used, they should be soaked for a day before planting, otherwise they may soak up moisture from the rooting medium to the detriment of the bulbs.

The depth of the bowls used will to some extent govern what is grown. The best types are those which are not less than 3 to 4 ins deep, particularly for hyacinths, daffodils and tulips. Smaller bulbs such as chionodoxas, *Scilla sibirica* and winter aconites will flower well in shallow containers.

Crocuses are different, for they seem to like a greater depth and the reason they are not always successful is due to the smaller amount of fibre drying out quickly, hence the need for more frequent watering. Some growers finish off the fibre flat, others mound it up slightly. While the mouding does give a larger area for the roots it is often difficult to water in such a way that moisture sinks in evenly. If the surface compost becomes dry, water will run off and some of the soil may have to be moved so that the roots do become properly moistened. It is certainly a great help if, before being planted, bowls are covered in the plunging bed or by some other means they are well watered.

It is most helpful in securing best results if, after planting, the bowls are immediately put into darkness, but it is a mistake to place them in a dry, airless cupboard. A cellar is suitable as long as it is not too damp, but a shed, frame or cold greenhouse can also be used. If the bowls can be placed close together at the base of a sheltered wall and are covered with well-weathered ashes or leaf-mould, this will be excellent. The covering prevents the fibre or soil from drying out whilst in the case of bulbs which are inclined to lift because of strong root growth, the ashes etc. prevent this happening.

It is not necessary to cover bowls or pots containing freesias, lachenalias, irises or winter aconites. Anemones, ixias and tritonias do better in pots of soil rather than in bowls of fibre.

Once the pots and bowls are removed from the plunge, or from wherever they have been kept after planting, they must remain under cool conditions. In addition, they need air and sufficient water. Slow progress in the early stages should be your aim. If the bowls are kept on a windowsill or near the greenhouse glass, they should be turned round very frequently. This will correct any tendency for the foliage to turn towards the light.

Make sure that the fibre or soil remains moist. In a warm room the surface of the bowls soon looks dry and it is necessary to make certain the fibre is really soaked rather than applying surface sprinklings, for when growing well, the bulbs will have formed a mat of roots which use up quite a lot of water. If you accidentally apply too much water, turn the bowls on their sides so that excess moisture can drain away.

Daffodils will naturalise in most fertile soils

Fritillaria imperialis, the crown imperial, the most
imposing of all the fritillaries

With practice it is possible to judge with some accuracy whether moisture is needed, by testing the weight of the bowls when they are lifted.

Indoor-growing bulbs may need supports. Certainly many of the taller-growing subjects are liable to flop over without warning. This is particularly disappointing if it occurs just as the flowers are reaching perfection. Often it is sufficient to insert a few twiggy sticks in the bowl or pot. These are usually soon hidden by the developing foliage. Alternatively, 3 or 4 sticks or thin canes can be used with a circling of soft string, raffia or green twine. The taller tulips can be similarly treated. The larger hyacinths also need help to keep their spikes upright. This can be done with individual sticks, although you can buy wire supports of several types specially for hyacinths.

Growing hyacinths in water is an old-fashioned method of obtaining colour. To do this, it is best to use the special hyacinth glasses which are narrow glass vases, cup-shaped at the top where the bulbs are placed, with a shaped neck to prevent the bulb going too far down. They are made of plain or tinted glass and sometimes of plastic, through which it is possible to watch the facinating growth of the roots. The glasses are filled with water until it reaches the point where it almost touches the base of the bulbs. A few pieces of charcoal will keep the water sweet and odourless. Stand them in a cool place so that the roots develop slowly and sturdily. Top up with water as necessary and turn the glasses periodically to prevent lop-sided growth.

When growing bulbs indoors the aim should be to secure a display over a long season. This not only means choosing a good range of subjects but the planting of the same varieties at different times. If, say, a few bowls are planted at intervals from August to November, it will be possible to have colour from November to April. Bulb specialists' catalogues will be helpful in

Many crocuses keep their flowers closed unless there is strong sunlight on them

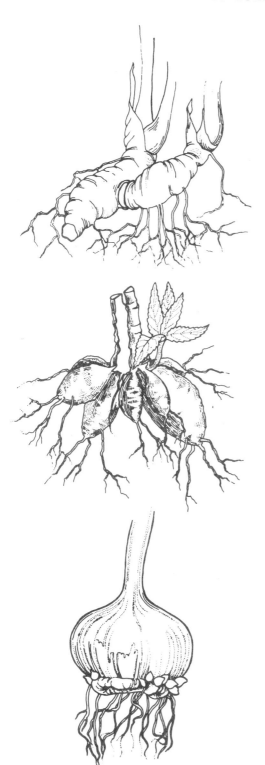

A typical rhizome *top* from a tall bearded iris.

A typical tuber *centre*, in this case a dahlia.

A typical corm *bottom*. This is a gladiolus.

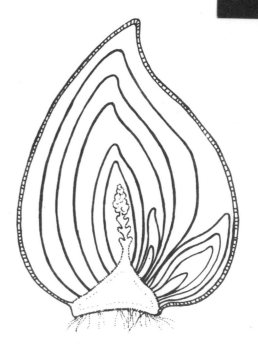

A cross-section of a typical bulb. A bulb is a
complete plant in embryo. The scales enlarge to become
leaves. Even the flower spike is perfectly formed,
though in miniature, in the centre of the bulb.
The section to the right is an off-set forming

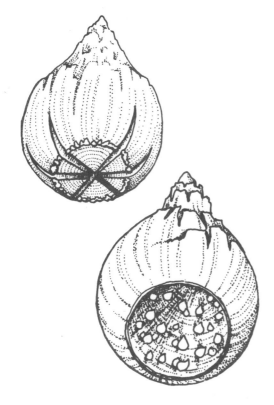

Professional techniques for increasing hyacinths.
The bulb may either be cross-cut or scooped out.
To produce the bulbils shown here the bulb must
then be kept in steamy, sterile conditions

Freesias, grown mainly for their delicious scent, need frost protection in most areas

more heat towards flowering time.

Most hyacinths for Christmas flowering are specially prepared bulbs, those for exhibition usually being known as top size. They can be purchased in splendidly wide-ranging colours.

Good named hyacinths include: White, 'Arentine Arendsen', snowy white; 'Edelweiss', creamy white, and 'L'Innocence', pure white. Yellow: 'City of Haarlem', creamy lemon-yellow; 'Prince Henry', lemon-yellow, and 'Yellow Hammer', rich, creamy-yellow. Orange: 'Orange Boven', apricot-salmon. Pink: 'Lady Derby', shell pink; 'Princess Irene', silvery, rose-pink; and 'Princess Margaret', soft, ice-pink. Red: 'Cyclops', rose-red; 'Jan Bos', rich crimson-red and 'Tubergen's Scarlet', deep scarlet. Blue: 'Delft Blue', porcelain blue; 'Grand Maître', deep lavender-blue; 'Marie', dark blue; 'Myosotis', light sky-blue; 'Ostara', dark blue and 'Queen of the Blues', azure-blue. Mauve: 'Amethyst', lilac-mauve; 'Amsterdam', purple and 'Lord Balfour', mauve-violet.

Narcissi for flowering early February are as follows. Yellow trumpet varieties: 'Golden Harvest', 'King Alfred' and 'Magnificence'. Large-cupped: 'Carlton', soft yellow; 'Fortune', yellow and orange; 'Brunswick', white and lime-yellow, and 'Mrs R. O. Backhouse', white and pink. Small-cupped: 'Barrett Browning', white and flame. Double: 'Texas', cream, gold and tangerine. Cyclamineus: 'February Gold', deep, golden-yellow; 'March Sunshine', deep gold and 'Peeping Tom', golden yellow. Poetaz: 'Cragford', white and orange-scarlet and 'Early Perfection', white and butter-yellow.

For flowering in late February: Trumpet varieties: 'Rembrandt', mimosa-yellow; 'Unsurpassable', buttercup-yellow; 'Celebrity', white and primrose; 'Beersheba', pure white and 'Mount Hood', pure white. Small cupped: 'La Riante', white and orange-red. Double: 'Irene Copeland', creamy-white and apricot. Tazetta: 'Cheerfulness', white and yellow; 'Gervanium', white and orange and 'Scarlet Gem', yellow and orange. Poeticus: 'Actea', white, yellow and red. Miniature: 'W. P. Milner', mimosa-yellow turning cream.

Tulips for indoor planting. Early single varieties: 'Bellona', gold; 'Mon Trésor', pure yellow and 'Vermilion Brilliant', dazzling scar-

giving information regarding flowering times, and by introducing some into greater warmth than others, you can do much to maintain a constant display.

There are several kinds of hyacinths available for growing indoors for flowering from November to March. The smallest and earliest is the Roman hyacinth often called French Roman. These produce several dainty spikes of loosely set, white bells from small bulbs and can be brought into flower as early as November. They may be set on pebbles, or planted in fibre or soil. Grow them cool and in the dark from planting time in early September to the beginning of November. Then remove them to full light. A temperature of about 50° F. towards flowering time is ample for their development.

'Rosalie', which is deep rose pink and 7 to 9 ins tall, and 'Vanguard', light blue and about the same height, are two miniature hyacinths of roughly similar habit to the French Roman, developed by growers to flower by Christmas. Grow them as Roman hyacinths but give a little let. Double: 'Marechal Niel', yellow and orange; 'Orange Nassau', orange-scarlet; and 'Peach Blossom', rosy-pink. Mendels: 'Athleet', pure white; 'Krelage's Triumph', rich red and 'Orange Wonder', orange-red. Triumphs: 'Bandoeng', mahogany-red; 'Merry Widow', red and white and 'Topscore', geranium-red.

Amaryllis or hippeastrums make a striking display and produce their flower spikes before the strap-shaped leaves appear. They are available in many separate colours as well as striped varieties. Bulbs are normally purchased in December when they are dormant. No water should be given and then the amount of water should be gradually increased in proportion to the top-growth. When the leaves turn yellow watering should be reduced and the bulbs dried-off completely.

Crocus species for indoors should not be confused with the large-flowered Dutch types, but are altogether daintier. In good light, the petals often spread out fully exposing the stamens and stigmata. Among the best for bowls are *C. imperati*, violet and lilac; and *C. chrysanthus* varieties including 'Blue Pearl', 'Cream Beauty' and 'Snow Bunting'. Of the large flowered crocus 'Queen of the Blues', silvery lilac; 'Remembrance', deep purple, and 'Snowstorm' are dependable.

Chionodoxa or glory of the snow is easy to cultivate indoors as it grows only 4 or 5 ins high. Chinodoxas are available in shades of blue. *C. gigantea* and *C. luciliae* are good, while the pink form of *luciliae* is attractive. All like little heat and should not be brought indoors until January.

Eranthis or winter aconites can be grown in bowls and they are best planted in September and left outdoors until January when they will soon produce their golden-yellow flowers surrounded by the green bracts in the form of a ruff.

Fritillaria meleagris produces its chequerboard flowers in various colours but must be grown in cool conditions.

Freesias and lachenalias make unusual pot plants and do best when grown in soil.

Galanthus or snowdrops are rather erratic whether grown in pots or bowls but the single form *G. nivalis* is the most reliable.

Iris tingitana, 15 to 18 ins high, with its blue flowers splashed gold will, if the bulbs are planted in August, be in flower by Christmas. The dwarf *Iris*, such as *I. reticulata* and others, are of value for their sweet-scented flowers which appear from late January onwards.

Of *Muscari* varieties 'Heavenly Blue' is inclined to produce long foliage if placed in heat too early. It is therefore best to leave the bowls or pots outdoors until January and then bring them into gentle heat.

Puschkinia libanotica with pale blue flowers, can be grown in the same way as chionodoxas.

Scilla sibirica 'Spring Beauty', with its china-blue flowers never fails to give a good display.

With all of these subjects once they are indoors they must not be kept in a dry atmosphere, otherwise the flowering period will be short and the plants will never look lively.

BULBS IN THE GREENHOUSE

A greenhouse not only extends greatly the scope for gardening, but enables the gardener to work comfortably whatever the weather. There are three types of greenhouse—cold, warm and hot —and what plants can be grown largely depends on the amount of warmth which can be provided. For most amateur gardeners a cool greenhouse is the most practicable and economical. This is one where a minimum winter temperature of 45° F. (7 C.) can be maintained.

Of the wide range of bulbs that can be grown without trouble, the following are among the best. Full descriptions will be found in the alphabetical list.

> *Amaryllis*, see *Hippeastrum, Achimenes, Begonia, Clivia miniata, Cyclamen* (Giant flowered), *Freesias, Gladiolus, Gloxinias, Haemanthus, Hippeastrum* (*Amaryllis*), *Hyacinthus, Hymenocallis*, see *Ismene, Ismene* (*Hymenocallis, Ixias, Lachenalia, Leucocoryne, Lilimus, Nerine, Polianthes tuberosa, Schizostylis, Sprekelia formosissima, Tigridia, Tritonia, Vallota speciosa, Veltheimia, Zantedeschia*.

Many lilies produce bulbils on their stems, known as axillary bulbils. These often start to produce roots even before they fall off the parent plant and afford a ready means of increase

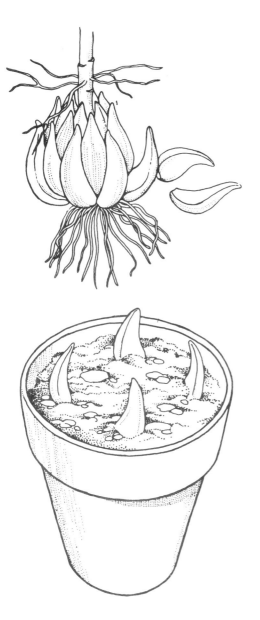

The scales of most lilies can easily be detached. If they are then potted up in a very sandy compost new bulbs will form at their bases. The photographs on the facing page show the sequence of development in full

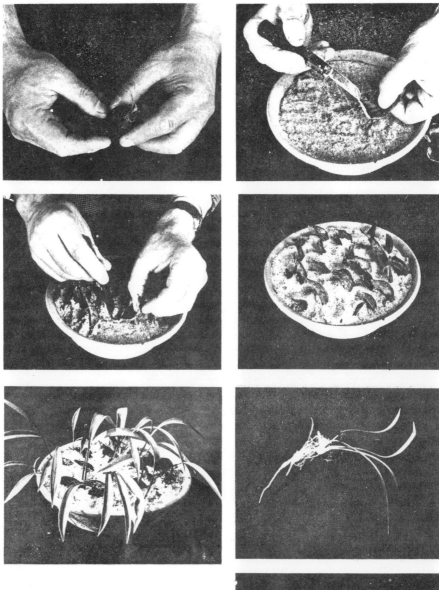

Propagating lilies from scales. First the scales are cleanly detached from the parent bulb and then they are inserted in a very sandy compost. New bulbs form at the bases of the old bulbs. Once several leaves have developed the individual bulbs can be moved into individual pots and grown on till large enough to plant out

BULBS FOR THE ROCK GARDEN

The rock garden can be kept gay for the greater part of the year instead of, as is often the case, being very colourful in early spring and lacking brightness for the remaining months. The smaller-growing or miniature bulbs will, without problems, provide a display year after year.

In a well-made rock garden containing crevices and interstices groups of 3 or more bulbs can be planted. After you have made a selection of the more usual subjects, look for some of the less familiar kinds, often listed in catalogues under the heading miscellaneous bulbs.

Given ordinary good culture they will multiply and spread yielding fresh dividends each year. It is worth remembering that some, including muscari and scillas, can be placed so that they eventually penetrate a carpet of growth made by plants such as *Mentha requienii*, *Veronica repens*, *Cotula squalida*, *Arenaria* and sedums which will ensure greenery on the rock garden when the bulb foliage has withered.

Most rock gardens are raised above the general garden surroundings so that little extra pre-planting cultivation is necessary, but in the case of rock gardens in lower positions, some effort must be made to ensure the bulbs do not become waterlogged.

Rock garden bulbs offer great variety in colour, form, and texture, ranging in height from a couple of inches to several feet. Their foliage is as diverse as their flowers.

> *Anemone blanda.*
> *Bulbocodium vernum.*
> *Chionodoxa.*
> *Cyclamen.*
> *Eranthis hyemalis.*
> *Erythronium dens-canis.*
> *Fritillaria.*
> *Galanthus.*
> *Iris.*
> *Muscari.*
> *Oxalis adenophylla.*
> *Narcissus, lobularis, cyclamineus, juncifolius, bulbocodium* 'Conspicuus', *triandrus* 'Albus'.
> *Puschkinia libanotica.*

> *Scilla siberica.*
> *Tecophilea cyanocrocus.*
> *Tritelia uniflorum.*
> Tulip species, *batalini, clusiana, eichleri, hageri, kaufmanniana, kolpakowskiana, linifolia,* and *persica*

NATURALIZING BULBS

Bulbs look particularly attractive when planted in an informal manner. Although it is easier to secure a more effective display where considerable space is available, artistic results can be achieved when only a small area is at your disposal.

Some bulbs are suitable for growing in permanent grassland. These, including crocuses and the smaller narcissi and daffodils, look best when seen as spreading drifts of colour. They are invaluable planted in this way in parklands and large areas, while in smaller gardens separate corners can be given over to growing groups of bulbs in grass. Difficult slopes and grassy banks can be brightened with spring-flowering bulbs.

Patches of a few dozen bulbs will give a striking display as is often seen in the case of bluebells under trees, hardy cyclamen around shrubs, crocuses and anemones on grassy banks and the smaller growing narcissi and tulips in shrubberies and in grassed-down orchards. Most of these bulbous subjects increase freely by making new bulblets or cormlets annually. In addition, many seed themselves freely, giving rise to numerous hybrids. While most seedlings may not compare favourably with the standard named cultivars, they often introduce different characteristics in the way of size, shape and colour.

One advantage in growing bulbs in this way is that they can be left in position for many years. Some gardeners split up clumps every 5 or 6 years but this is not necessary as long as growth remains healthy. It is probable that the size of the flowers may decrease but this is not really important, especially as the actual number of blooms produced normally increases.

The natural increase of bulbs planted in this way usually means that the shape of the clumps varies. This results in drifts of colour, giving a

Crocuses naturalised in woodland. Grass must not be mown till the leaves have died

magnificant display. As long as the ground is not badly drained, no special soil preparations are necessary.

Bulbs should not be planted in rows or even in specially shaped groups. It is the informal way in which they are seen flowering which adds to the effectiveness. They look much more pleasing seen growing informally. The usual method is to take the bulbs and plant them just where they fall on leaving the hands, making sure that all are properly covered with soil. In this way natural drifts will be produced.

There are two ways of planting bulbs in grass. You can cut round three sides of a square and use the fourth side as if it were a hinge and plant the bulbs in the exposed area. This is a simple method for the smaller bulbs. The other method is to use a trowel to lift individual pieces of turf, or better still, a bulb planting tool can be employed. This will cut out a 2 to 3-in circle for each bulb and as each fresh hole is made, the piece of turf previously cut out is ejected automatically for replacement in its former position. Larger bulbs should be given a covering of 3 ins and the smaller ones 2 ins. The grass should not be cut until the bulb foliage has died down.

The spring scene in the woodland garden or in grass plantings would be incomplete without the blue *Anemone nemorosa*, the wood anemone. *A. apennina* has narrower petals in shades of blue, rose or white, while in sheltered positions, the blue stars of *Anemone blanda* will appear from early March onwards.

Another smaller bulb flourishing beneath deciduous trees is *Chionodoxa sardensis*, blue, and *C. lucilae* which has a white eye. *Scilla sibirica* also produces a blue patch of colour. Flowering from February onwards is *Crocus tomasinianus*, which has slender, greyish buds opening to pale lavender.

The large-flowered Dutch crocuses in yellow, blue, white and striped will make a bold display, while for autumn colour choose *Crocus speciosus* and *C. nudiflorus* which, in the case of new plantings, need putting into the ground in late July or early August.

As long as the soil is not constantly dry or the shade very dense, the hardy cyclamens always create attention, not only for their fairy-like flowers, but because of their dark green, ivy-shaped leaves, often marbled in silver. *C. europaeum*, carmine, and *C. neapolitanum*, pink, are autumn-flowering. *C. coum* has crimson, pink or white flowers in winter, while *C. repandum* blooms in April and May.

The wild daffodil, *Narcissus pseudo-narcissus*, the Lent lily, has long been used for naturalizing, as has *N. obvallaris*, the Tenby daffodil. The old-fashioned double daffodil 'Van Zion' can endure adverse conditions, and *Narcissus poeticus* or pheasant eye increases annually.

For the semi-shade where the soil is moist and peaty, the dwarf *Narcissus cyclamineus* is excellent. Its frail-looking flowers with reflexed petals open in February and remain colourful for several weeks. *N. triandrus* 'Albus', known as Angel's Tears, also naturalizes well in short grass.

Lilies look particularly well among shrubs and small trees where shade is not dense. While moisture is needed, none like to be in stagnant water. Undoubtedly *L. regale* is one of the best, its white trumpets being marked brownish-red outside. *L. pardalinum*, orange; *L. rubellum*, rose-pink; *L. henryi*, orange and *L. tigrinum* 'Spendens', orange-red, look well growing on the margins of woodland areas. *L. giganteum*, now known as *Cardiocrinum giganteum*, grows 6 to 12-ft high and likes partial shade.

Of muscari, 'Heavenly Blue', 'Allium Moly', yellow and *Camassia esculenta*, blue, all create a fascinating display when seen flowering in large groups. It is perhaps, the bluebell, *Scilla nutans*, with which we are most familiar as growing in woodland areas. It is a great pity that they are so maltreated by those who go first to admire their beauty and end up by picking both flowers and foliage.

Ornithogalum umbellatum, the star of Bethlehem, produces numerous white flowers striped green in May. *Fritillaria meleagris*, the snake's head fritillary, flowers freely in moist grassy land and around shrubs, which provide the required shade. *Erythronium dens-canis*, the dog's tooth violet, is another bulbous subject with simple cultural needs.

Tulips are not really suitable for general naturalization but some species such as *T. batalini*, *T. clusiana*, *T. kaufmanniana* and *T. tarda* look attractive planted in groups of a dozen or more.

On a small scale it is possible to naturalize bulbs to fit in with the surroundings. Yellow daffodils seen flowering round the silver-steemed birches; muscari or chionodoxa growing under pink flowering cherries; these are just two very simple ideas.

Chapter 4

THE
PROPAGATION
OF BULBS

Many methods of propagation are known and practised by gardeners and the majority can be used in connection with increasing the stock of bulbous subjects. Layering and budding are usually reserved for woody plants, but only very rarely is grafting carried out, and then is confined to tuberous-rooted subjects such as dahlias rather than true bulbs.

Offsets are a ready means of propagating almost all bulbs and it is by this method that both professional growers and amateur gardeners work up a stock. The production of offsets is evidence of the strength and vigour of the parent bulbs, since these new plants arise as the result of nourishment taken from the soil, and through the air, by the healthy foliage of the growing plants. It is as if the food obtained and manufactured by roots and leaves has compelled the original bulbs or corms to build extensive storehouses to hold the extra energy.

Most gardeners hope or expect the natural propagation process to happen so that in course of time there is a great increase in their displays. This explains why, after a few years, some bulbs occupy much more than their allotted space. It also shows why occasionally, a batch of bulbs which have previously flowered well for some years, suddenly miss a year of colour. This is usually due to the bulbs' having produced an abundance of offsets or having completely divided into several sections, which are not big enough to bloom for a year a two.

Offsets vary greatly in size and it is wise to grade them when replanting since the best plan is to grow all offsets in beds where they can be left until of flowering size. Obviously the larger offsets, which will flower earlier, should be kept separately. Although there is this variation in size, every one has the makings of a complete, new and independent plant, which is of special importance in the case of those varieties that produce little or no seed. Almost all offsets are naturally attached to the parent bulbs but a few, notably liliums, montbretias and tulips,

Galanthus nivalis 'Flore Pleno', the double form of the common snowdrop

sometimes produce small bulbs at the end of a runner or creeping stem. These are known as 'droppers' for they develop lower in the ground than the mother bulbs.

Another means of propagation, particularly with gladioli, is from the tiny new cormlets usually referred to as 'spawn'. These are in addition to the full-sized corms which always develop. This spawn will attain flowering size after a couple of years or so, and, until this time, can be sown in drills like seed, and lifted before heavy frosts come.

Occasionally, roundish growths may be seen in the leaf axils of some subjects, particularly lilies and tulips. These growths are known as bulbils. They may be removed when the foliage is dying down and can subsequently be planted in the same way as ordinary bulblets.

Many subjects, especially those with rhizomatous roots, increase satisfactorily and quickly by simple division. In most cases this cn be done in autumn or spring. It must be performed with care, so as not to leave any ragged portions of root, thereby opening up the way for diseases to get a hold. This is a quick means of obtaining new plants which will flower in a short time. In many instances, divisions can easily be made by hand, while in others, a sharp knife may be necessary.

With lilies, scale propagation is often worthwhile. This is done by carefully detaching fleshy scales and inserting them more-or-less upright in trays of good sandy compost; peat moss and sand is another method, especially with the more rare kinds. These trays of planted scales can be placed in a fairly close frame or greenhouse, or stood outdoors in a sheltered, semi-shaded place. With the more common varieties, the scales can be placed in drills of sandy soil in an outdoor bed. Each scale normally produces one bulblet (sometimes two) which is grown on in the usual way.

In the case of hyacinths, in which bulblets

Chionodoxa luciliae, commonly known as 'Glory of the Snows' forms a veritable carpet of blue

do not always form freely, and where there are
no scales, fresh bulblets can be induced to form
by making several cuts across the bottom disc
or basal plate. This causes the formation of
vegetative buds, which develop into bulbs.

Yet another method of propagation is to take
leaf cuttings, particularly in the case of begonias
or gloxinias. The leaves are taken off the plants
during the summer and the stalks inserted,
almost to the leaf blade, in a mixture of loam,
leaf soil and silver sand, with additional sand
being spread on the surface of the boxes or
pans. Kept shaded in a temperature of 70 to
75° F., rooting will soon occur.

It is also possible to propagate from selected
leaves by carefully pegging these on to the
surface of sandy soil and making cuts along the
midrib, keeping it in close contact with the soil.
Roots will form where the cuts are made and
the separate portions can subsequently be potted
up and will then develop in the usual way.

Seed is the most important method of bulb
increase and is not as difficult as is sometimes
believed. Though a fairly slow process when
compared with propagation by offsets, divisions,
or bulblets, it affords unlimited possibilities in
that a good stock can be built up giving great
variation in size and colour. Sometimes too,
vigour, general constitution and hardiness can
be improved. In most cases it takes 3 to 5
years to obtain flowering bulbs from time of
seed sowing. In a few cases, the period is
longer. Even so, there is pleasure to be gained
while waiting in anticipation for the hoped for
results.

While seeds of hardy bulbous subjects are not
quite so easy to come by as the usual run of
flower seeds, there are several firms in Great
Britain and other countries who do supply many
interesting items. Seed should really be sown as
soon as it is ripe but this is not always possible
when it has to be bought.

Seed trays, boxes or pans of J.I. seed compost, or some other simple mixture, are quite
suitable for the purpose. Depth of sowing
depends on the size of the seed which varies
greatly according to the species being grown.
After sowing, sprinkle some coarse silver sand
on the surface soil for this will lessen the

31

possibility of moss appearing on the pots.

It is essential to start the seed under cool conditions in fact, it is quite usual to leave the sown receptacles exposed to frosts, if, after being sown in summer or autumn, seed has not germinated. The effect of frosts and snow on seeds of hardy bulbs seems to have a stimulating effect.

If seeds are left outdoors without cover it is best to place small mesh netting over the boxes or pans for this will not only keep off leaves and rubbish but give protection from mice which seem partial to the seeds. Some subjects, especially tulips, are extremely slow in germinating and it is not rare for certain items to take a year or more before starting into growth.

Slugs always seem to find young bulb seedlings and it is wise to use a good slug bait from the time the seeds are sown, for it is so easy to lose a good batch of seedlings in one night's attack.

Once growth is seen, the seedlings can be taken into the cool greenhouse or to the frame, but it is really best to leave them outdoors to encourage bulbs to form rather than promote much top growth. Do not prick out the seedlings the first year. This perhaps is the main reason why thin sowing should be practised.

Tender and half-hardy subjects are sown in the cool greenhouse and are kept under warm conditions, requiring rather more care than the hardy subjects.

It is possible for the amateur gardener to do a certain amount of hybridizing although it requires much patience. As a rule, the amateur hybridist will stick to crossing varieties in the same genus, but professional growers have attempted, with some success, to cross species of more than one genus. An example of this is an Australian success in crossing *Amaryllis belladonna* with *Brunsvigia josephinae* which, owing to the latter's influence, has produced a hybrid named *Amaryllis belladonna* 'Parkeri', with as many as 12 to 16 pale rose-coloured flowers on each spike. This hybrid may in some respects be a curiosity, but it is a pointer as to what is possible. Another such hybrid is known as Brunsdonna. An instance of simple cross fertilization is the appearance of *Eranthis* × *tubergenii*, the result of crossing *E. circlicia* with *E. hyemalis*.

The hybridizing of bulbous subjects is carried out in exactly the same way as with other plants, the flower chosen for the female parent being emasculated before its pollen sacs burst. The pollen from the male parent is transferred with a very fine-haired brush, just before it is ready to fall from the anthers. Even when seed is secured, it is often difficult to raise young plants, some seed, such as that of begonia, being very minute and having to be treated with great care.

Fortunately, there are several excellent seed sowing composts, such as the John Innes type, available, as well as various form of vermiculite, which does make seed sowing less of a gamble. In most cases several years elapse before a flowering size bulb or corm develops. There are exceptions such as gladioli seedlings which often flower in their second year. Many subjects hybridize themselves which accounts for the fact that in established colonies of bulbs or tubers such as anemones, several in-between shades of colour can sometimes be found.

Chapter 5

DEALING WITH DISEASES

Do not assume that in bulb growing you will encounter a large number of diseases, for no reputable firm would knowingly distribute unhealthy stock. Even so, the average gardener does sometimes come across conditions or symptoms in bulbs which cause concern. The information is intentionally presented in quite unscientific language and deals with troubles which have been met in growing bulbs and corms on both small and large scales. No pretence is made to deal with diseases in great technical detail, for this must be left to the plant pathologist and research worker, but, even so, there does not appear to be much literature on this subject, such as can be readily understood without continued reference to scientific publications.

Occasionally, diseases caused by undetermined species of the fungus *Botrytis* are found on chionodoxas, ixias, montbretias, muscari, ornithogalums and scillas. In these cases, badly affected bulbs are best burned. It is with the much more widely-grown subjects, on which disease sometimes makes serious inroads, that we are now concerned, since they are more likely to be met with in the average garden.

Colchicums sometimes have swollen, blister-like black spots and stripes on their foliage and occasionally on the corms, giving the plant the appearance of having been dusted with soot. These swellings eventually burst open distributing a black powder-like substance, which in reality contains the spores of the fungus commonly known as smut (*Urocytis colchici*). This fungus, however, is very rarely met with in the average garden and in any case does not appear

to prevent actual flowering, although naturally it disfigures affected bulbs. Smut has also been found on bulbocodiums and chionodoxas, although on these it is quite rare. Affected bulbs should be burned.

The most troublesome disease likely to be encountered in crocuses is *Fusarium* rot. This can be first seen by the premature discoloration and withering of the foliage, when the corms should be in growth. The disease seems to begin in the roots and gradually spreads to the corm, of which the base appears to rot, first showing a bluish colour. It spreads through the corm and eventually shows in the upper parts as rather sunken, dark spots, each with a small white centre. Such diseased corms are easily recognized at lifting time. When cleaning is being done or when seen in storage they must always be removed to prevent other corms becoming affected. Occasionally, too, instead of going soft, the corms harden and dry up, till they look like pebbles, hence the name 'stone disease'. Unfortunately there seems at present to be no cure beyond destroying all affected corms, whenever seen or suspected.

Fritillaria imperialis is sometimes attacked by a *Sclerotinia* fungus which eventually causes the bulbs to deteriorate into a nasty dark mess. The symptoms are yellowing of the foliage and the falling away of the flower stem, usually after the flowers have finished blooming. If diseased bulbs are not taken up and destroyed they will eventually disintegrate and the disease spores are left in the soil to increase and reappear on more bulbs the following year. On extremely rare occasions, the spores will also attack crocuses with the same harmful results.

Galanthus species are not prone to disease, in fact they rarely if ever suffer at all. However, grey mould (*Botrytis galanthina*) can cause damage and loss, particularly during mild winters or after great variations in weather conditions. The disease settles on the young green shoots, which become affected.

There is rarely any trouble with muscari, although rot spots may sometimes appear on the leaves and develop into streaks. Occasionally too, the foliage is patterned with light markings suggestive of mosaic disease, while bulbs have been known to exude a gummy substance. With all of these, the affected specimens are best burned to prevent the trouble spreading, especially since their origin and control are not as yet fully understood. They are most likely to occur in moist, shady places where growth is soft.

Botrytis narcissicola is often known as smoulder. Large numbers of spores are produced by the fungus but the leaves show no sign of unhealthiness; it is only the flowers which display spotting. Sometimes, however, as the leaves die off or if they are damaged, they may be attacked, where the infected scales cause rot to extend from the top to the base of the bulb. Occasional sprayings of a fungicide may prevent the onset of the disease while keeping the bulbs in a temperature around 90° F. while dormant helps to prevent the carrying over of the fungus.

Narcissus white mould shows itself by yellowish-brown patches near the leaf tips. In damp weather these patches extend and become covered with a white fungus which kills the leaves completely. If the disorder is suspected, spray with a good fungicide. Unfortunately, the spores can easily be carried by wind or water drops. This disorder is worse on later varieties such as 'Cheerfulness' and 'Actaea'. Spray with Bordeaux mixture which will usually prevent the trouble from spreading, and the ground should not be used for bulbs again for at least two years so that the fungus spores die out.

Basal rot is another well-known complaint of bulbs, again occurring most usually when the bulbs are in store. This works its way through the bulb from the base, therefore all bulbs which feel soft to the touch should be suspected, as well as any which appear to dry up. This is another case of avoiding high temperatures and a close dry atmosphere during storage. There appears to be no cure, but much can be done by avoiding injury to the bulbs at any time, while the use of some soil fungicide when preparing the ground is of great help.

Virus disease sometimes occurs in narcissi, and although it is not easy to recognize in its earliest stages it is usually first seen in the form of stunted, malformed growth in the leaves, which often display yellowish stripings. The flower stems fail to develop properly and any blooms which do appear are shapeless. The only thing to do when the virus appears is to destroy the whole of the infected stock, for even if individual bulbs appear to be free from the disease they may be affected.

Most tulip growers are familiar with the disease known as fire, but there is one with the same common name which occasionally spoils narcissi. These two diseases are not related and in the case of narcissi, the fire usually develops first on the flowers, showing as light brown spots on the petals. As the latter grow, particularly in moist conditions, the disease spores spread rapidly and the flowers are entirely spoiled. Only the flowers and foliage are attacked, and there is no record of the disease ever appearing on or being spread by the bulbs. Much can be done to stamp out virus troubles by insisting on the finest stocks from reliable sources, and avoiding the cheap lots which so often are of poor quality and disease-laden.

Freesias grown under glass are sometimes affected by a form of botrytis which causes the spotting of the flowers and foliage. Infection is worse under damp conditions. The remedy is to increase ventilation and avoid overwatering. Dead and dying foliage should be removed and there should be regular spraying with a fungicide containing thirom.

Gladioli are subject to several fungal diseases including dry rot. The first signs are seen after the plants have been growing for some weeks. The leaves turn yellow from the top downwards and eventually become brown and dry. New corms tend to become diseased from the shoot

Anemone blanda naturalises readily in sunny corners

The modern 'red' daffodils are rapidly increasing in popularity

Multi-coloured parrot tulips, one of the glories of spring

and should be burned when lifted. Do not grow gladioli on the same site for at least two or three years.

Neck rot (*Pseudomonas*) disease is usually first seen as small reddish specks on the foliage. These become larger and, as the rot gradually spreads, all the foliage becomes affected and wilts. The whole top growth may topple over. Often a clear, gum-like substance is emitted which eventually turns yellow and dries off. A control often practised is to tip the corms before planting in calomel solution. In this way an attack is prevented from developing.

Hard rot (*Septoria*) produces purplish-brown spots on the leaves of bulbous plants which are eventually destroyed. Growth is usually stunted, and no flowers produced. This appears to be a soil-borne disease more prevalent after a wet season. Avoid growing gladioli on the same site for some years.

Botrytis rot covers the tissues with a greyish mould which increases and causes decay often in the centre of the corm, producing the condition known as core rot. Affected specimens should be destroyed and a new site chosen.

Fusarium yellows is a common disorder. It attacks the roots leading to the yellowing of the foliage which is first seen as green mottling between the leaf veins. Clean growing conditions will help to avoid this trouble but affected corms should be destroyed and not allowed to contact healthy specimens.

Hyacinths are more likely to be affected by disorders than actual diseases. One of the most common is loose bud. Which is caused by the lack of balance between water intake and transpiration of the growing shoots. This causes a disorder at the base of the flower stalk resulting in an upward tension on the bulb causing the stalk to break. Good culture will minimize the possibility of this happening, while correct storage when the bulbs are dry will lessen the possibility of loose bud.

Iris reticulata and a few other irises are sometimes affected by ink disease which appears as black spots or patches over the bulb tunic. The disease spreads and eventually leads to the rotting of the bulbs which should be burned.

Lilium candidum is sometimes spoiled by *Botrytis elliptica*. The fungus first shows its presence as brownish-grey spots which spread so that the whole leaf is affected and droops. The problem with this is that the disease spores can over-winter in the rosette of leaves this lily forms in the autumn. All affected leaves, including those which fall, should be burned. An occasional spraying of a general fungicide helps to prevent the spread of the disease.

Tulip fire or mould is caused by a fungus known as *Botrytis tulipae*. The first signs of attack are numerous yellowish spots showing on the leaves; subsequently, a greyish-brown mould appears. Spores can be blown by the wind or splashed about by rain, thus spreading infection. Bulbs can become affected and may fall into entire decay. This is one good reason for lifting tulips annually, for any unhealthy bulbs can then be destroyed.

In a growing bulb, the presence of tulip fire is often indicated by malformed, stunted growth which must be burned and never allowed to lie about on the soil during the summer. Control is not easy, for spraying with Bordeaux mixture can damage the foliage. A fairly new fungicide known as Tulisan has given excellent results.

Grey bulb rot attacks bulbs in growth often before they break through the soil. Where the disease is known to occur, apply a dilution of formalin, say 1 part to 50 of water, to the soil before planting bulbs.

Shanking sometimes appears in forced tulips causing the bulbs to shrivel and the leaves gradually to fade. Sterilization of the soil is a good method of control. Some tulips show signs of featherings or flaming, often referred to as 'breaking'. This is caused by virus spread by greenfly. Several viruses are responsible, one adding colour, while another removes certain colour tones. The now established varieties of Broken tulips contain in some way a balanced mixture of the two viruses.

Virus disorders are perhaps the most difficult to trace and eradicate. These diseases sometimes cause the foliage and stems to twist and lead to discoloration of the leaves and flowers. Viruses are transmitted by insect carriers, particularly greenfly, so that if these pests are kept down there is less likelihood of trouble. Care is needed when handling affected plants or when using a knife blade to cut specimens, since it is through these means that the disease can be spread. Unfortunately there is no foolproof means of controlling virus diseases.

Chapter 6

SOME BULB PESTS

As long as healthy bulbs are obtained and properly grown under clean conditions, and preventative and remedial measures adopted at the first suggestion of the presence of pests, there is no need to be unduly concerned. The fact that several possible sources of attack are mentioned should not make you assume that they are usually encountered. They are described so you can recognize them and apply appropriate remedies before the pests gain a real hold.

The great garden enemy, *Aphis* or greenfly, will sometimes affect dormant bulbs as well as foliage and flowers, often crippling growth, and one bad attack can spoil a whole display. If dealt with early, a good insecticide will successfully eradicate the pests. Ants, too, are often troublesome although usually they only visit bulbous plants in search of aphids. The ordinary modern proprietary ant killers are most effective.

Root aphids are often the case of wilting and loss of plant vigour. If affected plants are lifted, the roots are covered with the typical grey aphids. While it is possible to wash the roots using malathion before replanting, to prevent spread of the pest, badly infested bulbs should be burned. Ants sometimes lead to the spread of aphids.

Birds, particularly sparrows, can be destructive to bulbs, especially when they mutilate crocus petals. The stretching of strands of cotton over the position appears to be the most effective way of discouraging birds.

The minute bulb scale mite, *Tarsonemus*, is not easy to identify in dormant bulbs when these appear to be firm. When cut open, affected bulbs show vertical streaks and patches and these, seen under a microscope, reveal large numbers of the pests present in the discoloration. In a warm, moist atmosphere they climb up the foliage and on to other plants. They breed at a tremendous rate and the foliage of affected plants becomes bright green and then distorted and flecked.

Immersion of the bulbs in hot water (at least 110° F.) for an hour or more, is the most effective method of control, since exterior spraying is ineffective. No bulb should be planted in infested ground for at least a year.

Two quite serious narcissus flies have been known for a long time. *Merodon equestris*, usually referred to as the large narcissus fly, is most active during May and June. It also attacks amaryllis, hyacinths, scillas and lilies. During the period when the foliage is dying away, the flies lay their eggs in the holes left by the shrivelled leaves and flower stems. The resulting maggot can then easily crawl into the bulb where it feeds, grows and eventually emerges, remaining in the soil during the winter. By the spring, it has wings and lays its eggs in other bulbs to continue the cycle of destruction. This large fly lays one egg annually, while the small fly *Eumerus strigatus* (*M. eumerus*) will lay up to a dozen. Badly affected bulbs are best destroyed.

Deep planting will lessen the chance of destruction, but other steps are also necessary. The flies can often be identified by the hum of their wings, so that catching them with a net is a certain means of destroying them. Immersion in hot water for an hour is effective, although keeping the bulbs in cold water for 48 hours has also been found to kill the grubs. Best of all is a three-hour soaking in a lindane solution and this is made even more effective if Captan is added. Do not ripen bulbs in sun, since this attracts the egg-laying flies. Dusting the planting holes with Gamma-BHC is wise if the pests are known to be in the soil.

Eelworms are responsible for a great deal of damage to many bulbous plants. Because they are so small, many gardeners know little about them. They are threadlike, about $\frac{1}{20}$ in. long and can rarely be seen except under a microscope. Their presence is identified by the little swellings or lumps on the leaves. They do not stop bulbs from flowering the same year, but when lifted, or if left in the ground, the tops of the bulbs will be soft and decay will spread rapidly. It is best to destroy the bulbs as soon as there is any evidence of eelworm. Professional growers apply the hot water treatment, but for the amateur the best course is burning and not to grow bulbs in the same site for two or three years.

Thrips are minute, but most destructive. They feed on the foliage of certain bulbous plants, sucking out the sap and making the foliage sickly-looking. They sometimes appear on gladioli and their presence is shown up by the long silvery lines in the leaves. These tiny pests are not easy to eradicate, since they both feed on croms while in store and damage the root points as well as attacking the leaves. The foliage of all affected plants should be burned, care being taken not to shake the leaves near healthy corms at lifting time, for this is one way in which the thrips are transported. If corms are stored during the winter in a temperature around 65° F., this will lessen the possibility of attack. As a further precaution sprinkle flaked naphthalene between the corms.

Leather jackets, cutworms, millipedes and other soil pests occasionally feed on the roots of bulbs, causing wilting. These pests are less likely to appear if the ground is kept reasonably clean. The use of a soil fumigant or vegetable traps will prevent soil pests gaining a hold. Slugs and snails are partial to the young shoots of bulbs as they emerge from the ground. Sometimes they bite deeply into the flower stem causing its collapse. Many effective slug killers are readily available. In open, exposed gardens or 'wild' areas, rabbits and hares may scratch up bulbs or occasionally actually eat into the young growth. Apart from destroying these animals, little can be done except to use netting or keep a dog.

Chapter 7

ALPHABETICAL LIST OF BULBS

However small or large your garden, you will find suitable species and varieties of bulbs to plant in every part of it. The following alphabetical list includes many of the less-common bulbs as well as the better-known ones, and reference to the list will disclose the characteristics of a wide and intriguing range of species and varieties which should encourage gardeners to be more adventurous in bulb cultivation.

ACHIMENES A most interesting genus of greenhouse plants closely related to gloxinias, chiefly from South America.

The long, tubular flowers are produced in many delicate colours, the attractive foliage providing a perfect foil. The flowering period is long, giving a bright display in the greenhouse or conservatory during the summer months when many other subjects have finished blooming With forcing, it is possible to bring plants into flower in the late spring and early summer. Particularly valuable for hanging baskets as well as growing in pots or pans, achimenes can be relied on to do well where a temperature of around 50° F. is maintained.

Plant the small rhizomes at the end of January or early February using a mixture of good loam, peat, silver sand and well-rotted manure, passing these through a fine sieve so that the roots can penetrate freely into the compost. Crock the pots well and place a little moss fibre over this material before any compost is added. Cover the roots with 1 in. of soil, keeping it nicely moist until top growth appears, when increased quantities of water and plenty of light are needed.

Rhizomes may also be planted in boxes and carefully transferred to their flowering receptacles when there is about 1 in. of top growth. As the season advances, give frequent sprayings of water night and morning. Shading during the hottest part of the day will keep the

Acidanthera bicolor 'Murielae' has strongly scented white flowers with a chocolate eye

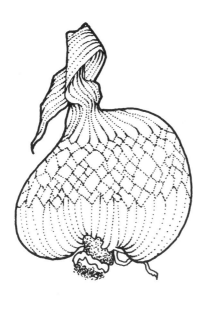

Acidanthera bicolor

foliage clean and discourage attacks by red spider mites. The small tubers may be increased by division or by stem and leaf cuttings, the stalks of the latter being inserted in a moist sandy mixture in late spring and placed in a shady position where they root freely. Seed, too, will germinate easily when sown in heat and just covered with a light sandy compost.

Varieties are a matter of personal choice, but many beautiful species can be had, including *A. longiflora* 'major, rich violet blue; *A. l.* Admiration', deep rose, spotted in carmine; *A. hoogeana*, lilac with a light centre. There are several charmingly striped and speckled varieties on a white ground, as well as self coloured, yellow, scarlet, crimson and blue.

Achimenes species grow 15 to 18 ins tall and, except when used in hanging baskets, should be provided with light supports. When growth has finished, gradually withhold water and dry off until next planting time.

ACIDANTHERA Graceful plants with narrow gladiolus-like foliage and distinctive flowers. This member of the iris family, noted for its beauty and fragrance, comes from the highlands of Ethiopia.

Acidantheras look well grouped in borders or by themselves. You can plant them in a mixed bed of summer flowering bulbs or grow them just for cutting. If picked in bud they will last a surprisingly long time in water. Spring planting should not be undertaken until the soil has had time to become warm about mid-May. The corms should be planted about 3 ins deep and about 6 ins apart in full sun and in sites sheltered from the wind. Acidantheras like light, well-drained soil and thrive with the addition of leaf-mould or thoroughly decomposed manure.

Acidantheras will not stand frost, so the corms should be taken up in October when the foliage becomes discoloured. After lifting, the leaves should be allowed to die back before laying out the corms in trays or boxes to dry off thoroughly and ripen. They should then be stored in a dry frost-proof place for the winter.

Acidanthera candida is pure white and *A. bicolor* is white with a purple blotch at the base of each petal, but the most vigorous form to plant is *Acidanthera bicolor* 'Murielae'. The large, tubular flowers measuring 3 to 4 ins across have segments that form a kind of star. There are 5 to 6 pure white flowers with maroon blotches at the centre on each 2 to 3-ft stem and they open in succession over a period of weeks from August to October. The flowers are fragrant, resistant to wet weather and rain does not spot them.

ALLIUM Alliums are very diverse in form, colour and height. Most are ornamental and have a long flowering season. Many are ideal for cutting. There are several hundred species distributed over various parts of the world, including Africa, Asia and America, and many grow easily in any good garden soil.

Although Allium is the family to which both garlic and onions belong, not all members of the family have strongly scented leaves or bulbs. Some varieties can naturalize themselves to such an extent that they become a pest. Many of the large-flowered species make excellent material for dried flower arrangements.

Planted in the autumn in groups of 6 or more, alliums are very showy and look well in borders,

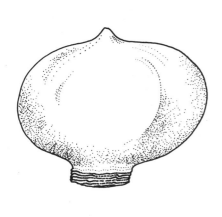

Allium karataviense

shrubberies or naturalized in grass, while some of the smaller sorts are most effective in the rock garden. When planting, the bulbs should be covered with 2 or 3 times their own depth of soil, and this varies greatly from species to species. Where happy, they will readily increase by offset or self-sown seeds. Seed of selected varieties may also be sown in pans in a sandy compost in the spring.

From the tunicated bulbs spring fairly wide leaves and strong stems at the top of which are lovely, well made umbels of semi-bell shaped 6-petalled flowers which open out in the sun.

The following are among the most ornamental and reliable species. *A. aflatunense*, growing 2½ to 3 ft with well-shaped umbels of purplish-lilac flowers, appearing at the end of May and during June. *A. albopilosum*, a particularly attractive species, growing to about 2 ft. The very large umbels of starry, lilac flowers, useful for cutting, develop early in June and the long, broad, downy foliage is most decorative.

A. azureum (*caeruleum*) is a charming species from the Altai Mountains with umbels of deep cornflower blue flowers on 2-ft stems. It is quite hardy and looks well when brought indoors. *A. cyaneum* is a miniature, growing only about 5 ins high and therefore ideal for the rock garden. The small heads of bluish-green flowers contrast well with the bright, grass-like foliage.

A. flavum, from the Caucasus, freely produces in June golden-yellow bell-shaped flowers grouped in dense umbels. *A. karataviense* grows 12 to 15 ins high, has glaucous, spreading leaves and greyish-lilac flowers which open in May. It is useful for growing in pots.

A. moly the golden garlic is a well-known species with bright yellow, starry flowers in compact umbels borne on 15-in. stems in June. It is good for naturalizing and will grow anywhere, but because of its spreading habit should not be planted among choice subjects which it might crowd out in time. It also makes good cut flowers and does well in pots. *A. neapolitanum* is the pretty, sweet-scented white garlic. Growing 15 ins high, it does well in pots.

A. roseum has loose umbels of 12 to 30 star-like, bright pink flowers. *A. rosenbachianum* is one of the most handsome and decorative species. Its round heads of purplish-violet or rosy-purple flowers on 2 to 2½-ft stems appear throughout June and July. *A. ursinium* is a white variety useful for naturalizing, although it has rather an invasive habit.

ALSTROEMERIA A native of South America, the root stock of *Alstoemeria* is really a kind of thickened fibre rather than a bulb, the stems varying in height from 2½ to 3 ft. Many species are hardy in all but the most exposed parts of Great Britain, and if given a light loamy, peaty soil, which is well drained and which does not dry out, they will flourish and increase fairly rapidly. The roots of alstroemerias are very brittle and great care should be taken not the break them when planting. Plants are usually sold as pot-grown, and should be planted with the minimum of disturbance. They will often not show above ground the first year after planting so do not assume you have lost them.

Nearly all alstroemerias flower from June onwards and although the normal method of propagation is by root division, they can rapidly be raised from seed.

Allium albopilosum, a very large flowered ornamental onion ideal for picking and drying

Of the species, *A. aurantiaca* is a well-known garden plant which grows in almost any sunny position, the bright orange flowers, spotted purple brown, being produced in umbels. *A. brasiliensis* from Brazil is also perfectly hardy, the good-sized flowers being reddish-purple, and spotted in brown and green.

A. chiloensis produces 12 or more reddish-pink flowers on each spike. *A. haemantha* grows $2\frac{1}{2}$ ft high, the bright red flowers being tipped green. *A. ligtu* produces, on its 2-ft stems, well-branched umbels of flowers which are white to mauvish-pink with purple streaks. The 'Ligtu' hybrids take in a very wide colour range.

A. pelegrina produces stout, leafy stems 10 to 14 ins high with umbels of large lilac flowers and is one of the most easy to grow, if given plenty of sun and good drainage.

A. violacea from Chile grows 18 ins tall and bears good-sized umbels of bright yellow flowers.

AMARYLLIS BELLADONNA. This subject has been known in Britain for 240 years as the belladonna lily. A native of South Africa, it is one of the most decorative of autumn-flowering bulbs and blooms freely when established. The stout stem, 18 to 24 ins or more high, carries at its top between 6 and 10 funnel-shaped flowers, which are a delightful shade of soft rose and sweetly fragrant.

There are several forms, although one rarely finds more than the type offered in catalogues. The form known as 'Kewensis' is particularly beautiful. It is bigger than the type and has a flush of apricot-orange with a suggestion of rose in the throat of each bloom.

A dry, sunny bank or the foot of a south wall will form an ideal site for the belladonna lily, for it likes shelter from severe frosts and cold winds, and a well-drained soil. If the bulbs are planted in August or early September they will

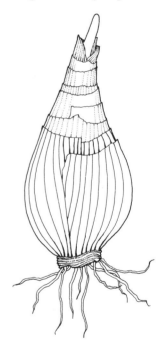

Amaryllis belladonna

produce their blooms within a few weeks. They should be set on a little silver sand and covered with not less than 4 or 5 ins of good quality, sandy loam.

If you leave belladonna lilies undisturbed for some years they will flower freely each autumn, especially if, in very severe winters, a little straw or bracken is placed over them. The dull green, strap-shaped leaves are produced in the spring and remain until late summer.

ANEMONE CORONARIA This plant comes from S. Europe and Asia Minor. One of the earliest records of the species arose in the latter part of the sixteenth century when corms were sent from Constantinople to Clusius, the renowned Dutch botanist of the period whose name has been commemorated in a number of bulbous subjects.

Well over a century ago, a special strain of single coronaria anemones was sent to France where a grower in Caen cultivated them with such success that they were soon listed as *Anemone de Caen*, under which name they are still officially grown although they are also referred to as giant French or poppy anemones. The large, saucer-shaped blossoms borne on 9 to 12-in. stems are most brilliantly coloured and valuable as cut flowers.

Apart from mixtures of magnificent single poppy anemones, these plants are now available in separately named sorts including the pretty 'Gertrude', rosy salmon with black central boss; 'His Excellency', bearing very large blooms of vivid velvety-vermilion with a blue-black centre, and often measuring 3 ins in diameter; 'Mr Fokker', true blue on strong stems which last well when cut; 'Sylphide', delicate mauve; and 'The Bride', with spotless white flowers.

The double poppy anemones are also greatly prized for cutting and many brilliant colours are to be found in the mixture. Among the separate colours are: 'Cornflower', a frilly double, dark amethyst-blue; 'Queen of Brilliants', with particulary vivid cherry-scarlet flowers and 'Scarlet King', having perfectly-formed, strikingly effective, scarlet blooms.

St Brigid anemones have a very graceful habit with large semi-double flowers all showing a dark-black central boss. Greatly prized for cutting they grow 10 ins high and the mixture contains very many hues. The 'Creagh Castle' strain is especially good.

Anemones appreciate a rich, deep sandy loam, which is essential if the tubers are left in the soil through the winter, for they are not so likely to rot as would be the case in a wet cold

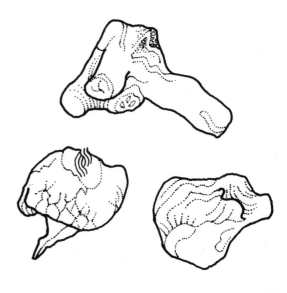

Anemone St. Brigit

soil. Many gardeners lift the tubers annually and store them in a dry, airy place until the next planting time. This certainly by-passes the untidy appearance of the plants as they are dying off.

Corms planted in autumn will produce flowers from early spring, while spring plantings will provide decoration from May onwards, although in a well-drained soil plantings may be made at short intervals during the winter months, thus ensuring a regular supply of blooms. They look most effective planted 2 ins deep in clumps of 6 or more. Bone meal dug into the soil before planting the tubers will prove greatly beneficial, and if a sprinkling of nitro chalk is worked around the plants when flowering begins, this will encourage the continuous production of a plentiful supply of long-stemmed blooms.

Propagation of *Anemone coronaria* is possible from seed which should be sown under glass in the early spring or later out-of-dors.

A. appenina is a showy, single, blue anemone often found naturalized in woodlands. There are less common pink and white forms, some being

Anemone 'de Caen', the popular garden anemones come in a very wide range of colours

double. The flowers appear on 6-in. stems during March and April and are often as much as $1\frac{1}{2}$ in. in diameter. The small cylindrical tubers, which are almost black, are easily identified because of their colour and can be increased by division. This is a good subject for growing on banks or in short grass where the soil does not dry out and where the anemones can be left undisturbed.

Use *A. blanda* for borders, the rockery, darkish corners of the garden that require splashes of colour, and for naturalizing in the wild garden. These delicate, yet extremely hardy Grecian windflowers produce small, starry flowers in March and April each made up of many rays of daisy-like gentian-blue petals in great abundance. The low, well-cut and pointed-leaved foliage provides a fitting background for the brilliant blooms borne on 4 or 5-in. stems.

A. blanda in mixed varieties includes dainty blue, pink and white flowers which open in early spring. For a deep blue effect try *A. blanda* 'Atroccarulea' a splendid free-flowering form. Set the fat, bulbous tubers of both 2 ins deep in rich, sandy loam, preferably where there will be light shade in summer but plenty of spring sun to open up the delightful flowers. Plant in October or November in large clumps of 12 or more. Anemones do require room, so plant them at least 4 to 6 ins apart. There are a few named varieties of *Anemone blanda* including the true blue 'Blue Pearl', the deeper 'Blue Star', the pure white 'Bridesmaid', the rosy-red 'Charmer', the deep cyclamen-pink 'Pink Star' and the rosy-purple 'Radar' although these are not always readily obtainable.

Among the many lovely species of *Anemone* in cultivation none is easier to grow than the hardy *A. nemorosa*, the wood anemone, which is a native of the British Isles. Whilst quite happy at the front of an ordinary flower border or rockery, wood anemones are really seen at their best growing on grassy slopes and banks, preferably where some shade is afforded during the day. Even the finely cut, hairy leaves are ornamental, and the flowers, growing on 5 or 6-in. stems, are often $1\frac{1}{2}$ in. in diameter. They thus make a really bright show during April and May.

Apart from *A. nemorosa* itself which has white flowers tinged with rose, there are several admirable forms, including 'Alba Major', single white; *A. n.* 'Allenii', soft lavender-blue; 'Royal Blue', rich lavender-blue; and *A. n.* 'Robinsoniana', with silvery, lavender flowers and prominent, yellow anthers.

All forms may be left to naturalize themselves, and in large colonies they present a really beautiful sight. A soil on the heavy side and an occasional mulching of leaf-mould prove beneficial.

ANTHERICUM *Anthericum liliago*, the St Bernard's lily, is easy to culture and most suitable for the hardy borders, but rarely seen in gardens. Theses bulbous-rooted plants thrive in any well-drained, porous soil which does not get too hot and dry; in fact partial shade suits them admirably. In such a place they will increase year by year and form really good clumps.

Although they do not like being disturbed, propagation can be effected by division of the fleshy roots in September or early October, or new season's seed can be sown, preferably as soon as it is ripe or in March. Provided with light soil in boxes in the cold frame, germination is fairly quick and the young seedlings must be pricked out in their early stages.

The St Bernard's lily grows about 2 ft high, while a superior form officially called *A. liliago* 'Mayor', commonly known as St Bruno's Lily, but also as *Paradisea lileastrum*, often reaches 3 ft and is perhaps more suitable for planting with the taller-growing border plants. *A. ramosum* is another such lily growing $2\frac{1}{2}$ ft high. It makes numerous underground stems which in turn produce spikes of bloom. For this reason, it is not suitable for growing in smaller borders.

All varieties have tufts of narrow, grass-like foliage and carry elegant, semi-pendulous white flowers from the end of June until August. The buds are tubular in shape and as they open reveal finely sculptured pointed petals.

ARISAEMA This is a genus of tuberous-rooted plants which owe their names to their likeness to arums. Most species attract attention by their oddity rather than beauty. Nevertheless, some of them are interesting. Chiefly natives of temperate and sub-tropical countries, arisaema are often known as pitcher plants on account of the shape of the flowers which are usually hooded, each hood ending in a long tail.

Although there are more than 50 species the following are among the easiest to obtain.

A. candidissimum of Chinese origin and known in the western world for over 30 years, can be grown outdoors in all but the coldest and most exposed places. It likes a good, rich site, and the tubers should be placed in a well-drained sand soil, under which there is a layer of manure or some other good feeding agent. In early summer, the tubers produce leaves up to 12 ins in length which as they unfold show a large white spathe sometimes tinged with green or pink. *A. fimbriatum* makes an ideal pot plant for the greenhouse, having a purple and white spathe, the narrow spadix emitting numerous purple hairs. *A. griffithii* has large, greenish-red flowers borne in June which are at least 5 ins in diameter. The big-hooded spathe which is brownish-red and veined or shaded green makes this a most decorative species which appears to be quite hardy in all but the coldest areas.

A. specoisum, which is also hardy, has a tall-growing pitcher flower often more than 2 ft high. The purplish leaves forming the spathe are beautifully striped and blotched creamy-yellow and are usually frilled or pleated, while the spadix, which appears in May or June, is anything from 18 to 24 ins in length and looks like a long purple tail, shaded green and white.

A. triphyllum known in America as Jack-in-the pulpit is hardy in a fairly sheltered place where there is leaf soil, and grows up to 12 ins high. The bright green hood shows up the pitcher, which is marked with green and purple, while the spadix is spotted and followed by scarlet berries in the autumn.

Plants growing indoors should be allowed to dry off after flowering, being potted up again in the spring in a rich compost. Propagation is by offsets or by seed sown as soon as ripe in a warm greenhouse.

ARUM Most arums are quite hardy and thrive in fairly moist, semi-shaded conditions. In the right place they are really ornamental and are inclined to suffer from the cold. Some need a sandy, peaty loam and a very well-drained warm situation, while others require cold-house treatment. All species are propagated by detaching offsets when the plants are dormant or seed may be sown when it can easily be separated from the pulpy matter which holds it.

Among the species easiest to manage are *A. crinitum*, growing to 18 ins or more, having a very large open purple-brown spathe, lined with hairs. Sometimes called dragon's mouths, the flowers emit an unpleasant smell. *A. creticum* is a native of Greece. It is hardy and produces its yellow flowers during March and April. *A. dracunculus*, the black dragon, has lobed leaves and fleshy stalks mottled black. Growing up to 3 ft high, the spathe is purplish-red, the spadix almost black. *A. maculatum* is the common cuckoo pint, and its scarlet berries, borne in the autumn, are most handome. *A. italicum* produces a large, pale yellowish-green spathe. Planted in a warm place it remains attractive throughout winter and is altogether superior to our native 'lords and ladies'. *A. pictum*, from Spain, is autumn-flowering, the spathes being produced before the leaves.

47

Growing 8 to 10 ins high, the colour is green and white both at the base and on the outside, and purple within, which is why it is sometimes known as the black arum. *A. palaestinum* (*sanctum*), has shiny green fleshy leaves. The spathe, blue and purple on the inside, is light green outside, the black spadix growing 8 ins long. This plant is particularly suited for pot work in the cold greenhouse.

A. elliottianum, *A. pulchrum* and *A. rehmannii* are listed under *Zantedeschia*.

BABIANA   Practically all the babianas come from South Africa and, in common with many other bulbous subjects from the same country, are most interesting and desirable. Baboons eat the bulbs, hence the Latin name.

The fibrous-coated bulbs, which should be planted 3 ins deep in a sheltered place out-of-doors in the autumn, or in pots and treated the same way as freesias, produce compact flowers of the most beautiful hues and vary in height from 6 to 10 ins according to variety. Whilst they are reasonably hardy in a light, well-drained sandy soil and sunny position, in a severe winter some protection should be given in the form of straw, bracken or similar material. They flower from May onwards and, if some bulbs are left unplanted until the early spring, it is often possible to have flowers as late as August. Propagation is by the offsets which form on the older bulbs.

Among the best of the named varieties are *B. disticha*, bearing particularly pretty spikes of pale blue on 7-in. stems during June and July; *B. plicata*, with violet-blue flowers in June, specially suitable for the rock garden; *B. rigens*, an earlier, brilliant scarlet species 4 to 5 ins high; and *B. stricta* 'Rubro-Cyanea', a most beautiful sort, not easy to obtain but worth seeking, growing only 4 ins high having deep blue flowers each with a small red eye.

It is possible to obtain a mixture of seedlings which take in a wide colour range, many sorts being delightfully scented. Whether grown in the open or in pots, the babiana is well worth any little extra attention needed in soil preparation and protection.

BREVOORTIA, see *Brodiaea*.

BRODIAEA   Despite their beauty, hardiness and the ease with which they can be grown, it is surprising that brodiaeas are so neglected even though the bulbs are so inexpensive. Catalogued at various times as *Tritelia* and *Milla*, but now definitely classed as brodiaeas, all varieties flower in June and July, doing best in a well-drained soil in the full sun, while they are admirable subjects for the rockery or front of the border.

B. ida-maia now known and catalogued under the name of *B. coccinea* and often referred to as the crimson satin flower and the floral, or Californian fire cracker, is, as its name suggests, Californian in origin. The corms produce drooping, scarlet-crimson flowers tipped in green on 20 to 24-in. stems. Five bulbs planted in a 5-in pot of sandy loam and leaf-mould in early spring and grown in cool conditions can be brought into the greenhouse where they will provide a good display. They are best potted up annually and stock can be increased by detaching offsets.

B. congesta grows 12 ins high and has small bluish-lilac heads; while *B crocea*, growing to only 6 ins, has small umbels of pale yellow flowers, and appreciates a gritty soil in a sunny position. *B. grandiflora* is a charming species for the rock garden or edgings, the light blue flowers showing up well on 6-in. stems. *B. ixioides* 'Splendens' is a rather rarer species, the yellow blooms being produced on 9-in. stems. With its tall umbels of purple flowers, *B. laxa* is excellent for cutting, while the newer *B. tubergenii* has most effective large umbels of pale blue flowers with darker shading on the outside.

B. uniflora, well known under the name of *Milla uniflora*, has been given yet another name, for it is now classified botanically as *Ipheion uniflorum*. However, it is retained here under its better-known title. This is among the most desirable of all brodiaeas, growing about 6 ins tall with flowers of substance which remain in bloom for a long time. Down the centre of each pale lavender petal runs a thin, faint, violet stripe and the flowers, which are highly scented, appear in such profusion that they hide the grassy foliage. This species is ideal for growing in bowls and may be gently forced in pots. A darker form known as *B.u.* 'violacea' is also to be had, and although less common, it is a very adaptable free-flowering sort which deserves to be widely cultivated.

BULBOCODIUM   The name of this plant comes from the soft, woolly coats of the small bulbs which are natives of Spain and other mountainous European districts. Although quite hardy they are rarely seen in gardens. This is probably because they are not vigorous growers or conspicuous when in flower, the narrow petals spreading out untidily.

The only species in the genus is *B. vernum*, sometimes referred to as *Colchicum vernum*. The flowers closely resemble the crocus in habit and appearance, and this subject is also related to *Merendera*. On stems of 4 to 6 ins the longish, rosy-purple, funnel-shaped flowers appear early in the year, the strap-shaped ribbed leaves developing later. There is also a rare form with mottled leaves.

Given a rich fairly light soil either in the rock garden or at the front of the border, *Bulbocodium* soon establishes itself. Offsets, detached during late summer, form a ready means of increasing stock and are best planted 3 to 4 ins deep.

CALOCHORTUS   Natives of N. America, Mexico and Guatemala, *Calochortus* species are sometimes known as mariposa or butterfly tulips and on other occasions as star or globe tulips. Their graceful growth and brightly coloured flowers make them very attractive.

The flower consists of 6 petals, the 3 outer ones being shorter and narrower than the remainder, and many varieties are striking in colour with vivid markings. They are valuable for cutting, having tall stems and, when established, many blooms are produced over a long period. Calochortus are hardy, although they do best in a sunny position where the soil is light and sandy and drainage good. A bed raised above the surrounding soil is helpful in preventing moisture from settling around the bulbs in winter.

The plants are divided into several sections botanically and those known as mariposa tulips should be planted during October and November, and covered with 3 ins of soil, and placed 4 ins apart. It is a good plan in the winter, especially when there are heavy rains, to cover the beds with straw or similar material which can be removed in the early part of the year. This gives protection and keeps the surface soil from caking. The flowers are upright, mostly several to a stem, the leaves being narrow and linear.

Named varieties include *C. clavatus*, large golden-yellow expanding flowers; *C. kennedyi*, dazzling orange-scarlet with black central blotches; *C. nuttallii*, white, tinged in lilac with brownish-red markings; and *C. venus* 'Eldorado', a large strong growing sort, of unusual colouring, varying from creamy white to lilac, through to pink and rosy purple, the centres of all being blotched brown.

The species known as globe tulips are best planted in March. They like partial shade, with porous soil. They flower from June until August and during dry spells should have occasional soakings of water.

The best of the globe tulips include *C. amabilis* with beautiful pendent, golden flowers and *C. amoenus*, having drooping blooms of delightful rose, both growing about 8 in. high. Of those described as star tulips, *C. benthami*, clear yellow with dark central blotch, and *C. maweanus* 'Major', a most delightful species with large cup-shaped white flowers and prominent blue central hairs, are among the finest. Although it is normal to increase stock by the young bulbs which form at the base, calochortus may also be propagated from seeds, which should be sown as soon as they are ripe, either in pots or in the cold frame and then planted out the following season.

Eucalochortus is the name of a group of species which differ from the mariposa tulips in that the flowers are usually pendulous and less showy, while they also have larger foliage. Growing 8 ins high, they are sometimes known as fairy lanterns. The species includes *C. albus*, white; *C. caeruleus*, pale lilac-blue; *C. pulchellus*, golden-yellow flowers on well-branched stems and *C. uniflorus*, lilac-pink, marked in crimson.

A third section of the genus is the cyclobthra, of which most species have campanulate nodding flowers. They are best planted each spring and lifted in November so that they have winter protection.

Calochortus make charming pot plants and are easy to grow in the cold greenhouse or frame. Three or four bulbs in a 5-in. pot provide a really remarkable display. Plant in a compost consisting of loam, peat, leaf-mould, and coarse silver sand with sharp drainage. Stand the pots outdoors and cover with peat fibre. Bring the plants into the greenhouse when top growth can be seen.

CASASSIA These beautiful North American members of the lily family are reminiscent of the European asphodel, producing a profusion of starry flowers. Soaring gracefully to 2 or 3 ft, camassias bloom from May to July before the herbaceous subjects are at their height. They require no special treatment and grow vigorously, increasing if left undisturbed. They need lifting and dividing only about every third year, and only then if they have become overcrowded. All species should be planted in autumn about 4 ins deep and 6 to 9 ins apart, in moist soil,

Camassia esculenta, a strong-growing plant with blue flowers and large, edible bulbs

in sunny or semi-shaded positions.

Among the first to bloom in May is *C. cusickii*, which produces tall 2-ft spikes of pale lavender, star-shaped flowers with pale golden anthers above a rosette of broad, glaucous foliage. This is an elegant species with the small flowers borne freely in loose racemes.

Long before the first colonists arrived in America, the Indians used to gather the bulbs of some species of *Camassia* and fry them for food. One of the species is *C. esculenta*, often referred to by its Indian name of quamash or the descriptive name of 'bear grass'. *C. esculenta* produces, as early as May, graceful, 18 to 24-in. spikes of showy, rich blue flowers and is particularly effective if planted in groups in the border or naturalized. From a distance, groups of this species create the illusion of a blue haze.

For later flowering from June into July plant the species *C. leichtlinii*. There is a lovely white form. *C. leichlinii* 'Alba' which grows up to 3 ft tall but even more striking is *C. leichlinii* 'Atrocoerulea'. The flowers, on vigorous 3-ft spikes, are brilliant aster-blue and will even flourish and spread if planted in clumps in grass.

CARDIOCRINUM This is one of the most stately of bulbs which for many years has been included in the genus *Lilium* to which it is so obviously related. It is now regarded as a different family and must therefore be dealt with separately. The main botanic differences between the two are that the bulbs of *Cardiocrinum* are made up of few scales, formed from the base of leaves of previous season, whereas liliums have scales arising at the base of the stem axis.

Cardiocrinums have broad, cordate, basal foliage with smaller stem leaves, while liliums have basal leaves which are almost identical with those on the stem and which disappear when the bulbs are fully mature. The best and finest cardiocrinum is *C. giganteum*, a Himalayan plant which produces, in July, noble spikes 8 to 10 ft high, with up to 18 trumpet-shaped flowers 5 to 6 ins long. Each is white outside and is marked in red on the inside.

After flowering, the main bulb dies but not before producing several offsets. These should be separated and replanted. A stock can also be

secured by sowing seed preferably into flowering positions. Seed-raised plants take at least 7 years to reach maturity.

This is a fine subject for woodland gardens, associating well with shrubs, including rhododendrons. A lime-free soil and one which does not dry out at any time is best for the bulbs, which should be planted shallowly, 2 ins being deep enough.

CHIONODOXA This name means glory-of-the-snow in Greek, and that was exactly how these flowers appeared to their discoverer, George Maw, who found them less than a century ago in the high mountains of Asia Minor, blooming in great sheets of blue just as the snows were melting away. They look most effective when planted in a similar fashion, that is, naturalized in great numbers. A few hundred will give you a good start, for chionodoxas seed themselves readily and also increase by offsets, choosing the spots they like best and spreading quite rapidly in the course of a few years.

The dainty, sky-blue flowers of *Chionodoxa* are a most welcome sight in late March or early April, appearing soon after the snowdrops and

Chionodoxa sardensis has smaller but more richly coloured flowers than the commoner *C. luciliae*

along with the deeper blue scillas which they resemble somewhat. Once seen together, however, you will never mistake them, for the chionodoxa's cluster of blue flowers, each with its starry white centre, always faces up to the sky, while the early scilla nods its head and is deeper blue.

For your first planting, choose a sunny location in light, sandy soil which retains its moisture during the growing and flowering season. The plants are especially effective at the base of spring flowering shrubs such as the bright yellow forsythias or the creamy-white magnolias. Plant them, too, at the edge of light, open woods, along woodland paths, in the rockery, on corners of a stone retaining wall, in the lawn or even under deciduous trees. They can be used in windowboxes too.

Set the small, pear-shaped bulbs about 3 ins deep and as close as an inch from each other. If you are a patient gardener you can set tham 2 to 3 ins apart and after a few years they will have increased to give their true 'patches of sky' effect.

51

The Cambridge-blue *C. luciliae*, whose flowers have a clear, snow-white centre, is perhaps the most popular of all species. There are 6 to 12 flowers on each 4-in. stem, and the 3 or 4 broadly linear leaves appear at the same time as the flowers. This species has a delightful form 'Pink Giant', which produces large, sturdy spikes of cattleya-violet flowers.

C. gigantea is taller, upwards of 6 ins high, with somewhat fewer flowers to each stem, but each flower is definitely larger, almost 2 in. across. The colour is a glorious lavender-blue with a clear snow-white centre.

Chionodoxa sardensis is the earliest species to flower. The small flowers are true gentian-blue and have a very small, barely noticeable white centre.

Once planted, chionodoxas need little care, but will benefit from a top dressing of really old, well-rotted manure, or good soil and leaf-mould mixture, every 3 or 4 years.

Through proportionately small in stature, the flowers last well when cut. Arrange them in small bowls by themselves or with other spring blooms of similar size to brighten up your home.

CHLIDANTHUS

CHLIDANTHUS *Chlidanthus*, whose name means 'delicate flower' is related to *Hippeastrum* and *Sternbergia*. The bulbs succeed out-of-doors in warm, sheltered gardens, in favoured parts of Great Britain.

Of the two species generally grown, *C. ehrenbergii*, from Mexico, flowers in June and July. The large bright yellow blooms have a central tube 2 ins or more in length and are flushed green, being produced on 10-in. stems. *C. fragrans*, from Chile, is very similar to *C. ehrenbergii* but has sweet-scented flowers on taller stems, the foliage being glaucous blue.

Only in the mildest districts can *Chlidanthus* be grown out of doors, where they need a fairly rich sandy loam with some peat. Planting is best done during March or early April at which time offsets may be detached to increase stock.

Take up the bulbs in autumn and store them in sand until spring, although in very warm, well-drained situations they can be left outdoors so long as they are given extra protection with bracken or strawlitter.

CLIVIA Of South African origin, these plants are easy to cultivate, with attractive clusters of funnel-shaped flowers on sturdy stems. There are several species, all flourishing in the cool greenhouse or on a window sill, so long as they are kept free from frost.

Often referred to as *Imantophyllum*, many useful hybrids have been raised. The best known is *C. miniata*, which has several forms and is a native of Natal; the bright green, strap-shaped leaves grow from 18 to 24 ins long and the 15 to 18-in. stem is surmounted with an umbel of 12 to 18 campanulate, scarlet flowers. Each one has a yellow throat, making an effective display during the winter. *C. nobilis* is not quite as large as *C. miniata* and has orange-red flowers, the petals of which are tipped with green. *C. gardenii* is a less usual species, the orange-red petals being green-tipped. The flowers of all varieties are scented and followed by large bright red berries.

Plants can be raised from seed sown in the spring, but this is a long process and it is usually easier carefully to divide the fleshy roots. A compost of 2 parts loam, 1 part decayed manure, plus silver sand and a dusting of charcoal, suits the plants which like plenty of moisture during their growing period. They should only be disturbed when it is necessary to divide, in fact they seem to flower better when pot bound. Well-established plants will benefit from a few applications of liquid manure when in full growth.

COLCHICUM These boast larger and more spectacular flowers than the autumn crocus for which they are sometimes mistaken. They are not crocuses at all but belong to quite a different family. The most noticeable difference is in the leaves. Autumn crocuses have narrow, strap-shaped leaves, which appear shortly after the blooms and die down in due course. Colchicums, however, produce their gorgeous blooms in late summer and autumn, before the leaves develop, which is why they are sometimes known as naked ladies. In early spring they flaunt stems, usually with four of five broad gleaming leaves, sometimes stretching a foot or more long. These must be left to ripen and die down before they are cut back in July.

A well-established group of *Anemone blanda*

Clivia miniata 'Citrina'

Iris reticulata 'Joyce'

Erythronium dens-canis

These leaves are showy and prominent which means colchicums must be carefully sited in the garden. They are not suited to a rock garden or the front of a border, but are lovely in grass which does not have to be cut in spring, or when employed in bold groups in shrubberies or in drifts under shrub roses. Seen among autumn-flowering heathers such as *Erica cinerea* or *E. vagans*, their goblet-shaped blooms of white, lilac or mauve provide excellent colour harmony. They may also be interplanted with spring-flowering narcissi to give autumn colour.

Colchicums should be planted in late July and August not less than 4 ins down. Flat dwellers will also find that colchicums can be grown for indoor bloom without any soil or water. Simply place the corms in saucers on the window sill and wait for the flowers to open.

C. agrippinum has medium-sized flowers with narrow, pointed, rosy-lilac flowers, chequered in purple. It blooms during September and October but unfortunately is not a strong flower, and is inclined to topple over once the petals develop.

C. alpinum produces medium-sized, rosy-purple flowers from early August onwards. It is not as vigorous as most other species. Few, but long leaves are produced after the flowering period.

C. autumnale is native to Britain and other European countries. The long, narrow, starry petals are a rosy-lilac colour. It grows rapidly once sap actively begins and is often used 'dry' for an indoor decoration, since it will soon come into flower if placed on a saucer in a cool room in early September. The species has several forms including *C.a.* 'Roseum', double rosy-purple. This, however, is not so robust as *C. autumnale* which, once established, flowers freely every year.

C. bornmuelleri, see *C. speciosum*.

C. bowlesianum is a handsome species, which shows colour in November. It has bold flowers, the long rosy-lilac petals being tessellated or chequered purplish-violet. The large leaves appear in the New Year.

C. byzantinum related to *C. autumnale*, is one of the best free-flowering species, being larger than many others. The rosy-lilac flowers are succeeded in early spring by large, broad leaves.

C. giganteum produces really large rosy-purple flowers, notable for the fact that the petals open widely, almost flat.

C. luteum is a scarce species which produces its yellow flowers in spring, usually in early March. The short petals are narrow. This is not a spectacular species and is best grown in the alpine house.

C. sibthorpii has large, rosy-lilac flowers lightly tessellated, with darker lines. The larger bluish-green leaves appear in the spring, spreading out horizontally.

C. speciosum is one of the best-known species and very suitable for general garden culture. The good-sized, globose flowers up to 12 ins high appear in September and October and vary in colour from rosy-lilac to reddish-purple. There is a white form known as *C.s.* 'Album'. The large leaves appear in spring so that planting should not be done too near the lawn.

A number of hybrids have been raised, chiefly in Holland, by using *C. speciosum*, *C. giganteum* and some of the tessellated species. The following are among the very best hybrids which are readily obtainable. 'Autumn Queen', purple-violet with large, cup-shaped flowers; 'Disraeli', deep mauve-blue, well tessellated; 'Lilac Wonder', deep pinkish-violet with thin white stripe; 'The Giant', huge, violet-mauve flowers each with a white base; 'Violet Queen', deep mauve with thin white stripe, mottled; and 'Water Lily', enormous, lilac-mauve flowers.

All hybrids last well in water indoors, and can be grown in saucers without soil or water.

CRINODONNA This is a bigeneric hybrid between *Crinum moorei* and *Amaryllis belladonna*, the latter being the female parent. It has been known for over 50 years and is sometimes referred to as *Amarcrinum howardii*.

Autumn-flowering, the soft pink flowers are reminiscent of *Amaryllis belladonna*, although this hybrid is best grown in the cool greenhouse preferably in large tubs or even in the greenhouse floor. The bulbs are large and therefore not very suitable for pot culture. On stems 2 to 2½ ft high, the large funnel-shaped flowers open during September and October, the leaves being long and persistent similar to those of *Crinum*. This is a very fine subject.

Crinum x powellii

CRINUM   The name of these bulbs comes from a Greek word meaning 'lily'. The genus contains species native to several tropical parts of the world. The biggish bulbs produce ornamental, evergreen, strap-shaped leaves and umbels of funnel-shaped flowers on sturdy stems. They like a rich, loamy sandy soil containing peat or leaf-mould. Firm planting is essential, and potting-up should be done in March, although established plants can be left 3 or 4 years undisturbed, and will benefit by occasional applications of liquid manure during the summer. A few sprayings of clean water will keep the foliage clean and fresh. Propagate by offsets at potting-up time, or seed sown in heat in the spring.

C. moorei is pink, although the shade of pink varies as does the flowering time from late spring to summer. The well formed, campanulate petals are often 4 ins wide. Tender.

C. × powellii is a splended hybrid of which *C. moorei* is one of the parents. On stems $2\frac{1}{2}$ to 3 ft high, it produces up to 10 large pink flowers varying in shade. The long, strap-shaped leaves are bright green. This is probably the best

known *Crinum* which will flourish outdoors, in unexposed places, especially if planted against a south wall, where the flowers open in September. One established, the bulbs will increase, all the more so if left unmoved for some years. It has a pure white form, *c × p.* 'Album', while there are one or two less common named cultivars in varying shades of pink.

CROCOSMIA   This small genus of South African plants is closely related to the tritonias and includes species for long catalogued and thought of as montbretias. The pointed, sword-like leaves combine with the spikes of flowers to make a valuable garden subject as well as providing first-class cut flowers.

Give a deep, well-drained, loamy soil to which leaf-mould has been added. Fresh plantings of these large-flowered corms should be made in February or March. A surface covering of leaf-mould or peat fibre not only gives some immediate protection but provides a summer mulch which is beneficial later in the year. When established, the 'Earlham' varieties are hardy, although if similar mulching to that already advised is given annually in the late autumn, it will afford winter protection and assist in the production of good flower spikes.

The corms should be planted 2 to 3 ins deep, preferably in groups of a dozen or more, allowing 5 or 6 ins between each.

C × crocosmiiflora is the group name of the plants we know best as montbretia. Varying in height from 20 to 36 ins, according to variety, the flowers appear in August and September.

C. masonorum, a particularly beautiful species, produces stems of 2 to 3 ft carrying, in July and August, arching sprays of orange-flame and reddish flowers, the prominent stamens adding to their attractiveness. When cut, the spikes last 10 days or more in good condition, the lower buds continuing to open. The corms are best lifted once the foliage has discoloured and can be replanted again the following spring.

C. pottsii (*Tritonia pottsii*) grows up to 4 ft high. In August its yellow-flushed, orange-red flowers are most attractive. It is one of the family which includes *Montbretia*, although the species itself is not always easy to obtain. It is doubtfully hardy.

Of comparatively recent introduction are the new 'Earlham', large-flowered hybrid montbretias, originated at Earlham Hall, Norwich. They are a great advance on the older types in every way, being taller and stronger in growth, with larger flowers which often measure 3 or 4 ins in diameter. Always decorative in the border, they are first class for cutting.

Choice 'Earlham' varieties include: 'Comet', golden-orange with a band of crimson; 'Fiery Cross', brilliant orange; 'Hades', bright vermilion-scarlet, golden markings; 'His Majesty', velvety scarlet, shading to gold; 'Lady Wilson', bright yellow, shaded in orange and 'Mephistopheles', scarlet petals with crimson-maroon markings. A mixture of 'Earlham' hybrids provides a most charming display.

CROCUS For most gardeners the crocus is one of the earliest spring flowers, but many do not appreciate that it blooms both sides of winter.

There are about 80 species native to central and southern Europe and to many parts of Asia Minor. Most of them are hardy and so easy to grow, and there is a fine selection available for planting in the summer for autumn colour. These are similar in appearance to the spring-flowering crocuses but have striking styles, which divide into numerous stigmatic branches.

Autumn crocus species are hardy and, left undisturbed, increase readily from self-sown seed and cormlets. A small patch in borders, rock gardens, shrubberies, woodland or in grass, soon spreads into into an ever-widening colony of glorious blooms. Autumn crocus grow in any well-drained soil, and they should be planted 3 ins deep and 2 to 4 ins apart in late July and August for best results. They also do well in window boxes or in pans or 'flats' in the cold greenhouse.

The mixed autumn-flowering species are an excellent bounty for those gardeners who want a really good show in naturalized conditions. For a continuous, long-flowering period choose from among the named species. Many flower soon after planting and before producing foliage.

Among the first to bloom in September is *C. zonatus* (*kotschyanus*), a hardy species from the mountains of the Middle East producing large, but dainty, pinkish-brown flowers each with a gold base and orange-gold anthers and borne on slender stems. Its leaves appear after the flowers.

Very early, sometimes flowering even before *C. zonatus*, is *C. banaticus* (formerly known as *iridiflorus*) from the Carpathians. The flowers are pure lavender with light purple stigmata. This crocus is different in that the inner segments are little more than half the size of the outer ones. Plant it in the rock garden in full sun for dramatic display.

About two to three weeks later, the long, broad-petalled flowers of *C. speciosus* burst into bloom bearing bright blue goblets with violet veinings and orange stigmata. The entire

Crocus chrysanthus

speciosus group comes from the Middle East including the pure white form, *C. speciosus* 'Albus', with rich red stigmata. This free-flowering crocus blooms from late September into October, and is delightful when planted with groups of *C. pulchellus* which boast big sky-blue flowers, each silvery-blue at the base and with white anthers. This species originated in Turkey.

C. speciosus 'Globosus' is sweetly-scented

Crocus chrysanthus will spread readily in any fertile soil

segments oblong in shape, and gradually tapering to a short point. The fine flowers are enriched with yellow throats and red stigmata. Grassy leaves are produced at flowering time. The corms are large, some measuring as much as 2 ins across and should be planted in sheltered spots.

The winter-flowering species are quite exceptional in their habit and are free-flowering, and often produce 4 or more flowers at a time. Planted 3 to 4 ins deep in August and September the corms may be left undisturbed and will increase rapidly over the years. In addition to brightening the garden they are ideal for window boxes and terrace containers and can even be gently forced in pots or bowls under cool conditions.

C. chrysanthus is a most variable species and there is now a fine collection of named varieties that begin flowering in January.

If you want indoor blooms during the dark days of winter, plant any of the *C. chrysanthus* varieties in shallow bowls; keep them outside, bringing the bowls in only when the flower buds are showing.

Reliable winter-flowering species include: *C. imperati*, sweetly-scented flowers with violet inner petals and fawn feathered lilac outer petals; *C. korolkowii*, star-shaped, corn-yellow flowers with the exterior striped bronze-purple; *C. ancyrensis*, the golden bunch crocus with 18 to 24 brilliant orange flowers; *C. aureus*, rich orange-yellow flowers; *C. fleischeri*, star-shaped, white flowers with red stigmata.

Also appearing in February is *C. tomasinianus*, a silvery-lilac species from Dalmatia. This species has yielded a quantity of named varieties in shades of pink, mauve and purple. Ideal for naturalizing, it sows itself naturally and spreads rapidly. The most choice varieties include 'Ruby Giant' with long, slender heads of gleaming purple, silver throats and brilliant orange stigmata and 'Whitewell Purple', producing masses of slender tiny flowers of rich, violet-purple which is softer inside, with bright marigold-coloured stamens.

C. biflorus from Asia Minor, the Scotch crocus, blooms in March. The handsome flowers are cream with well-defined, striped markings of purple. When they open in the sun they

with almost spherical small flowers of blue-purple and is the latest of the *speciosus* group to flower. Both, *C. speciosus* 'Cassiope', with silvery petunia-blue flowers and silvery white base, and *C. speciosus* 'Conqueror', with large, rounded blooms of soft violet-blue with a gold flush, enliven the October garden.

In October, too, *C. karduchorum* from Kurdistan reveals its lovely broad-petalled, tulip-shaped heads of silvery violet blue with a creamy base and anthers. Still later, the scented *C. longiflorus* (*odorus*) which comes from Sicily and Malta has slender, pointed soft-lilac petals with orange stigmata. Grass-like leaves are produced at flowering time.

C. ochroleucus is a lovely species growing 4 ins tall with longish, milk-white flowers, a bright orange base and white anthers. This crocus from the rocky districts of the Lebanon and Galilee produces its leaves before it blooms and does well in both rock garden and border. Showiest of all the late-flowering crocus is *C. medius*, with pretty oval flowers of lilac-blue with brilliant flame-coloured spreading stigmata.

C. salzmannii hails from the Tangier area and boasts lovely rosy-lilac flowers with outer

58

reveal shining white segments with a yellow base and emit a honey-like fragrance. The unusual *C. balansae*, orange-yellow within and marked faintly on the outside with rich mahogany-brown, comes from Turkey, and blooms in March.

A late species, flowering in March and April, is *C. vernus* from the Swiss and Italian Alps. Buy *C. vernus* 'Vanguard' which has large flowers of silver-grey which are clear lavender within. *C. vernus* is the source of the magnificent, large-flowered crocus which blooms late in March and in April. Many named varieties are available including: 'Enchantress', lilac-mauve with conspicuous orange stigmata; 'Grand Maitre', lavender-violet with a silvery gloss; 'Kathleen Parlow', pure white; 'Purpureus Grandiflorus', glorious deep purple; 'Queen of the Blues', silvery-lilac with really large flowers; 'Remembrance', rich deep blue; 'Striped Beauty', white with rich purple markings; 'The Bishop', deep purple with a satiny sheen and 'Yellow Giant', bright golden-yellow.

All the large-flowered crocus can also be grown in pots, pans and bowls in the greenhouse or indoors and need very little attention.

CYCLAMEN This is a genus of distinct and beautiful plants with fleshy, corm-like tubers. The name itself comes from a Greek word *kyclos* meaning 'circular' and refers either to the rounded tubers and leaves or to the spirally twisted leaf stalk. The common name of sowbread sounds much less pleasant.

The long-stalked leaves are more or less ovate-heart shaped, each slender flower stem carrying a single, nodding bloom. As the flowers pass over, the stems twist spirally and if left, the seed capsule becomes pressed into the soil, and this is the plant's natural method of sexual reproduction.

The cyclamen can be conveniently divided into three groups, those which flower in autumn, and the spring-flowering species, both of which are hardy, and the large-flowering *Cyclamen persicum*, which requires greenhouse treatment. Several forms of the latter are sometimes known as *C. latifolium*.

Beginning with the hardy species, by careful selection it is possible to have flowers in bloom from August to May. These dwarf-growing plants require a well-drained position where they are sheltered from ground winds and do not get the early morning sun. They are well adapted for growing at the foot of a north wall or under the shelter of trees or shrubs, where they look charming. They also naturalize well in grass where the site is cool and shady, or in the rock garden in a prepared place which has good drainage and partial shade, but do not naturalize too well on highly acid soils.

The most suitable soil is a mixture of good, fibrous loam, well-decayed leaf-mould, and a generous proportion of old mortar rubble. The corms should be covered with about 1½ ins of soil and a top dressing of old leaf soil will prove beneficial, especially in exposed districts.

C. africanum likes a warm situation, with blush flowers during September and October, while

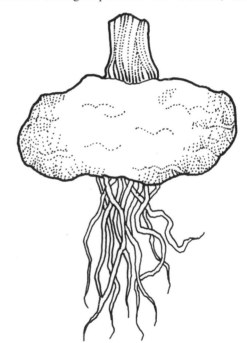

Cyclamen atkinsii

the large heart-shaped leaves, zoned with silver, are fully developed in December. This fine variety is somewhat similar to *C. neapolitanum*, but with larger foliage.

C. cilicicum is a compact grower, the rounded, marked leaves showing at the same time as the fragrant, whitish-pink flowers, which have a purple basal blotch. It does best in a warm situation.

C. europaeum shows its fragrant rosy-red flowers from August to October, the pretty silver-marbled leaves appearing at the same time as the flowers–in fact this variety frequently retains its foliage all through the year. Plant the corms about 4 ins deep.

C. fatrense is a newly introduced species that is rapidly becoming available. It is very similar to *C. europaeum* but has matt green leaves and flowers from June until August, thus linking the flowering seasons of *C. repandum* and *C. europaeum*. It fills a gap and means that one can now have cyclamen in flower all the year.

C. graecum bears pure white flowers each with a purple spot at the base in September and October, followed by beautifully marked leaves.

C. mirabilis is a newly re-introduced species and is very similar to *C. cilicicum* but differs in its fringed petals.

C. neapolitanum (sometimes known as *C. hederaefolium*), produces abundant rosy-pink flowers during August and September, each bloom having a violet-purple spot at its base. The leaves, which develop just before the flowers disappear, are ivy-shaped and marbled in silver. This particular sort is most valuable in that its foliage acts as ground work for such spring-flowering bulbs as scillas, snowdrops, and the like *C.n.* 'Album' has white flowers which are succeeded by marbled foliage.

C. rohlfsianum produces large, corky tubers and, in September and October, reddish-pink flowers. Not really hardy, it is best grown in the frost-free greenhouse.

The spring-flowering species include some which show colour as early as February. Taking them alphabetically, we start with *C. atkinsii*, which was once regarded as a separate species, but is now considered to be a form of *C. orbiculatum.*

C. creticum has scented, white flowers with narrow, rather wavy petals. There also appears to be an uncommon pink form. It needs a sheltered warm spot and it does well in pans in the cool greenhouse.

C. libanoticum has pink flowers which show from late February onwards following the foliage, which is an attractive deep green colour, marked with a lighter shade and usually crenulated. This species is best grown in the alpine house or frame.

C. orbiculatum is the name under which quite a large number of spring-flowering species are grouped. Most have the habit of producing flower buds which seem to develop horizontally before growing upright as they begin to show colour. They are very hardy, the flowers frequently unfolding during really bad weather.

Anyone who has seen these flowers making their colourful display in the early part of the year, particularly when planted beneath winter flowering shrubs such as *Hamamelis mollis*, will know how attractive they are.

The flowers of all forms appear on stems of 2 to 3 ins and especially in the case of those usually sold as *C. atkinsii*, *C. coum* and *C. ibericum*, it is almost impossible to see any difference particularly in the case of the pink or purplish-magenta forms. *C. coum* is still offered in catalogues, distinction being made of the forms given, including *C.c.* 'Album', white; *C.c.* 'Roseum', pink; and *C.c.* 'Rubrum', crimson. The white forms show up well especially if planted where they are not splashed with soil.

A variety of *C. orbiculatum*, known as 'Hiemalis', often flowers in early February. Each magenta-carmine petal has a dark spot at its base. The leaves are prettily zoned in silver.

Though most varieties produce a continuous display of colour, occasionally some are a little intermittent in their blooming but, when this is so, the length of the flowering period is extended.

Hardy cyclamens are propagated by seed which is best sown as soon as ripe and freshly gathered, in pots or boxes in a cool frame, using a good, open compost. When big enough to handle, the seedlings may be planted in their flowering positions, preferably sheltered by some straw or bracken during their first winter.

Whenever possible, a top dressing of fine leaf soil, with a sprinkling of bone meal, will be greatly beneficial to all cyclamen and should be applied in mid-summer, before the new growth appears. Cyclamen seed will not generally come true to type.

Whatever variety is planted, once the corms are established they will grow close enough to form a carpet which will prevent weeds from developing, and the brightly coloured flowers will be freely produced in all weathers. Thus they provide an invaluable ground covering of foliage and also colour in positions which often remain bare and uninteresting.

Cyclamen persicum is among the best of the winter-flowering bulbous subjects and very popular for Christmas decoration. The root is actually a corm and not, strictly speaking, a bulb. These cyclamens are usually raised from seed which can be sown either in August or early in the New Year, since this plant requires a fairly long growing season, and good flowering plants cannot be obtained from late sowings. It is important to keep the plants growing well through their first winter, giving good ventilation to maintain healthy specimens of good colour.

For seed sowing, use well-drained pans or shallow boxes of light, rich compost, placing the seed $\frac{1}{2}$ in. apart and $\frac{1}{4}$ in. deep. Keep these in a temperature of around 60° F. and cover them with glass and paper until growth is seen, or use a propagating case. Germination may take 4 or 5 weeks. When 2 or 3 leaves have formed, transfer the seedlings to small pots, using a compost containing plenty of leaf-mould and sand. Keep the seedlings near the glass and in full light in a warm place until June, when they can be moved into their flowering pots, which should be the $4\frac{1}{2}$ or 5-in. size.

Do not damage the roots and take care not to bury the corms too deeply, for moisture must not settle on the top surface. Keep them shaded for 3 or 4 days so that they settle down quickly. Gradually harden off the plants and stand them in the cold frame for some weeks during the summer, where they have shade from bright sunlight, but are well ventilated. Give feeds of liquid manure at 10-day intervals. At the end of September, the plants can be taken into the cool greenhouse or living room.

Discoloured foliage and dying flowers should be pulled off with a sharp twist so that a stub is not left. Never overwater or let the pots stand permanently in water. Keep them out of draughts and away from gas fires.

The corms can be kept for subsequent years and for this purpose moisture should be gradually withheld so that the compost becomes almost dry. In early August, the corms should be started into growth either by giving them new pots or simply soaking the compost. August, too, is the time to buy new corms for planting up and the same growing process is required as for seed-raised plants. This should result in flowers developing from the end of November onwards.

There are few disorders likely to affect cyclamens but the condition sometimes known as windmill flowers, in which the petals are misplaced, is usually due to irregular watering. When the flowers have exceptionally long stems, or when the stems are extremely short, this is caused by a phosphoric acid deficiency. Cobbled or distorted leaves are caused by attacks of aphids, while the withered edges on the foliage occur where the roots have been allowed to dry out for a period, although occasionally lack of potash will produce the same appearance.

A number of first-class mixtures are offered by the leading seedsmen including *C. persicum* 'Giganteum' and 'Giganteum' fringed mixed; 'Papilio' mixed are sometimes known as butterfly cyclamens because of their beautifully frilled petals. The new 'Puppet' mixed is a miniature counterpart of the 'Giant Flowered' type producing a wealth of sweetly scented flowers on strong stems. 'Puck' mixed grows only 6 ins high and is an early-flowering mixture, the colours being mainly in pastel shades. This mixture has the advantage of flowering about 6 or 7 months from time to sowing. A fairly new variety known as 'Grandia' is a spectacular development since the plants produce immense pink flowers with very waved petals.

DIERAMA   The name of this small genus of South African plants means a funnel which is an indication of the shape of the flowers. The most popular species, *D. pulcherrima*, is sometimes known as *Sparaxis pulcherrima*, or, more familiarly, the wandflower, owing to its habit of swaying gracefully in the wind. It is a perennial, bulbous plant growing 4 to 6 ft high. The foliage is strap-like, and the slender but strong flower stems produce many gracefully pendent, funnel-shaped, tawny-red blooms during August, September, and frequently well into October.

D. pendula, growing 3 to 4 ft high, is a most dependable species with lilac flowers. Although more easily procurable in mixture, it is possible to obtain seedlings to colour and named varieties are also available. Among the best of these are: 'Merlin', with fine large purple blooms; 'Heatherbell', pink flushed with rose; 'Magic Wand', pale lavender-pink; 'The Dove', soft shell-pink; and 'Alba', pure white.

The corms should be planted 3 or 4 ins deep in early November, which will be almost as soon as the long-ribbed foliage has died down. Give them a favourable, well-drained, sandy but not dry position where there is shelter from early frosts, which otherwise might mar the later blooms. A covering of straw or bracken during winter will protect the corms and prevent damage in the event of a prolonged spell of severe weather.

A newer, dwarf variety, growing about 3 ft high has flowers of deep carmine. It blooms during June and July and is a welcome addition to the number of bulbous subjects suitable for the herbaceous border.

DRACUNCULUS Closely related to the arums, and at one time grouped with them, *Dracunculus* has now been officially recognized as a small separate genus. This is because of some particular botanical differences, including the fact that some leaves are divided.

D. canariense, from the Canary Islands, is rare and, if obtainable, needs to be given winter protection. The narrow spathe is pale greenish-white and the spadix is bright yellow. *D. vulgaris*, sometimes known as the dragon arum, grows 18 to 24 ins high. The fleshy stem is prominently spotted, the spathe being purplish-green on the exterior and reddish-maroon inside. When fully open in May and June, it is as much as 10 ins long and 6 or more ins wide. The tapering spadix is almost black.

The strong, nasty smell this plant emits is made worse by the flies and other insects which have been attracted to the plant. The large leaves are the most attractive asset this subject has, although as an ugly curiosity which always draws attention it is worth growing in a warm position away from the house!

ENDYMION This name is unfamiliar to many gardeners but as the result of a change of nomenclature it is now the title of the plants we know so well as bluebells which at various times have been classed as hyacinths and most familiarly as the taller scillas.

British woodlands are decorated in spring by bold displays of bluebells which are seen at their best under the light shade of trees where the soil does not dry out.

E. non-scriptus is the common English bluebell and is still generally catalogued as *Scilla nutans*. It looks best planted in groups. The bulbs should be placed 3 ins deep and can be left to form really large clumps, when they can be divided as necessary.

E. hispanicus is the Spanish bluebell frequently catalogued as *Scilla hispanica*. It has larger spikes, with bigger florets than the English bluebell, and will grow as well in the open garden as in semi-shade. The colour is variable from deep to pale blue, while there are pale pink and white forms. Some of the best have been selected and given names such as 'Excelsior', deep blue; 'Mount Everest', white; and 'Queen of Pinks', lilac-pink. All of them flower in May.

ERANTHIS Much better known as winter aconites, these are dwarf-growing, tuberous-rooted perennials each crown producing solitary yellow flowers with from 5 to 8 petals or, more correctly, sepals, since the actual petals are quite small and insignificant.

Where well placed the small tubers increase freely, although winter aconites may also be propagated by seeds. These should be sown as soon as ripe in a sandy, porous loam which does not dry out too quickly. The seed is frequently very slow to germinate, often remaining quite dormant until the following spring, and it will take at least 3 years before such seedlings are large enough to flower. The compost should therefore not be disturbed if seedlings are a long time in appearing.

All species do well under trees and shrubs where little else will grow, or in moist places.

Eranthis hyemale

or shrub border. Although not strictly a bulb, the dormant crown consists of a series of thick and fleshy white roots, arranged in a star formation round the centre. They have been likened to an octopus. These should be planted in humus-rich soil in September or October, the crown covered with only $\frac{1}{2}$ in. of sand with the spider-like roots only 2 to 3 ins deep. Plant them in groups about 2 ft apart in sunny, sheltered borders with a background of shrubs for maximum impact, and leave them undisturbed for 3 years or so, simply adding dried manure and leaf-mould.

The huge, round shoot appears in spring, the glossy-green foliage developing rapidly to a full rosette. The floral stem of round, stiff and fleshy sections rises from the centre of the clump, the upper half bearing the massive floral raceme with hundreds of star-shaped flowers. For May flowering, choose *Eremurus bungei*, a species with bright golden-yellow flowers with orange-coloured anthers and narrow leaves, about 3 to 4 ft tall. The flowers are long lasting and make excellent and unusual cut flowers. The crowns should be mulched in winter as a protection against frost.

For June flowering, *E. robustus* bears superb racemes of lovely rosy-pink flowers on giant 8 to 9-ft stems. The race of 'Shelford' hybrids raised by F. G. Preston have long handsome spikes 4 to 5 ft tall, bearing flowers in a wide range of beautiful shades varying from soft salmon, orange, sulphur-yellow through to golden brown. They do best in sunny positions sheltered from winds.

E. elwesianus (*nobile*) is strikingly beautiful with huge spikes up to 10-ft tall, the flowering portion being 3 to 4 ft and light pink. *E. himalaicus* produces, in June, elegant, large, snow-white flowers on 6 to 8-ft stems, the leaves looking like green swords dropping acutely under their weight.

When established they provide an attractive, green ground cover. Plant the tubers 2 ins deep in autumn or early winter and they can be left to naturalize where the soil is fairly well drained. Autumn is the best time to divide the roots, when necessary, and a good show of early colour over a period of may years can be ensured with the minimum amount of trouble.

E. cilicica is golden-yellow, and the much-divided leaves have a bronzy tinge. *E. hyemalis* has bright, glistening golden-yellow flowers resting on emerald-green irregularly lobed leaves. *E. sibirica* is late blooming, in fact, it often does not flower until March or April.

As a result of hybridization mainly between *E. hyemalis* and *E. cilicica* several good hybrids have been raised including: *E. × tubergenii* having deep yellow scented flowers; and *E. × t.* 'Guinea Gold', a later flowering variety, is deep yellow, with bronzy foliage.

EREMURUS Known as the fox-tail lily or desert candle, this is a spectacular garden flower. The blooms look like giant candles or huge hyacinths and make a focal point of any flower

ERYTHRONIUM These are most graceful spring-flowering bulbs, the flowers having attractive reflexed petals. The prettily blotched leaves add to the value of this subject.

There are many species, although some are to be found only in North America, either in the wild or in specialists' collections. Botanically,

Erythronium dens-canis, the dog's tooth violet, so-called from the shape of the corms

Erythronium tuolumnense, a dog's tooth violet with large yellow flowers

they can be divided into several groups, although the distinguishing features of each group are of most interest to plant breeders and botanists rather than to practical gardeners.

The following list includes the best known and most readily obtainable species.

E. albidum has narrow leaves and white sometimes tinted blue, nodding flowers on 8 or 9-in. stems.

E. americanum is yellow, varying in depth, the petals usually being flushed or marked red. Although growing only 5 ins tall, the flowers are as much as $2\frac{1}{2}$ ins in diameter the thick leaves being blotched brown.

E. californicum grows happily in British gardens where the soil does not dry out. Growing 9 to 12 ins high, the stems carry wide-spreading, creamy-white reflexed flowers and heavily mottled leaves. Reports show that this species grows much larger in its Californian home.

E. dens-canis is the European dog's tooth violet and a favourite with British gardeners. The common name is derived from the likeness

of the small tubers to dog's teeth. Fortunately, this species will grow well under widely differing soil conditions but prefers an open woodland site, flourishing in the dappled shade provided. The flowers, which appear in March and April, vary in colour from white to pink and pinkish-mauve, all with orange-red markings at bases of petals. There are several first-class named forms including 'Frans Hals', reddish-violet; 'Rose Beauty', pink, and 'Snow-flake' white.

E. grandiflorum has golden-yellow flowers and deep green leaves. Not so strong growing as most species, several forms are known, the distinguishing feature being the different coloured anthers.

E. hendersonii is a strong grower with 6 to 10 mauve flowers on each stem. Flowering in April, it gives a good display once established.

E. revolutum, sometimes known as the trout lily because of its heavily mottled leaves, is a first-class species. The colour varies from white to lavender-white through to pink, 1 to 3 flowers with boldly recurved petals being produced on each 5 or 6-in. stem in April and May. Among the various forms the best one is 'Pink Beauty', a fine hybrid with rich pink flowers.

E. tuolumnense has golden-yellow flowers and light green, unmarked leaves. Left to become established in a rich, damp soil with plenty of leaf-mould, and where there is semi-shade, it will increase freely and give a pleasing display. The star-shaped flowers appear on stems 10 to 12 ins high. All should be planted 3 or 4 ins deep.

EUCHARIS A native of Colombia, and known as the Amazon lily, this is a warm greenhouse subject of stately appearance, not grown as often as it deserves. The bulbs, best planted in the early summer, are of medium size, and although it is possible to grow one successfully in a pot with a $3\frac{1}{2}$-in. diameter, 3 or more in a larger receptacle prove the most effective, especially as the foliage is evergreen. A temperature of not less than 65° F. is needed when the plants are in growth.

The best mixture for potting consists of 2 parts rich loam, 1 part each of leaf-mould and rotted cow manure, and a little bone meal and silver sand. The pots should be well crocked for thorough drainage, and a lump of charcoal added.

Eucharis dislike frequent potting and a good plan with established plants is to remove the top soil from the pot annually, replacing it with fresh, rich compost and feeding with liquid manure when growth is in full progress. This aids the production of good blooms. Except during the late autumn and early winter, the pots should be freely watered. In fact, it is possible to keep the plants in constant growth by watering them according to season. Plenty of light should be given, and if the leaves are sprayed frequently this will keep down attacks by mealy bugs and thrips whilst providing the humid atmosphere this plant likes. When division is necessary, this should be carefully done in the spring. It is occasionally possible to obtain seed.

There are many species, all bearing umbels of fine white scented flowers, of which the best known is *E. grandiflora*, or *amazonica*, each 18 to 24-in. stem producing 5 or 6 pure white sweetly scented flowers 4 in. or more in dia-

meter. This is a favourite market variety and is often grown in very large receptacles, where the bulbs remain and go on flowering for many years. Other good species are *E. sanderi*, which is rather smaller than *E. grandiflora*; *E. lowii*, of which the petals curve slightly back; and *E. candida* of which the drooping white flowers are flushed yellow at the centre. To keep the plants in good order a minimum winter temperature of 65° F. is necessary. Flowers can be had in succession by planting batches of bulbs at different times, although the main flowering period is from December to March.

EUCOMIS This small genus from South Africa, known as the pineapple flower or king's flower, is still not grown as widely as it deserves. The large bulbs produce oblong, lanceolate, wavy leaves sometimes 2 ft or more long and 2 or 3 ins wide, spotted purplish-brown underneath. At the top of each stout 12 to 14-in. flower spike is a densely-packed head of waxy-looking flowers surrounded with a little tuft of leaves or, really, bracts.

Eucomis like a light, rich, well-drained, gritty soil. A warm, sheltered position at the base of a wall suits them admirably. A winter mulching of leaf-mould or weathered ashes will prove beneficial in giving protection.

There are several species, but *E. comosa* or *punctata* is the best known, its spiky, creamy-yellow, star-shaped flowers appearing in July and continuing into September. The pleasing scent emitted by the blooms, which have deep violet centres, gives rise to the name pineapple flower. Other good species include *E. robusta*, with narrow, pointed leaves and greenish-brown, bell-shaped flowers; *E. autumnalis*, better known as *E. undulata*, greenish-yellow; and *E. bicolor*, a vigorous sort with greenish-yellow petals edged purple. *E. pole-evansii* is rare, the flower stem growing as much as 5 ft high. The yellowish-green flowers are often tinged white when young.

Stock is increased by offsets, which frequently form around the main bulbs and may be detached at planting time in early spring, or seed may be sown under glass as soon as ripe, in pots or boxes of good compost, although the resultant seedlings will not reach flowering size until about 4 years old.

Eucomis make excellent pot subjects and should be planted early in the year, using a rich rooting medium.

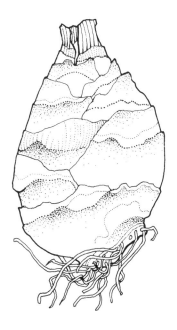

Eucomis punctata

FREESIA Among spring flowering greenhouse bulbs none is more graceful than this subject. Of S. African origin its elegance, beauty and fragrance make it most popular. It forms fibrous coated corms which produce narrow leaves and attractive tubular flowers on strong wiry stems up to 2 ft high.

Plant the corms an inch deep during August and September. A pot with a 5-in. diameter will accommodate 5 or 6 corms which, with proper management, will flower from February until April. A suitable planting mixture consists of 4 parts good loam, 1 part each of silver sand, rotted manure, leaf-mould and a sprinkling of lime rubble.

Place the pots on cylinders or ashes in a cold frame or sheltered place until growth is seen. Keep the soil moist and give cover and ventilation as necessary. Wherever possible, cover the pots with coconut fibre or peat.

Remove suckers should they appear, and give the slender shoots the support of twiggy sticks to keep them erect.

About the middle of October, transfer the pots to a greenhouse, in which the temperature is about 55° F. Once the flower spikes are seen, feed with liquid manure at 10-day intervals. This will encourage the production of good blooms and aid the formation of offsets, which is a reliable way of keeping stock true to character, for corms raised from seed vary considerably from the parent plant.

As the flowers wither they should be removed, although it is best to avoid cutting the foliage at any time. Gradually withhold supplies of water to encourage the new corms to dry off and rest until the following August when they can be potted again. Freesia corms can also be planted in the greenhouse border.

There is now a strain of freesias which can be planted directly into the garden, placing them 2 or 3 ins deep in April or early May. Plenty of moisture should be available, and the sweet scented blooms provide colour for 7 or 8 weeks. The colour range is wide, but these corms cannot be grown for more than one season in the garden so that a new supply must be obtained annually.

Freesias are known to have been in cultivation for well over 170 years, but they have only been grown on a large scale since the beginning of this century. The highly perfumed, white *F. refracta* 'Alba', was for many years the most-widely grown sort, but tremendous advances have now been made. As the result of much hydridizing there are now dependable strains which produce large flowers on strong stems.

A further great advance is that very many varieties now come fairly true from seed, and the most beautifully coloured varieties can be brought into flower by the gardener without any technical knowledge. If seed is sown at fortnightly intervals from April until June a succession of flowers can be obtained from early December until April. The best sowing mixture for freesias consists of clean light loam, good peat, silver sand with a sprinkling of bone meal. Large pots or fish boxes may be used for sowing the seed, which should be spaced about 2 ins apart and covered with a $\frac{1}{4}$ in. of soil. Sowings can also be made directly into the greenhouse floor. Germination of seed is not always reliable and can be helped by 'chitting' the seed in advance. To do this, lightly chip the hard seed coat, then mix the seed with damp peat and keep in the warm until there are signs of germination when the seed can be sown in compost. Or the seed can be soaked in warm water before sowing.

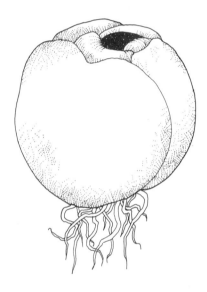

Fritillaria imperialis

FRITILLARIA This is a large genus with a wide distribution reaching from the Mediterranean to China and through to North America, although there are many species which are not in general cultivation, and some are quite rare. They are diverse in size and appearance but almost all the species in cultivation are easy to grow, while the few that are not so are well worth cultivating for their subtle beauty.

Fritillaria like moist soil containing plenty of leaf-mould which, however, should be well drained so that the bulbs do not rot in winter. The dwarf varieties are suitable for the rock garden or the front of the border, while the

tall Imperialis forms look well when properly placed in the border or with shrubs.

F. acmopetala is an easily grown species suitable for a shaded position. It grows 4 to 6 ins high, according to situation, and produces lovely translucent bells of pale, brownish-green shading to yellowish-green, while the petals are often marked in brown.

F. bithynica species grows only 6 to 8 ins high and, in May, produces on slender stems flowers of citron-yellow often shaded in green. The outer petals are faintly marked with red.

F. camschatcensis is a North American species notable for its deep maroon-purple, bell-shaped flowers which appear in May and June. It does well in most districts and soils but should be grown in semi-shade in confined, hot gardens. It is now properly known as *Sarana camschatcensis*.

F. cirrhosa produces 1 to 3 flowers in April

The pure white form of the freesia is among the most exotic of all white flowers

and May on 2 to 2½-ft stems, the main colour being purplish-brown with varied greenish or yellowish shading.

F. citrina see *F. bithynica*.

F. imperialis well known under the name of crown imperial, is an old-fashioned plant quite distinct from all other species. On stems up to 4 ft high, it produces in April clusters of pendent bells of terra-cotta capped with a tuft of bright green leaflets. There are several named varieties bearing flowers in shades of yellow and orange, and of which the height varies from 3 to 3 ft.

The large bulbs, 3 to 4 ins in diameter, are hollowed at the top and it is therefore advisable to plant them on their sides to prevent moisture from entering. If bruised, these bulbs emit an unpleasant smell. A sunny situation where the soil is on the moist side is advisable.

F. meleagris is the snake's-head fritillary, a native of Britain and other European countries. The 8 or 9-in. slender stems bear 2 or 3 pendulous flowers in varying shades of rosy-purple with chequered markings giving rise to another popular name–guinea-hen flower. It flourishes in moist (but not wet) soil and is excellent grown in pots under cool conditions.

Some of the finest forms have been named. These include 'Artemis', with smoky-purple chequerings; 'Charon', deep purple and 'Contorta', a form of *F. meleagris* with united perianth segments.

F. pallidiflora is an uncommon species which, in May, bears greenish-white flowers on stems of 18 ins or more.

F. persica is a little-grown species with stems of 2 ft or more which, in March and April, carry bell-shaped flowers of purplish-maroon, flushed in green and sometimes with pinkish shading.

F. pontica produces, in April, on stems 12 to 18 ins high, moderately large greenish bells tinged in brownish-red. The glaucous green leaves are produced in tufts.

F. pudica is most valuable for the alpine house or can be grown in the open in a well-drained position. On stems of 5 to 8 ins, there appear in April 3 to 5 large, golden-yellow nodding bells.

F. pyrenaica is a hardy species which is easy to grow. This has stems of 8 to 18 ins on which appear, in April, flowers of deep purplish-brown chequered crimson-purple and yellow; the exact colouring varies with the specimen.

F. roylei, see *F. cirrhosa*.

F. recurva is a beautiful but very scarce species producing, in summer, on 1½ to 2½-ft stems, many sharply recurved orange-scarlet flowers with yellow fleckings. The large bulbs like moisture during the growing season but should be kept dry in winter. Difficult but rewarding.

There are many more species most of which are not easy to obtain. Some are unlikely to flourish in British gardens but if an alpine house or cold greenhouse is available, there should be little difficulty in securing good results particularly if the bulbs are allowed to ripen in their pans during summer.

GALANTHUS The snowdrop is one of the most popular of winter and spring flowering subjects. The meaning of the name *Galanthus* is 'milk flower' which is a fair description. Many

Galanthus elwesii

68

people do not realize how many species and varieties there are in cultivation. Some species are similar, varying in the shape of the flowers, the size of the notches and the green markings of the three inner segments.

All the species are remarkably hardy and stand up to the roughest weather. Even when prolonged, severe frosts cause the flower heads to bend, they soon become upright again when conditions change. They will flourish in sun and semi-shade and even in quite shady positions. The common snowdrop, *G. nivalis*, always produces its blooms freely. Snowdrops are not particular about soil, but do best where moisture is available. In very dry ground, the addition of peat and leaf-mould is of great help. Avoid planting where fresh manure has been applied. Organic fertilizer is much more suitable.

Although most gardeners plant snowdrops in the autumn, which is when they are usually offered by bulb merchants, they are really best moved when they are in growth. They come to no harm if lifted and divided as necessary just as they are passing out of flower. Apart from division and the removing of offsets which can be found on the dry bulbs, galanthus can be propagated from seed, the seedlings flowering when they are 3 or 4 years old.

Botanists have placed the species in groups and the following are among the best species and varieties.

G. nivalis is the common English snowdrop. Now naturalized in Britain, it is found in many European countries as well as in Asia Minor. Flowering from January onwards, it has a number of forms including a double, usually listed as *G. nivalis* 'Flore-plena'.

G.n. reginae–olgae flowers in October, the leaves usually following the blooms.

G.n. 'Flavescens' has yellow markings on the inner segments.

G.n. 'Scharlokii' is distinguished by the two leafy spathes, the flowers hanging like a white bell between donkeys' ears.

There are a number of garden forms and varieties of *G. nivalis*. These include 'Atkinsii' a strong tall grower and an excellent garden plant, the flowers first appearing in January. 'S. Arnott' or 'Arnott's Seedling' is another well-formed variety of high merit while the 'Straffan'

Galanthus nivalis 'Lutescens Flore-pleno', the rare double yellow snowdrop

is a vigorous grower and late flowering.

G. corcyrensis begins to flower at the end of November. It does best in a sunny position.

G. graecus, from Greece, has glaucous-green leaves and flowers from January onwards.

Another group of galanthus is that known as the *plicatus*. In this the species usually have flatter, broader leaves than *G. nivalis* varieties. *G. byzantinus* produces large flowers, the markings on the inner segments being deep green.

G. plicatus has large flowers and foliage. Known as the Crimean snowdrop it is not now very common. A variety know as 'Warham' produces double flowers.

The so-called 'Latifolia' group of snowdrops have rather twisted broad leaves, sometimes of a distinct greyish-green.

G. allenii is late flowering on tallish stems.

G. caucasicus flowers from mid-January and is a first-class, vigorous grower.

G. elwesii is one of the best of all snowdrops. Rather late flowering, it has several well-known forms including 'Whitallii' with really large blooms and 'Maximus', with attractive twisting foliage. A variety known as 'Merlin' is a splendid garden plant.

G. fosteri is rather tall growing, although its flowers are small: it does best in unexposed sunny positions.

G. ikariae has broad, shiny green leaves and globular flowers with bright green markings, while *G. latifolius*, sometimes known as *G. platyphyllus*, has wide, strap-like leaves and slender petalled green-tipped flowers in March.

GALTONIA CANDICANS Introduced into Europe about 1870, this subject was named after Frank Galton the British anthropologist. Often known as the summer hyacinth it comes from South Africa and is a member of the lily family.

The large bulbs produce tufts of bold, strap-shaped leaves and strong, erect flower spikes on which, in July and August, appear loose

Galanthus latifolius ikariae is a form of snowdrop with exceptionally large flowers

racemes of 15 to 20 delicately scented and large drooping milky-white bells often tipped in green. The stems, in contrast to those of the spring flowering hyacinth, grow $2\frac{1}{2}$ to 4 ft high.

Galtonia candicans likes sunny, well-drained positions, and if not lifted, appreciates a winter mulch of peat or leaf-mould. An excellent subject for the back of borders, for planting among shrubs and for siting in groups, it looks well among colourful subjects. According to soil conditions, bulbs can be planted from late February into April, 5 or 6 ins deep, and between 6 and 8 ins apart. If you do not intend to lift them after the foliage has died down, double the space between the bulbs.

Summer hyacinths make excellent cut flowers and they can also be grown in pots in the warm greehouse. If potted in early spring they will flower in the late summer. Bulbs should be placed individually in 5 to 6-in. pots in John Innes potting compost No. 2 or a similar mixture.

There are 2 or 3 much less common—almost rare—varieties, *G. clavata* and *G. princeps*, both smaller than *G. candicans*, and not so good for garden decoration.

GLADIOLUS The gladiolus has a history covering several centuries but undoubtedly the ancient species were very different to the varieties in cultivation today. Among the species which have had an influence on modern varieties are the following.

G. byzantinus is often referred to as the hardy gladiolus as it can be left in the ground undisturbed. The colour is an attractive crimson-wine.

G. blandus has been nicknamed the painted lady, its white or pale pink flowers being blotched maroon.

G. cuspidatus is a dwarf growing species suitable for the rock garden, the white flowers being flaked purple.

G. nanus is another dwarf species whose colour varies from white to pale pink and sometimes into carmine. It is noteworthy because it can be planted in the autumn in pots and be plunged out of doors until December, when if brought into the cool greenhouse it will flower during May and June.

Crocus sativus flowers in October

Tulipa kaufmanniana 'J. Strauss'

Crocus chrysanthus form

A Spanish iris

The Kaufmanniana tulips are brilliant in leaf and flo

The early-flowering 'Nanus' group were originally raised from a cross between *G. tristis*, scented, creamy-primose and marked brownish-green, and the red *G. cardinalis*. This group is sometimes identified as *G. × colvillei*. There are many named forms including 'Amanda Mahy',

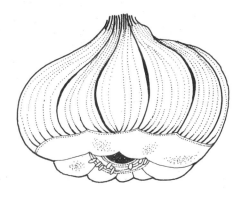

Gladiolus byzantinus

salmon pink; 'Blushing Bride', white flaked carmine; 'Peach Blossom', shell pink; 'Spit-fire', salmon-orange marked violet; and 'The Bride', white.

G. oppositiflora is white with a red band.

G. papilio is greyish-buff, blotched in maroon.

G. psittacinus is rich salmon marked yellow.

G. segetum is rose pink.

Although many gladiolus species are in cultivation, none has had a greater influence on the production of the best modern varieties than *G. primulinus*. The first record of its existence is 1887. Then at the beginning of the century, it was seen growing wild near where a bridge was being constructed over the Zambezi river in Rhodesia. Corms were collected and sent to England. Soon hybridists saw its value and it

was largely used in breeding new varieties, for introducing a wide colour range, and to impart a more dainty appearance to the older, larger-flowering varieties then in cultivation.

All varieties are superb for cutting for indoor decoration, particularly since they are so light and dainty. For a riot of colour in the garden and a succession of spikes for cutting, few flowers compare with the gladiolus. And many varieties are inexpensive for producing excellent flowers for the home and garden from July to September.

Today there are types of gladioli available for all purposes ranging from special beds and mixed border clumps, to cut flowers, flower arrangements and exhibitions. The successful cultivation of all types of gladioli is the same. Almost any soil will do, but to produce the best flower spikes soil should be well enriched and contain plenty of humus, supplied by compost, organic matter or peat. Prepare the ground well in advance, digging at least 8 ins deep, working in a complete organic fertilizer such as Maxicrop or fish manure at the rate of 3 oz. per square yard. Gladioli do not like freshly-manured ground; soil enriched for a previous crop is ideal.

A sprinkling of streamed bone flour along the rows (first removing the mulch) when the lowest flower buds can be seen brings great response from the plants.

When choosing planting sites, select sunny situations and avoid wind-swept positions. Gladioli make excellent decorative plants in beds or borders, especially if grown in irregular groups, but do not plant them among tall plants in the herbaceous border or among shrubs. Those you want for cutting purposes can be planted in separate beds or in rows in the vegetable garden.

Planting can begin at any time after frost is out of the ground and it is dry enough to work easily, usually from mid-March onwards. Successional planting may continue at intervals of 2 to 3 weeks, until mid-May for fine spikes in the autumn. Place the corms 5 or 6 ins deep, and about 8 ins apart, in groups or clusters of a dozen or more. If your soil is heavy, some sand placed underneath the corms will assist their drainage, but on lighter soils this will not be

E

The Gladiolus 'Butterfly Hybrids' are brilliantly marked with contrasting colours at the centre

Types of gladioli. *Left* large-flowered, *centre* 'Butterfly' type, *right* Primulinus type

necessary. Shallow planting will lead to a lot of staking, and many good spikes may be lost in heavy winds, particularly in the case of the large-flowered varieties.

By mid-May, the young shoots of the early plantings will begin to show above the soil. From then on, the soil around the plants should be lightly hoed, taking care not to snick the young shoots. If there is a dry spell in June or July, you should water the gladioli regularly. One good soaking is much more effective than a number of sprinklings, for gladioli like an abundance of moisture. Mulching with compost or moist peat from June onwards is helpful and also keeps down weeds.

Cut the spikes when the first floret shows colour and always leave at least three leaves when you cut gladioli, so that the developing young corms for the following season obtain sufficient nourishment to complete their growth. To produce healthy corms, gladioli like a spell of dry weather for a couple of weeks after they have finished flowering, by which time the foliage will begin to turn brown, and they will be ready for

lifting, which in any case should be done by mid October.

When lifting, save all small corms and cormlets. Label each sort carefully, then cut off the tops an inch or so above corms. Dry off for a few weeks, then discard the husks and old remains and place the new corms in open paper bags or ventilated boxes for the winter, keeping them in an airy but frost-proof place. The very small cormlets can be planted in spring close together in rows about 2 ins deep to produce specimens for the following year.

The large-flowered gladioli provide the widest choice and are generally the most satisfying to cultivate. Easy to grow, the plants reach $3\frac{1}{2}$ to 5 ft in height, and range in colour from white to almost black. They are equally suited to garden decoration and cutting, being particularly valuable where large arrangements are needed.

The following is a list of a few of the most reliable varieties. 'Albert Schweitzer', salmon-orange; 'Flowersong', yellow; 'Purity', white; 'Dr Fleming', salmon-pink; 'Blue Conqueror', violet-blue; 'Eurovision', vermilion-red; 'Uhu', ash grey, salmon and brown.

'Butterfly' gladioli varieties are available in separate colours, all with central markings, producing the appearance of exotic butterflies. The so-called Miniatures grow about 3 ft high, the florets being attractively ruffled. This group contains very attractive varieties. The name is a little misleading since they are not dwarf growing but about the same height as the 'Primulinus' hybrids, and it is the florets which are somewhat smaller. They are first class for bridging the gap between the large-flowered and 'Primulinus' varieties.

'Primulinus' gladioli can be grown in exactly the same way as the large-flowered types but the appearance of the flowers is much less formal. They are almost as attractive and graceful as sweet peas and therefore lend themselves to easy and attractive indoor decoration. The colour range is extremely wide and takes in many art tones not to be found in any other groups, and a mixture will give a very satisfying display.

Introduced in 1968 is the new star-flowered gladiolus, 'Salmon Star', which is a beautiful orange-salmon shade and ideal for cutting. The new 'Early Peacock' hybrids are another distinct race resembling the 'Primulinus' ones but with pointed reflexed petals, and this again is an ideal strain for cutting.

An entirely new race of gladioli raised by Konynenburg and Mark has recently been introduced. Known as 'Coronados' they are the result of a cross between the 'Butterfly' strain and various early flowering varieties as well as the species *G. nanus*. The result is a combination of early-flowering characteristics and the unusual markings of the 'Butterfly' varieties. Most remarkable is the fact that each corm produces two or three spikes.

There is no doubt that the gladiolus is one of the best flowers for summer display, and if the stems are plunged in water immediately they are cut the florets will last in good condition for a long time.

GLORIOSA A native of Central Africa and Rhodesia, sometimes known as the Mozambique lily this, as the name suggests, is a genus of beautiful flowering plants, ideal for growing in the warm greenhouse. From the tuberous roots erupt climbing stems with stalkless, deciduous leaves, not plentiful in number, each with a tendril-like appendage at the point. The lily-like flowers are borne singly towards the tops of the stems, the 6 narrow, slightly crinkled petals reflexing as the flower opens, revealing the 6 prominent stamens.

Although they can be planted direct in the greenhouse border, the best plan is to grow gloriosas in good-sized, well-drained pots of loam, peat and well-decayed cow manure with a sprinkling of bone meal; this should be done when there are signs of new growth early in the year, usually in February. Gradually increase water supplies as growth develops and provide supports while the stems are small. Eventually, the growths will prove decorative on the sides and roof of the greenhouse, especially when the flowers appear from the end of June until August.

Leaves and stems die down in the late autumn and water should then be gradually withheld, so that the tubers remain dormant in winter and have an opportunity to ripen. As far as possible, aim to secure a temperature of 65 to 75° F. from February to September, and about 20° F. lower for the remainder of the year.

G. rothchildsiana, from East Africa, is one of the best known being ruby-red, shaded yellow. *G. superba*, growing up to 8 ft tall or more, is very reliable, and has reflexed orange and red petals. This is the best known and probably the hardiest species. *G. simplex* (*virescens*) bears on $3\frac{1}{2}$ to 4-ft stems, flowers of deep, reddish-orange with yellow bases. A larger form, var. 'Grandiflora' is bright yellow. All these species have varieties of slightly different colouring.

Propagation is by offsets at potting-up time, or seed can be sown in a temperature of 70 to 75° F. in March.

GYNANDRIRIS This genus was formerly included in the iris family but is now classed separately as a monotypic genus.

C. sisyrinchium, a native of Southern Europe, produces in spring and summer showy lilac-blue flowers marked yellow and white. These flowers, borne on 6 to 8-in. stems, rarely last more than a day but this is compensated by the succession of blooms produced.

The corms are very much like those of *Iris reticulata*, being attractively netted. The foliage is similar too. For best results they need to be planted in well drained soil and they like plenty of sun, in fact, in dull seasons they are shy to bloom. Propagation is by offsets.

HABRANTHUS   Closely related to the hippeastrums and zephyranthes, this South

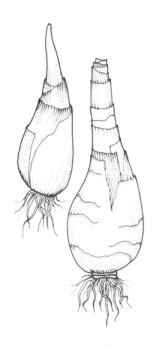

Habranthus robustus

American subject has the common names of knight star lily and batchelor's lily. The magnificent flowers are distinguished botanically by having stamens of unequal length. Although not hardy in all districts they will flourish in warm, sunny, well-drained positions. They seem to like lime and are easily grown in the cold greenhouse. September and October is the right planting period. The funnel-shaped flowers, usually one to a stem, open from May to July according to species. Overpotting should be avoided as the finest flowers are produced by slightly pot-bound plants.

H. advenus see *Hippeastrum advenum*.

H. andersonii is sometimes listed as a *Zephyranthes*. The flowers are golden-yellow, flushed a rich coppery shade with red streaks. The solitary flowers, borne on 6-in. stems, develop from dark-coloured, rounded bulbs. This is the same as *H. texanus*.

H. brachyandrus has solitary, funnel-shaped, violet-rose-pink flowers carried on 12-in. stems. The long leaves often reach a length of 1 ft before the blooms develop.

H. cardinalis bears in June light scarlet, large, funnel-shaped flowers.

H. pratense which has yellow flowers is now known as *Hippeastrum pratense*.

H. robustus is particularly fine and in warm, sheltered places can be grown outdoors although it is at its best in the cool greenhouse. The large pale pink flowers are veined and flushed a deeper pink with green throat markings. Keep dry in winter.

H. versicolor is a fine greenhouse species and usually flowers from October onwards. The red flower buds open to vary pale pink.

HAEMANTHUS   This large genus of African plants has the common names of blood flower and shaving brushes. Ideal for the cool greenhouse, they make a good show when grown in large pots or tubs. The flowers, which are produced in umbels, have long petals and prominent, protruding stamens. The large, coloured bracts at their bases make the flowers even more showy. As with many other members of the *Amaryllis* family, the roots need moisture until the leaves discolour when much less water is needed. This allows the bulbs to rest for a period although in some cases some of the foliage is inclined to persist. Some liquid feeding while the plants are in growth will be helpful but re-potting should e avoided. Too much root room leads to leafy growth at the expense of flowers. Take care not to bruise or damage the fleshy stems. Stock is increased by means of offsets.

H. albiflos, growing to 1 ft has greenish-white flowers in July. *H. coccineus* has huge bulbs producing, from June to September, on 9-in. stems, large heads of bright red flowers with upright stamens.

H. katherinae carries, on 1 to 2-ft stems, during July and August, long umbels of salmon-red flowers. The individual florets are small and thin petalled. This is a handsome plant worth any trouble to cultivate.

H. magnificus is indeed magnificent. The umbels or orange-scarlet flowers borne on 15-in. stems, have given this species the nickname of paint brush. The flowers usually appear before the wavy-edged leaves.

H. multiflorus, with ball-shaped heads of scarlet on 12-in. stems in late spring, is splendid for the greenhouse.

H. natalensis growing to 15 ins has heads of red in spring although it is scarce in cultivation.

H. puniceus is distinct in that leaves and flowers appear together. The colour is a showy vermilion and it makes an excellent greenhouse plant.

HEDYCHIUM Sometimes known as the ginger lily, other common names for this plant include the scented garland flower, or butterfly lily. Most species come from the Himalayas and its surrounding regions. The rhizomes or small tubers produce erect stems on which appear biggish, ornamental, evergreen leaves somewhat like a *Canna*, and in fact the plants may be treated similarly. Although really best in the cool greenhouse during the summer, they will flourish out-of-doors in certain warm southern and western districts, especially if grown in rich sandy loam. Most reach a height of 3 to 4 ft, though on occasions some flower spikes will attain 5 ft. They make good, bold specimens in large pots and should always have plenty of moisture when in growth.

Of the species which flower in summer, *H. coccineum* is bright red; *H. coronarium* is white; *H. densifloram* is orange and *H. gardnerianum* has scented, clear yellow flowers. The last two are hardy out of doors in warm, sheltered positions in the garden. All are propagated by division in the early spring. The roots have a strong ginger smell.

HERMODACTYLUS TUBEROSUS A monotypic genus from Mediterranean districts, this is closely related to the irises. Until recently it was listed as *Iris tuberosa* and is still named as such in some catalogues. This plant has divided, tuberous root-stocks from which bright green, four-sided leaves appear and slender, erect flower stems 12 to 18 ins long. The unusual flowers, which appear in March, have green standards and black falls. Although not showy, it is attractive in its own way and has the two common names of snakeshead iris and mourning iris.

The plant likes a warm, dry soil and a sunny situation. It can easily be increased by division or seed.

HYACINTHUS Although there are several dozen species of hyacinthus, only a few are in cultivation or can be obtained today.

H. amethystinus is one of the loveliest of dwarf bulbs. The 8-in. spikes carry the pale, porcelain-blue flowers in March and April. There is also a white form.

H. azureus forms clustered heads of deep azure blue on 7 or 8-in. stems, the leaves being quite broad.

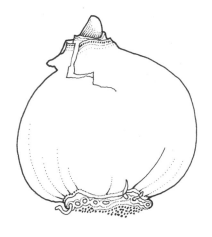

Giant flowered Hyacinth

H. dalmaticus produces, in spring, 6 to 8-in. spikes of pale blue. Not easy to obtain, it is well worth hunting for.

H. orientalis, which varies in colour from white to mauve and purple, is the main parent of the well-known, large-flowered florists' hyacinths which are both decorative and fragrant. It grew wild in Eastern Mediterranean countries centuries before the birth of Christ.

H. romanus is the Roman hyacinth, referred to in old literature as *Bellevalia romana*. Growing up to a foot high, it has spikes of loose, whitish bells.

Hyacinths are amongst the most perfect of all bulb flowers. They have been at home in British gardens ever since that noted English herbalist John Gerarde introduced them to his garden in 1596. During the Victorian era, formal plantings of vast beds of hyacinths were all the rage. Mass plantings are carried out in parks and stately gardens throughout the country, but as private gardens shrink in size, terrace-living becomes fashionable and flat-dwellers multiply in both urban and rural districts, hyacinths are being employed in a host of informal ways.

Bulbs can be planted any time from September to December in Britain, 4 to 5 ins deep and 5 ins apart. But never plant the bulbs when the ground is wet. No special preparation is required for hyacinths and any ordinary well-drained soil in good condition is suitable, although the bulbs prefer a light, rich soil. They like sunny positions and plenty of nourishment but do not allow fertilizers to come in contact with the bulbs.

For outdoor use, 'bedding' grades give excellent results and are more economical than the top size 'exhibition' grades used for indoor forcing. The 'bedding' hyacinths are specially selected, second-sized bulbs, hand picked and healthy; they will produce flower spikes almost as large as the top-size bulbs because they grow more slowly outdoors and have a longer time to make a strong root development.

Hyacinths do not require lifting, but after they have bloomed, cut off the flower stalk and allow the foliage to ripen so that you will have good blooms the following year. The ripening foliage can be concealed with an overplanting of annuals or by loose-growing ground cover. Hyacinths left in place should be given an autumn and spring feeding or top dressing of well-rotted manure or bone meal.

Some gardeners, particularly those who want the space for other plants, prefer to lift hyacinth bulbs each year, replanting the old bulbs in a cutting garden or border and using new bulbs of different varieties in choice spots. It is advisable to lift hyacinths grown in window boxes, tubs or urns to ensure against frost and in any case these receptacles are invariably wanted for other flowers after the hyacinths fade.

Good named varieties include: White—'Arentine Arendsen', 'Carnegie' and L'Innocence'.

Yellow—'City of Haarlem', 'Prince Henry' and 'Yellow Hammer'.

Orange—'Orange Boven'.

Pink—'Anne Marie', 'Lady Derby', 'La Victoire', 'Marconi', 'Princess Margaret', and 'Pink Pearl'.

Red—'Cyclop', 'Jan Bos', and 'Tubergen's Scarlet'.

Blue—'Bismarck', 'Delft Blue', 'King of the Blues', 'Marie', 'Myosotis', 'Ostara', 'Perle Brilliante' and 'Queen of the Blues'.

Mauve—'Amethyst', 'Lord Balfour' and 'Purple King'.

HYMENOCALLIS This large genus of South American plants includes species which were once regarded as a separate group known as *Ismene*. One or two species have in the past been known as *Pancratium*—notably *H. narcissiflora*.

Most species are normally cultivated in the cool greenhouse although one or two are almost hardy. Occasionally, they are grown outdoors in a warm border during the summer and then lifted in early October and kept in the greenhouse, where they need little water, so that the bulbs become almost dormant during the winter. As permanent greenhouse subjects they respond well to good treatment. Regular watering and feeding will usually result in a striking flowering display.

The bulbs, not unlike those of large narcissi, produce strap-shaped leaves and, on strong stems, from 2 to 5 rather spidery flowers. Since the narrow 'trumpet' or cut edged parianth tube is surrounded by spreading, outward curving

Hymenocallis festalis

petals, the shape varies with the different species.

Outdoors, they need planting at least 5 ins deep. Select a sheltered position where the soil is rich in humus matter. The flowers last a long time when cut.

H. amancaes, from Persia, bears bright yellow flowers in June and is a most striking plant for the cool greenhouse.

H. calathina, see *H. narcissiflora*.

H. harrisiana has white, spidery flowers with narrow wavy petals.

H. narcissiflora was once widely known as *H. calathina* and has the common name of chalice-crowned sea daffodil. The white flowers, with long perianth tubes and reflexing petals, are very fragrant.

Several varieties are generally available. A particularly good one is 'Sulphur Queen', in which the pale yellow flowers show green markings.

IPHEION This is now the official name of the early spring flowering South American bulb which was previously known by a number of other names. These include *Brodiaea, Milla* and *Tritelia*. It has the common name of spring starflower. It is however, comparitively minor botanical differences that keeps this genus of one species separated from the brodiaeas.

The pretty, small, pale porcelain-blue (often almost white) flowers borne on 6-in. reddish stems above grassy leaves, are easy to cultivate and very rewarding whether grown in sun or semi-shade. The most common species is *Ipheion uniflorum*. In time, if left undisturbed, the bulbs will increase fairly rapidly to form really large clumps.

Seedlings of *I. uniflorum* show considerable variation, and the two extremes have been selected and grown on for commerical distribution. One is a pure white form, *I.u.* 'Alba', the other a very dark violet form known as *I.u.* 'Violacea'. In gardens where this plant seeds freely it is better to keep the forms separate otherwise seedlings will produce inferior forms.

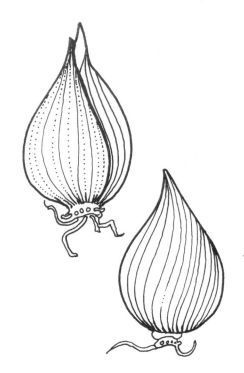

Iris reticulata

IRIS This name means 'rainbow' and these subjects are among the most colourful and

Ismene festalis, known as the sacred lily, has pure white deliciously scented flowers in summer

ornamental of all bulbous plants. They have always attracted amateur gardeners and iris societies have emerged everywhere, especially in Britain, Germany and the United States.

The family is a large one containing nearly 200 species some bulbous, other rhizomatous and they come from virtually all corners of the world.

For convenience the bulbous section can be split into three divisions; the Reticulate group which includes the low-growing *I. reticulata* and *I. danfordiae* blooming in February and March; the Juno irises which are noted for their small standards and the Xiphiums which include the Dutch, Spanish and English irises. The rhizomatous or non-bulbous section includes the beardless, bearded and crested divisions of the family.

Among the best-known and most widely grown of the Reticulate division is *I. reticulata* which grows only 6 to 10 ins tall and flowers in February and March. The sweetly-scented flowers are deep purple-violet with prominent yellow blotches and the thin, pointed foliage is dark green. They grow easily out-of-doors in a

rock garden or in pots indoors. These dwarfs need planting 3 ins deep in a warm sunny position outdoors and prefer light, sandy soil with good drainage.

The Reticulata irises do not need to be grown in a rich soil. Indeed, they do better in a poorer soil. In rich soils the bulbs increase by offsets at a phenomenal rate, and seem so concerned with increasing in this way that they hardly ever bother to flower.

There are a number of *I. reticulata* hybrids available in named varieties. 'Cantab' has dainty flowers of cobalt blue with deep Cambridge-blue falls and tongues of orange. 'Joyce' is a sky-blue variety 5 ins tall with distinctive crest and ivory tongue while 'J. S. Dijt' has sweetly-scented reddish-purple blooms with narrow swords of orange on the falls. Harmony is royal blue with a yellow blotch.

I. reticulata 'Purple Gem', also 5 ins tall, is wine-purple with an ivory-white tongue flecked purple-blue. The sweetly-scented blooms stand erect on 5 in. stems. Just 4 ins tall is *I. reticulata* 'Velvet', in rich, velvety purple tinged bronzy-violet with bright orange crests on the falls.

The sweetly-scented flowers of *I. bakeriana* have slender, lavender-blue standards and unusually marked falls of ivory, heavily dotted deep blue-purple. They grow 4 ins tall and bloom in January and February, the stiff leaves being distinguished by 8 ribs.

I. danfordiae is early-flowering, producing rich golden-yellow flowers on 3 to 4-in. stems from February onwards. Named after Mrs Danford who discovered them in the Taurus Mountains of Turkey less than a century ago, they are as hardy as *I. reticulata* and like warm, sunny positions in the garden. They have a habit of breaking up into small bulbs after flowering and the bulblets will not flower for a year or so. For continuity of bloom fresh bulbs should thus be planted annually.

I. histrio is an early-flowering plant of varying habit. Growing 4 to 6 ins high, the main colour is lilac-blue to reddish-blue with white markings often spotted in gold. Like *I. danfordiae* it sometimes splits to form a number of bulblets after flowering.

I. histrioides 'Major' is clear, nemophila-blue

with a golden yellow crest and flowers as early as January. It likes sunny nooks in the rock garden and withstands frost, hail, rain, and snow successfully despite its 3-in. stature. It is also excellent for growing in pots in the alpine house.

I. vartani is a tender species, its slaty lavender-scented flowers which have a yellow ridge on the falls appearing in December. The white form is the one usually offered in commerce, and is noted for its strong almond scent.

Dutch irises. Botanically classified as *Iris hollandica*, these plants evolved over many years and involved using multiple crossings to broaden the colour range to take in whites, yellows, blues, mauves and purples. They are called Dutch iris, not because they come from Holland, but because they are a distinctly different breed, obtained in 1909 by a famous Dutch breeder of Haarlem.

To develop such a distinctive and handsome group in a family that comprises nearly 200 species in 12 different sections is no mean achievement. But new breeding advances have resulted in improved varieties and a whole series of modern cultivars with noticeably larger flowers.

Today, Dutch irises are by far the largest culti-vated group of the huge iris genus, popular not only with gardeners who like them best in clumps in the rockery, in borders or to set off evergreen shrubs, but with housewives who find them invaluable for floral decorations in the home. They are particularly fine plants with larger flowers than the somewhat similar Spanish iris, and are sturdier and stronger in growth. Compared with English irises, Dutch irises are not only more colourful (there are no yellows among English irises) but produce exotic and delicate blooms with graceful stems and foliage.

Dutch irises produce large flowers of great substance on tall stems ranging from 20 to 24 ins in height. They are long lasting, and among the first of cultivated irises to bloom. Planted in September and October, 3 to 4 ins deep and about 5 to 8 ins apart they will flower from mid-May onwards. Spanish irises bloom at least a fortnight earlier and English irises do not flower until June.

Dutch irises are hardy and accommodating,

flourishing in well-drained soil and under almost any conditions. For best results, plant the bulbs in sunny positions in soil containing plenty of humus. They need little care and attention. Unless overcrowded they need not be lifted and the bulbils that develop round the mother bulbs will flower after 2 or 3 years. When necessary, they can be lifted when the foliage dies down and the bulbs kept dry until it is time to replant them in September.

Dutch irises provide welcome colour for late May or June Clumps of 6 to 12 irises of one or a number of varieties will brighten your rock garden, border, shrubbery or narrow bed along a fence. They are effective clustered around the base of trees and shrubs and will enliven sunny corners beside steps or walls. A selection of named hybrids or mixtures now available are ideal for cutting. The varieties 'Wedgewood' and 'Imperator' are par-

The dark blue *Iris reticulata* makes a good companion to the yellow *I. danfordiae*

ticularly easy to force in the cool greenhouse.

Make your choice from any of the following or a good mixture of these named varieties. 'Golden Harvest', golden-yellow, shaded in orange; 'H. C. Van Vliet', dark violet-blue standards, falls of grey-blue blotched in orange; 'Imperator', indigo-blue with an orange blotch; 'Mauve Queen', standards of mauve-violet, pearl-grey falls with narrow yellow blotches; 'Melody', standards sulphur-white, falls lemon-yellow with orange blotches; 'Princess Beatrix', standards rich yellow, falls buttercup-yellow; 'Princess Irene', standards creamy-white, saffron-yellow falls, each with a golden-orange blotch; 'Wedgewood', standards lobelia-blue, falls flax-blue with yellow blotch; 'White Excelsior', an old favourite, pure white with yellow blotches and 'Yellow Queen', golden-yellow with orange blotches.

Spanish irises. There are many curious and interesting colour blendings in the Spanish irises, which come from Spain and Portugal and flower in about the second week of June. Excellent for beds and borders, not the least of this division's value is the fact that if the flower spikes are cut when in bud they will open well and last a long time in water. Bulbs of Spanish irises should be planted about 3 ins deep during September and October, and like an open, sunny position with a lightish, well-drained soil in which they will multiply rapidly and bloom freely, especially if the soil is given a dressing

Iris reticulata produces its rich violet-purple flowers often as early as February

of bone meal in the late autumn.

Varieties include: 'Cajanus,' large blooms of clear yellow; 'Hercules', purplish-blue, bronze shading, orange blotch; 'Prince Henry', purplish-brown, and bronze-yellow blotch; 'Innocence', pure white and 'King of Blues', rich blue with yellow blotch.

English irises. These plants are hybrids of *Iris xiphioides* and flower 10 to 14 days later than the Dutch irises. They have rather bigger flowers of more solid appearance. It is strange, as they are natives of the Pyrenees, that they should be called English irises though they have some-times been referred to as *Iris anglica*.

The bulbs have loose, rough skins compared with the fairly smooth coats of the Spanish and Dutch varieties. The seed pods and seeds are much larger, though fewer in number. Growing 18 to 24 ins and flowering well into July, bulbs of English irises should be planted from October onwards. As with the Spanish irises, cover them with 3 ins of soil and provide a moist, but not waterlogged position. Sufficient moisture should be available during the spring and early summer, or the foliage will be poor and the flowers scarce and weak. Whereas the foliage of the Spanish and sometimes the Dutch iris begins to show through the soil in the late autumn, there is no sign of the English varieties until early spring. Where the soil is on the dry side, the Spanish and Dutch irises will always thrive, while in heavier positions the English ones will provide a charming display, so that whatever the make-up of the soil it will be possible to have a supply of these indispensable flowers during the early spring.

Although bulbs of all sections of irises are frequently left in the ground for several years, best results undoubtedly come from lifting them about every second season.

Among the good varieties of English irises are: 'Baron von Humboldt', rosy-lilac splashed and flaked in ruby; 'King of the Blues', dark blue with darker flaking; 'La Nuit', reddish-purple with white markings; 'Mont Blanc', pure white; 'Princess Juliana', deep blue with yellow blotches and 'Rosa Bonheur', white, flaked rosy-purple. All make admirable cut flowers.

Ixia paniculata

IXIA Natives of South Africa, the corn lillies are most graceful in appearance. The wiry, yet strong stems grow 15 to 18 ins high and in June and July produce 6 or more flowers of striking beauty. Most have a prominent dark centre and make ideal cut blooms, the narrow foliage being an added attraction. They can be given the same pot culture as freesias, except that the receptacles are best plunged up to their rims in weathered ashes or peat and left in a

sheltered position until February, when, if brought into the cool house, they will soon produce a fine show of blooms.

Delay outdoor planting until October or even November so that the leaves do not start growing before winter. They require sunny positions and are best planted in groups, 3 ins deep and 3 ins apart in sandy soil to which peat and leaf-mould has been added. A winter mulch to protect the top growth should gradually be uncovered in spring to accustom the young shoots to light and air.

Separate varieties are: 'Afterglow', orange-buff with a dark centre; 'Azurea', violet-blue; 'Bridesmaid', white, red centre; 'Hogarth', creamy-yellow, dark eye and 'Vulcan', scarlet, shaded in orange. A good mixture gives a bright display.

Ixias are best increased by offsets, while seed can be sown in heat in the spring.

IXIOLIRION A small genus of bulbous plants native of Central Asia, these plants are sometimes confused with the ixias. They are, however, members of the amaryllidaceae whereas the ixias belong to the iridaceae family, and come from South Africa. Each *Ixiolirion* flower has petals divided at the base which is a distinguishing feature.

Amid the grey-green long, narrow leaves, arise slender, wiry stems about 15 ins in length, on which a number of semi- funnel-shaped flowers are produced in May and June. They like to be grown in warm, sheltered positions, with a rich, well-drained sandy soil. The bulbs, which should be planted 3 ins deep in autumn or early spring, can be left to become established, although during a severe winter, a surface covering of bracken or peat is advisable. Offsets can be detached to increase stock, or seed can be sown in the greenhouse as soon as ripe.

I. kolpakowskianum grows a foot high. The flowers are pale blue, almost whitish-blue, appearing in April and May. This is a rare species.

I. montanum, better known as *I. ledebourii*, growing 15 to 18 ins high and flowering in May and June, varies in colour from lilac-mauve to a deeper blue. The leaves are narrow and grass-like. There are several forms including

I.m. 'Macranthum' which is rather larger-flowering, the colour being a darker shade.

I.m. pallasii is often given specific rank. It is rather later flowering, the flowers being a distinct pinkish-lilac shade.

I. tataricum is a synonym of *montanum*.

LACHENALIA This family of South African plants bears the name of a Swiss botanist and has the common name of leopard lily. When planning for colour in the greenhouse in the early spring, the lachenalias or Cape cowslips should not be forgotten.

Pot the bulbs toward the end of August or in September using a good compost of loam, leaf-mould or peat, silver sand and decayed manure. Place 5 bulbs in a 48 size pot so they are covered with about ½ in. of soil. Set the pots in an airy, cold frame or unheated greenhouse making sure to exclude draughts. Do not over-water, particularly in the early stages of growth.

Before winter weather arrives, say about the middle of November, transfer the pots to the greenhouse where the temperature can be maintained between 45 and 55° F. As growth proceeds, water more frequently but do not

Ixia hybrids are among the most graceful and gaily coloured of all cormous plants

subject the plants to too hot an atmosphere. As soon as the flower stems show, occasional applications of liquid manure will help to bring out the colour and size of the blooms. The flowers appear from January until early May and are produced on spikes 10 to 12 ins high. The foliage is fleshy and strap-shaped, often mottled or spotted, while the drooping tubular flowers, made up of 6 petals, the 3 inner ones frequently being longer than the others, are carried on erect scapes.

A number of species and varieties are normally obtainable. *L. aloides* is frequently offered as *L. tricolor*. This is a tall-growing species and most showy having bells of red, yellow and orange, many being edged in red. This has a number of forms including: *L.t* 'Apricot Flame', rich apricot, on strong stems; 'Boundii', a particularly good sort, bearing large coral-red bells tipped purple, and one of the earliest to flower; 'Lutea', bright yellow tipped red, with a stiff stem which does not require staking. 'Nelsonii' is another very early, free-flowering hybrid with golden-yellow bells marked in greenish red. A number of hybrids have been introduced during recent years and one of the most highly valued is 'Burnham Gold'.

After flowering, when the leaves begin to wither, the pots can be moved to the cold frame or other sheltered place, so that they get plenty of sun. This, with the gradual withholding of water, allows the bulbs to ripen. Keep them dry until the time arrives for re-potting in the autumn.

If the flower heads are left, seeds are produced and may be saved for sowing as soon as ripe in the greenhouse, using pots or pans of sandy, gritty soil. Under normal conditions one may expect the resultant seedlings to make flowering-size bulbs about 3 years from the time of sowing.

LAPEYROUSIA This is a South African plant long known and catalogued as *Anomatheca*. An attractive subject, ideal for the cool greenhouse, it is only likely to come through the winter unharmed in warm sheltered gardens where the soil is well drained.

The best-known species in *L. cruenta* which has been widely grown for many years. The smallish corms produce leaves 6 to 8 ins long

Leucojum pyramidata

come, bring the pots into the cool greenhouse, where they will continue to develop freely. The tunicated bulbs produce umbels of salver-shaped flowers. Two of the earliest-known cultivated species are *L. alliacae* with white blooms and *L. purpurea* with lavender and dark crimson flowers. Of comparatively recent introduction, however, is *L. ixioides* 'Odorata' which produces heliotrope-scented blooms on 18-in. stems during February and March. At the top of each flower spike 3 or 4 sky-blue flowers are produced which are often well over 1 in. in diameter.

LEUCOJUM   The name leucojum has its origin in two Latin words meaning 'white fragrance'. Containing few species, the genus takes in forms which flower in spring and autumn. All have tunicated bulbs, long, narrow leaves and bell-shaped flowers similar to snow-drops with which they are frequently confused.

with slender stems of the same height, each being formed into a dense spike of many red flowers with pretty red anthers. There is a less common, pure white form, '*L.c.* 'Alba', which is hardier than the type. The two forms planted together are most useful for producing a bright splash of colour in the rock garden in July and August, when most other plants have finished blooming.

Lesser-known species include *L. grandiflora*, bright scarlet; *L. juncea*, a pinkish-red; and *L. speciosa*, bright red. Seed is produced in small quantities or offsets form a ready means of propagation.

LEUCOCORYNE   Coming from Chile, this is the name of a small genus of bulbous plants with narrow foliage. The name literally means 'glory of the sun'. This subject, not as well known as it deserves, should be cultivated in much the same way as ixias and freesias and potted up during September and October using a compost of good loam, silver sand and some well-decayed manure or bone meal. In each 5-in. pot place 5 bulbs about 1 in. deep, stand the pots in a sheltered sunny position outdoors and apply moisture as necessary. Before frosts

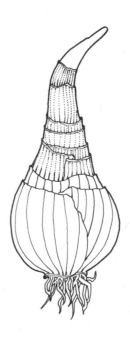

Lapeyrousia cruenta

They are distinct in that they have 6 segments of equal length whereas snowdrops have 3 longer, outer ones.

The leucojums or snowflakes as they are often known, are of easy culture, thriving in good, moist, well-drained sandy soil. The smaller varieties are ideal in small groups in the rockery or in the front of borders. They are seen at their best growing in grass or among some dwarf carpeting subjects.

The taller sorts look fine in the shrubbery, flowering freely when established. They resent disturbance and do not always bloom the first season after planting. New bulblets are produced annually and these can easily be separated as necessary. Seed is sometimes available.

L. aestivum, known as the summer snowflake, is the widest-grown of all species. Sometimes to be found growing wild in Britain, it forms a handsome plant with 18-in. flower spikes which appear in April and May. The elegant, drooping, white flowers are about 1 in. long and have green tips, being greatly prized for cutting.

Of the same height, and blooming at the same time, is *L. aestivum*, 'Gravetye', a greatly improved form, the large flowers being more refined than the type. It does best when planted in a shady position. A rare variety sometimes offered as *L.a. pulchellum* is similar, the only apparent differences being smaller flowers and narrower leaves.

L. vernum, the spring snowflake, is probably the finest of all lilies. It can be found naturalized in some parts of Britain where it blooms from February to April. It grows 6 to 8 ins high and is sometimes mistaken for a snowdrop. The sweet-scented flowers of this *Leucojum* are more open and of better shape, each pointed petal being tipped with green, making it most attractive. True to its name, it flowers in February and March, and, in established clumps, blooms can sometimes be found in late January. Another characteristic is that it has roundish, green-skinned bulbs in contrast to the long-oval-shaped specimens of other species.

L. autumnale, growing to 8 ins, comes from Portugal, Sicily and parts of Africa and therefore is not so hardy as those previously mentioned. It is best planted in warm, sunny positions. The bulbs are quite small, and the thin leaves do not develop until the time the flowers are passing off in August and September. The white, 5-petalled flowers are lightly tinted in pink.

Another species which is autumn-flowering and which has very narrow foliage, is *L. roseum* which has rosy-pink blooms on each 3 or 4-in. stem, which appear in August and September. The leaves develop just as the flowers are dying.

The scarce *Leucojum hiemale* (*nicaense*), although small, is a species with a right to a place in cultivation. It thrives in sun-baked positions, but not in wet and cold, so that it is best grown in the alpine house or the cold frame. The bulbs are very small and have smooth brown skins, while the greyish-green leaves form close to the ground. The pure white, cup-shaped flowers are produced on 3 or 4-in. stems during the late winter and early spring.

LILIUM *L. amabile*, a native of Korea, grows 2 to 3 ft high, has been in cultivation for nearly 50 years and produces, from late June onwards, showy red nodding flowers. The colour varies, and sometimes appears to be

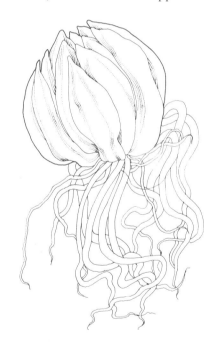

Lilium pyrenaicum

distinctly orange-red, the sharply reflexed petals being spotted black. The stem is quite hairy, and the upper surfaces of the narrow leaves are also hirsute. It likes a well-drained, loamy soil and succeeds when planted among shrubs. A stem rooter, it should be planted 5 or 6 ins deep.

Its somewhat unpleasant odour is the only apparent reason why this lily is not more widely grown.

Lilium auratum, the golden-rayed mountain lily of Japan, has often been acclaimed as the queen of lilies. It is undoubtedly one of the most beautiful and magnificent species in cultivation. The claim is made that this lily was introduced to Europe from Japan by the once-famous firm of Vietch in 1862, but there is some evidence that it was known in France in the seventeenth century.

L. auratum should be planted in a sunny position where it flourishes and regularly builds up energy for the following year. In the shade there may be good-looking foliage, but there will never be regularity of flowering. While a windy aspect should be avoided, an open, airy situation will lessen the possibility of mildew and allied troubles. Good drainage is another necessity. A moderately acid soil seems to suit the bulbs which should be planted 3 or 4 ins deep.

This variety and its forms flower during August and September and the spikes can, of course, be cut. It is best to do this after the buds reveal their whiteness, but before they open. Do not cut off all the leaves for from these the bulb gains its energy for the next season's display.

L. auratum will, when established, grow 6 or 7 ft high and produce, from August onwards, 15 to 25 or more lovely bowl-shaped scented flowers which are waxy white, golden-rayed and spotted crimson. Often they are as much as 10 ins or more in diameter.

L.a. 'Apollo' has a maroon central band to each petal with large light red spots and grows 3 to 4 ft high.

L.a. 'Crimson Queen' is said to be a hybrid from *L.a.* 'Blatyphyllum' and *L. speciosum* 'Melpomene'. It is a most lovely flower, having a wide streak of rich crimson down the centre of each petal with flashes of red over the whole surface of the bloom.

L.a. 'Flore-pleno' is a double form growing about 5 ft high. It is not very popular or easy to obtain.

L.a. 'Pictum' is a fine form in which the flowers are heavily spotted with crimson and the tip of the yellow band is crimson flushed.

L.a. 'Pink Hybrids' are typically *auratum* in character, the pink shading varying in depth from plant to plant.

L.a. 'Platypyllum' is a vigorous plant with wide, handsome leaves and appears to be hardier than the type, although usually somewhat shorter growing. The very large flowers have fewer spots.

L.a. 'Rubro-vittatum' is another very well-marked variety, the band or stripe being yellow at the base of the petals and changing to crimson as it reaches the top.

L. bakerianum from China and Burma is a good lily to grow, and appears to be variable in habit and colour. It was first found about 70 years ago and was named in honour of the famous lily authority J. G. Baker. Most graceful, it is not altogether hardy and excepting in really warm, sheltered districts should be grown in the cool greenhouse border. It likes really sharp drainage and should be covered with 5 or 6 ins of fairly rich, sandy loam. The stems are usually 3 to 4 ft high though sometimes higher while the number of flowers, which at first are a greenish colour, varies from 1 to 6 or 7.

Lilium bolanderi, from the western coasts of America, was first known in cultivation as long ago as 1890 but it has never become a well-known species because it fails to survive for any length of time in British gardens. Named in honour of Dr Bolander, a well-known American botanist and lily grower, this is a small and dainty species which is not always easy to establish.

There are usually two or three pendulous, bell-shaped, wine-red flowers which have a yellowish-pink colouring inside. A good deep, well-drained soil is best so that the stem roots are never checked and ideally one should give the bulbs a nicely moist, rather shady position where they can be planted at least 4 ins deep.

Lilium brownii is another lily whose origins are uncertain. It is generally believed that the original stock came from China to England in 1935 and was possibly sent here by a missionary, who may have been the brother of Mr F. E. Brown, a nurseryman of Slough who first flowered this species in 1937. This man is said to have given bulbs to a grower in France.

Whatever its origin, *L. brownii* is one of the

loveliest of the trumpet-flowered group. Its strong, 3 to 4-ft stems are clothed with dark, glossy foliage and each bears, in July, 2 or 3 large, funnel-shaped, fragrant flowers of great beauty. These are creamy-white, heavily shaded in chocolate brown on the outside with anthers of the same colour. Stem rooting, it should be planted 8 ins or more deep in sharply-drained soil which is rich in humus matter. A top dressing of leaf-mould should be annually.

Lilium bulbiferum is the orange lily which has been cultivated in Europe for many years. Widely known as *L. croceum* and also as *L. aurantiacum* it is one of the easiest of all lily species to grow. The colour in various stock certainly seems to vary but the 'true' *croceum* is distinctly orange while some bulbs sold under this name have flowers with a reddish tinge. This species grows 4 to 5 ft high, and thrives in almost any soil, doing well in sun or partial shade. It seems not to like or dislike lime. In June, the leafy stems bear pyramidal heads of 12 to 15 upright, wide-open flowers which look magnificent in the herbaceous border or in groups on their own. This lily can be raised easily from seed. A form known as 'Giganteum' grows 5 to 6½ ft high, and there are a few other forms sometimes to be seen in botanical gardens, although there does not appear to be much difference between them.

Lilium × *burbankii* is one of the many hybrids of Luther Burbank the famous American hybridist. It is a hybrid between *L. pardalinum* and *L. parryi*. On stems from 4 to 6 ft high it usually carries at least 20 deliciously fragrant flowers. These are bright orange-yellow, flushed crimson towards the petal tips and spotted dark brown. They appear in July. Plant the bulbs 4 or 5 ins deep, in well-drained, lime-free loam containing plenty of leaf-mould. This lily likes partial shade and does well among shrubs or herbaceous plants.

Lilium canadense, known since 1620, is a North American species with several common names including the Canada lily, meadow lily and wild yellow lily. Well suited to European gardens, it flourishes in the open and under woodland conditions. On stems 3 to 5 ft high it produces loose heads of dainty open, bell-shaped flowers from late June onwards. The colour is predominantly orange-yellow but varies from golden-yellow to reddish-orange, but all are heavily spotted dark brown inside the petals. This lily likes a deep, moist loam containing plenty of leaf-mould or peat and as long as the humus content is high it does not greatly resent lime. Plant the bulbs at least 5 ins deep.

Lilium candidum is probably the oldest and best known of all lilies and has been in cultivation for well over 350 years and while it is sometimes known as St Joseph's lily or the Annunciation lily, it is more usually referred to as the Madonna lily. *Lilium candidum* is found growing in southern Europe and Asia Minor and is the lily most commonly found in the cottage gardens of Britain. It appears to thrive with little or no attention.

While it is sometimes seen growing in fairly dry positions, *L. candidum* prefers a rather heavy, yet well-drained loam, especially where there is a fair amount of lime present and where the bulbs will not become waterlogged at any time. A little coarse peat or leaf-mould mixed with the soil where the lilies are to be planted will be of great help.

Unlike most lilies, the Madonna should be planted as soon as flowering has finished, August being the best month, for as soon as the flower stem dies down, fresh leaves are produced from the base, which means that there is foliage to be seen for practically the whole of the year. When planting, use a trowel and cover the bulbs with only an inch or two of soil, in fact, with well established clumps it will be noticed that many of the bulbs are half exposed which certainly seems to have no adverse effect upon them. From this, it will be evident that *L. candidum* is not a stem-rooting variety, for these require quite deep planting.

Surround the bulbs with coarse silver sand, as this will not only aid drainage, but will keep away soil pests which might attack the fleshy bulbs. Builders' sand is no use; it becomes 'clingy' which does not allow the water to pass through. A dusting of yellow sulphur will discourage any tendency to rotting in the bulbs. When in full growth, fortnightly applications of liquid manure will ensure the production of good spikes of bloom, and the stateliness of the Madonna lily grown in this way will surprise

Lilium 'Golden Splendour,' a striking, large-flowering
hybrid

Dahlias have a vast variety of flowers shapes, sizes and colours

those who have only seen them planted in the garden.

The worst enemy of *L. candidum* is botrytis, a fungus disease which first appears as a reddish-brown spot. Unchecked, it rapidly spreads over the foliage, stems and flowers. All affected parts must be destroyed by burning and the whole plants sprayed with a good fungicide making sure to contact the under as well as the upper surfaces of the leaves.

There are a few, little-known varieties of *L. candidum*, the most important one being the 'Salonika' form collected in Macedonia which flowers earlier than the type, with narrower and more spreading basal leaves: the flowers too, are wider. It has the distinction of setting seed which the type rarely does. The variety 'Cernuum' ('Peregrinum') is difficult to secure and to grow, and another old and rare form is 'Purpureum', of which the flowers and bulbs are marked with red. It is quaint rather than beautiful, as is the double form, 'Plenum'.

Lilium centifolium, see *L. leucanthum*.

Lilium cernuum is a beautiful species from north-east China, Korea and the borders of the USSR. Its general habit is much like that of *L. pumilum* except that the stems are more rigid. *L. cernuum* grows up to 3 ft high and bears, during June and July, up to 9 and occasionally more nodding, lilac-pink, scented flowers with purplish spots, the long segments being sharply reflexed to produce a Turk's cap-like appearance.

This stem-rooting lily should be planted at least 4 ins deep and is very much at home growing among low shrubs and plants while it looks well properly sited in the rock garden. Good peaty soil suits it but avoid lime.

Lilium chalcedonicum is sometimes known as the scarlet martagon. A native of Greece, this species forms a large bulb from which arise leafy stems 3 to 4 ft high. Each of these stems produces in July 6 to 10 rather pendulous, showy orange-red flowers with pollen of the same colour. When really established this lily is very effective. It can be raised from seed which, for preference, should be sown in the autumn. Primarily a base-rooting lily the bulb should be planted 4 ins deep and it does best in partial shade.

Lilium columbianum is the Oregon lily or Columbia tiger lily, a native of NW America where it grows in open woodland. The bulbs should be planted 4 or 5 ins deep in partial shade preferably where the soil is on the light side. Leaf-mould and good drainage are other requirements, while a little lime is not a disadvantage. The flowers vary in colour from orange-yellow to reddish-orange, spotted deep crimson particularly on the throat. From July onwards many of the flowers, which make a pyramidal shape, appear on 3 to 5-ft stems.

Lilium concolor is a native of China and Korea. A most dainty species, it usually grows about 18 ins high, though it sometimes reaches 2 ft. Very easy to grow and hardy, it does best when given a sunny position, sheltered from north-east winds, and looks ideal in the rock garden. The bulbs should be planted about 4 ins deep in good, loamy soil where the roots can have a cool run in leaf-mould and sand. The flowers appear in June and July, being distinctly star-shaped and of a brilliant scarlet colour entirely unspotted and slightly fragrant. It is easily raised from seed sown in the spring when it germinates within a month. Various forms of *L. concolor* are sometimes available and have slightly different colouring.

Lilium cordatum is a Japanese species which takes its name from the large heart-shaped leaves. In July it bears funnel-shaped, white flowers tinged with green on the outside, with a yellow blotch and brownish spots on the inside. It is not the easiest of plants to grow and should be planted in a sheltered position in the shrubbery or woodland. *Lilium cordatum* is not as fine as *L. giganteum* which it much resembles. Both of these plants have now been moved to the sub-genus *Cardiocrinum*.

Lilium dauricum is a native of north-eastern Asia, and is said to have been discovered in Siberia from whence it came to England in the middle of the eighteenth century. It grows from $1\frac{1}{2}$ to 2 ft high, the stem being furnished with narrow, dark-green leaves, and in June it bears several (occasionally one) large, open erect, reddish-scarlet flowers with brown spots. A hardy lily, it should be planted in well-drained, good, sweet soil up to 5 ins deep, since it is a stem rooter. It is most successful in the full sun.

F

Lilium davidii is a fine species from China and named in honour of a French missionary-naturalist who first collected the bulbs almost 90 years ago. This lily has been known by other names at various times, but the name now used has been established as correct. In some respects *L. davidii* is not unlike *L. tigrinum*, although seeing the two together ones not confused.

The strong stem reaches a height of 4 to 6 ft and is clothed with graceful, narrow leaves which become smaller as they reach the tip. It carries, during July and August, up to 20 nodding Turk's cap-like flowers of bright orange-red, marked with black spots. It is a stem rooter and should be planted up to 8 ins deep in sandy loam and leaf-mould in a sunny or partially-shaded position.

Lilium elegans, see *L. maculatum*.

Lilium excelsum, see *L. testaceum*.

Lilium formosanum was once thought to be a variety of *L. philippinense*, but has since been accorded specific rank. It should not be confused with the variety of *L. longiflorum* known as 'Formosum', although both are indigenous to the Island of Formosa.

L. formosanum is graceful in appearance. The

Lilium 'Enchantment', a rich orange-pink hybrid now widely available

long, tubular, funnel-shaped flowers open widely at the mouth. The petals are pure white, irregularly marked on the exterior with wine-purple shapes and they reflex sharply at the tips. Although the fragrant flowers are 6 to 8 ins long they are posed horizontally and show up beside the narrow, dark-green foliage. Stem-rooting, it should be planted deeper than 6 ins. It grows $5\frac{1}{2}$ to 6 ft high in well-drained, lime-free loam.

Excellent for potting or the greenhouse border, *L. formosanum* will only grow well outdoors in the most favoured parts of the country. The form known as 'Price's variety' or *L. pricei* grows $1\frac{1}{2}$ to 2 ft high and flowers from July onwards. It will usually come true from seed. The white flowers are shaded in purple on the outside of the petals. The plants seem to like lime and a lightly shaded position. A winter mulch of bracken or peat is advisable and every effort made to keep the bulbs fairly dry during the winter. It can be raised from seed in spring, the seedlings being given glass protection until they are two years old.

Lilium hansonii, the yellow martagon lily, will thrive in any position in well drained soil. Lime-tolerant, it has pendant flowers of bright golden-yellow with crimson-maroon spots and reflexing petals of good substance. It blooms during June on robust 3 to 4-ft stems and does best in sunny situations.

Lilium henryi is a graceful, tall, vigorous lily from northern China which is very hardy and attains a height of 6 to 8 ft. It flowers profusely in August and September with up to 18 large, orange-yellow flowers with back-curving petals and prominent stamens. For best results plant the bulbs 6 to 8 ins deep. They like lime and do equally well in sun or partial shade. Once established, they form good-sized clumps which are best divided every fourth year.

L. × hollandicum is now reckoned to be the correct name of a group of lilies of garden origin which have for long been known as *L. umbellatum*. This lily is easy to culture and valuable for making a show in the garden. According to variety, height varies from $1\frac{1}{2}$ to $2\frac{1}{2}$ ft a few reach a height of 4 ft. It is hardy, decorative, long-lived, and increases freely.

Stem-rooting, the bulbs should be covered with at least 4 ins of good, loamy soil, containing well-decayed manure and leaf-mould. All bloom during June and July, having erect flowers. Since they are liable to mosaic disease they are not always long lived and every effort should be made to start with healthy stock.

Good forms in general cultivation include: 'Apricot', delicate apricot; 'Erectum', reddish-orange; 'Golden Fleece', golden yellow, tipped in scarlet; 'Grandiflorum', orange deepening to red at the tips; 'Incomparable', rich crimson spotted in dark red; 'Invincible', large, orange with reddish petal tips; 'Moonlight', clear yellow; 'Orange Brilliant', tall-growing, brilliant orange shading to crimson; 'Sappho', orange, flushed red; 'Satan', deep blood-red, and 'Vermilion Brilliant', intense red, dotted blooms.

L. humboldtii is a lovely Californian lily named after a noted German scientist. It is sturdy-growing and usually reaches a height of 4 to 6 ft. Established plants produce many blooms in pyramidal heads and usually from 8 to 18 flowers appear on each spike. The nodding, recurved flowers which appear in July, are bright orange-red, prominently spotted in maroon. This lily does best in light shade, or in the open where there is ground cover, for cool, moist soil conditions are essential during the summer. Plant the bulbs at least 6 ins deep in good, loamy soil containing leaf-mould, where drainage is good.

L. humboldtii 'Bloomerianum' is a more dwarf form with smaller flowers usually growing 2 to 3 ft high.

L. humboldtii 'Ocellatum' is a particularly fine lily. Stem-rooting, it is easier to cultivate than the type. The rich golden-orange flowers are spotted maroon often tipped red.

L. × *imperiale*. The first hybrids to be given this name were found in 1916 by Dr E. H. Wilson in a bed of seedlings of *L. regale* which were growing next to some *L. sargentiae*, in the nurseries of Messrs. Farquhason in Boston, USA.

Stock of the original hybrids appears to have become lost and further crosses were made, notably by Miss I. Preston of Ottawa Agricultural College who used *L. regale* as the male parent and it would seem that most of the *L.* × *imperiale* now in commerce are from these Canadian crosses. For about 20 years from 1925 this lily or group of hybrids was known as *L.* × *princeps*, but it is now recognized that *L.* × *imperiale* is the correct title. They grow 4 to 6 ft high according to culture and climatic conditions and have greyish-green, wiry stems.

One of the best of Miss Preston's crosses was named after Dr George E. Creelman who was President of the Ottawa Agricultural College for some years. This fine form was given an award of merit from the Royal Horticultural Society in 1934. 'Crow's Triumph' is another excellent hybrid of the same parentage and was named after Professor Crow, also of Ottawa. *L.* × *imperiale*, 'Pride of Charlotte' is another excellent American seedling.

L. × *imperiale*, which is planted in July, is easy to cultivate, thriving in good, loamy soil rich in leaf-mould and well drained. Plant the bulbs 4 to 6 ins deep preferably in a semi-shady position.

L. japonicum is the Bamboo Lily of Japan. While the charming, funnel-shaped fragrant flowers are delicate rose pink, the segments are slightly and prettily recurved. Growing $1\frac{1}{2}$ to 3 ft high, the slender, glabrous stem bears 1 to 5 of the large trumpets that are thrust out horizontally and made more attractive by the orange-brown pollen on the anthers.

Stem-rooting, the bulbs should be planted at least 6 ins deep in fairly moist, light loam where drainage is good. A position sheltered from winter rains should be provided. In really cold districts this is a lily for the unheated or cool greenhouse. Fresh seed sown in the early autumn will usually provide fine young plants. If the seed is not fresh, germination can be slow.

L. kelloggii is a fragrant North American species which was once regarded as a form of *L. rubescens*. Now it is rightly recognized as a distinct species. Of dainty habit, this charming lily is not among the easiest to grow, it is well worthy of more general cultivation. A good, deep, well-drained soil is needed, but on no account must it dry out during the summer. Lack of moisture at that time is probably the reason why this lily has not always proved successful. An ideal spot is among low-growing shrubs. It varies in height from $1\frac{1}{2}$ to $2\frac{1}{2}$ ft and produces dainty, reflexed, pinkish-mauve flowers which deepen with age, each petal being dotted maroon with a yellow central stripe.

L. kesselringianum is a native of Russia and a fairly rare species not in general cultivation. Growing about 2 ft high the stems have lanceolate leaves and carry up to three, pale straw-coloured flowers having minute brown spots. The rather spreading petals recurve towards the tips. It was once thought to be a form of *L. monodelphum* and it is obvious that it is allied to both *L. monodelphum* and *L. szovitzianum* and it can be given the same culture as these two lilies.

L. lankongense is a native of Western China. It was for many years regarded as a form of *L. duchartrei*, but it is now recognized as a distinct species. Although they are obviously similar, colour is different, the flowers of *L. lankongense* being flushed purple-rose with deeper spots. Growing from 2 to 4 ft high, the stems have few leaves, although there is usually a cluster of foliage at the base. This lily likes a light, porous loam containing leaf-mould and coarse sand but little lime, whilst a moist root run and semi-shade are appreciated.

L. leichtlinii commemorates Max Leichtlin the famous German lily specialist who died in 1910. It was discovered as a stray plant in a bed of *L. auratum* the bulbs of which Messrs. Veitch had imported from Japan. This species forms underground growths or stolons and such growths may appear some distance from where the bulbs are planted. This is why it is best to grow it in the greenhouse border rather than in pots. A stem rooter, it should be planted up to 6 ins deep. Even when it grows well, it never exceeds a height of 3 or 4 ft and is often shorter. From 1 to 5 large, reflexing flowers are produced in August, their colour being citron-yellow heavily spotted in purple-brown.

L.l. 'Maximowiczii' named after the Russian botanist, is a form which is sometimes accorded specific rank, and in July it produces leafy stems from 3 to 6 ft high. These bear up to a dozen showy reflexing orange or orange-red flowers spotted purplish-brown, which look something like those of *L. tigrinum*. Plant the bulbs deeply where there is plenty of leaf-mould in a moist, yet well-drained position. Lime is disliked.

L. leucanthum is a lily which has been subjected to much botanical confusion and has been known as *L. brownii* 'Leucanthum' and also *L. sargentiae*. A native of China it was discovered by Dr Augustus Henry who sent bulbs to Kew Gardens in 1888.

This lily grows from 3 to 4 ft high the stem being well furnished with long leaves and bearing 4 or 5 large, sharply recurved trumpets. The milk white petals are tinted pale yellow on the inside with a greenish band on the exterior.

L.l. centifolium is the form most likely to be obtained, and it is generally agreed that this is the one seen by Reginald Farrer in China about 1914. Seed was obtained, and once the bulbs were established in Britain they attained a height from 6 to 8 ft. The stems are very leafy and from late July onwards produce many large, fragrant trumpet-shaped flowers of which the insides are white with pale yellow shading at the throat, the outside of the trumpet being shaded dull purple, often marked with green. Although it has done well in the open garden, generally speaking this is not an easy lily outdoors and should always be planted 6 to 9 ins deep and be given sharply-drained, loamy soil containing plenty of leaf-mould.

L. longiflorum is probably the most important of the commercial species being grown in large quantities for all kinds of floral work. Otherwise known as the Easter or Bermuda lily, it is of Japanese origin and has been grown in Britain for over 140 years. The bulbs are still imported in large quantities, although many now come from various sources including Bermuda, St Helena and the USA.

L. longiflorum does not object to lime, and although it is chiefly grown as a pot or greenhouse plant, in warm sheltered south and south-western districts it can be cultivated in the open ground, but must have protection from early frosts. It is a good plan to start bulbs in pots in the greenhouse and then put them out at the end of May. It is rarely if ever that open ground plants produce seed, unless hand pollinated.

This species and its forms are stem-rooting, so that deep planting is needed and up to 7 or 8 ins is about right. The flowering period for imported bulbs is July and August although, when forced, they can be had in bloom from

March onwards. From 5 to 6 large, fragrant, pure-white, funnel-shaped flowers are produced on 2 to 3 ft stems. The leaves are quite big, being 6 or 7 ins long and more than ½ in. wide. Both stigma and anthers are prominent and an abundance of yellow pollen is produced.

Bulbs used for forcing must be selected with care, and at one time stocks were frequently found to be disease-laden, but nowadays special care is taken and bulbs from Bermuda and St Helena may be depended upon as being disease free. Special strains have also been raised in the United States to secure healthy stocks, selected for forcing and cutting.

There are now many forms and strains in cultivation, the following being among the best known and reliable. *L.l.* 'Albo Marginatum' known for about 90 years has leaves having a broad white margin. *L.l.* 'Creole' is a form largely grown in New Orleans and is of fairly dwarf habit. *L.l.* 'Croft' first came into cultivation in 1931 being introduced by Sydney Croft of Oregon for forcing and for pots.

L.l. 'Eximium' is the well-known Easter or Bermuda lily which is frequently referred to as *L. harrisii*. This is a form having narrow flowers which are larger than the type.

The RHS journal reported some years ago that the origin of this strain was from bulbs given by a missionary homeward bound from Japan, to a clergyman in Bermuda some time during the middle of the eighteenth century. This lily soon became widely grown in Bermuda but unfortunately, virus disease caused a great deterioration. Subsequently, it was found that aphids were largely responsible for the rapid spread of the disease from affected to healthy plants. Under Government supervision, there is now a system by which bulbs exported from Bermuda and elsewhere are examined and certified as disease free and true to type.

There are now many other strains of *L. longiflorum*; some, however, are not readily available. Among the best are the following: *L.l.* 'Holland's Glory' producing 4-ft stems which carry 6 to 12 flowers having very long trumpets. It can be raised from seed without difficulty. *L. longiflorum* 'Insulare' is a Japanese selection which is said to be somewhat hardier than the type. It holds its flowers at right angles.

L.l. takeshima is particularly strong growing. In July and August the tall, purplish-brown stems bear from 5 to 10 large white blooms. Particularly good for forcing, this form is known in the trade as *L. longiflorum* 'Giganteum'.

L. mackliniae. Seed of this lily was sent home from Manipur in 1946 by Capt. Kingdon Ward. This seed germinated quickly and seedlings flowered under glass in 1948. In Britain, the plant grows about 2 ft high. The very leafy stems, terminating in a group of 2 or 3 nodding and bell-shaped flowers, about 2 ins long, are white, flushed externally with rosy-purple.

These flowers are reminiscent of those of a *Nomocharis*, and in fact this plant was once thought to belong to that genus. Originally regarded as suitable only for pot cultivation under glass, subsequent experiments have shown that it is hardy and will flourish in the open. It does well in fairly deep soil where drainage is good, being most successful when the lower part of the stem is shaded by dwarf growing plants.

Propagation is by means of seed or scales and there are instances of bulbs flowering within two years of seed sowing.

L. × maculatum is the correct name of the range of lilies long grouped together as *L. umbellatum* or *L. thunbergianum*, and which have been known in Japan for many years, although their exact origin is unknown. The flowers of all varieties face upwards and some have a distictive creeping stem-base, showing the influence of *L. dauricum*. Growing from 12 to 20 ins high, they are excellent for pots or the rock garden, and equally suitable for the sunny garden border. They flower in June and July and being stem-rooters, the bulbs should be buried 4 or 5 ins deep. The conspicuous, cup-shaped blooms sometimes appear singly but there are usually several in an umbel.

There are many splendid varieties including: *L. × m.* 'Alice Wilson', clear lemon-yellow, spotted dark red.

L. × m. 'Alutaceum', deep apricot-yellow, is a dwarf lily 9 ins high. It is sometimes known as 'Kirkak'. *L. × m.* 'Atrosanguineum', crimson-red with dark spots. *L. × m.* 'Mahogany', broad petalled flowers of mahogany crimson. *L. × m.*

'Wallacei', apricot, spotted maroon in the centre.

L. × marhan was originally raised by the well-known Dutch firm of Van Tubergen as long ago as 1896 and among good seedlings this one was outstanding. In July, the thick-petalled, rich orange reflexed flowers spotted in brown, appear on stems reaching up to 7 ft, although often they are shorter. A stem-rooting variety, bulbs should be planted 6 to 8 ins deep.

L. maritimum has been grown in Britain for over 70 years, and this graceful Californian species has its home in coastal districts. For the finest results it should be given a place where the roots are well supplied with moisture during the growing season, and yet where the bulbs remain fairly dry during winter. At the same time, the ground should be well drained. The rather small bulbs should be planted 4 ins deep and, apart from silver sand, the presence of leaf-mould or peat will be helpful. Although *L. maritimum* is quite tall when growing in its native habitat, it rarely attains even 3 ft in Britain. It is well worth the special attention needed to obtain good results. The small, bell-shaped, deep reddish-orange flowers appear in July, the slightly reflexed petals being spotted purple on the inside.

L. martagon is one of the oldest and best-known lilies, the name apparently having been originally given because of the sharply recurved petals. It is native in Britain and some other European countries as well as in parts of Asia. This lily has a rather unpleasant smell which makes it unsuitable for growing very near the house, but it is useful in woodland places. Both the type and its many varieties thrive in sun or shade and look well among shrubs and in grassland. Left to become established in a suitable place the bulbs will increase both by the production of offsets and by means of seed, which falls to the ground and grows freely. Seedlings take some years before they bloom.

The quickest way to secure young flowering stock is to separate the offsets from the bulbs or carefully to detach and pot up scales, but the former method is the quicker as far as blooming is concerned. Not particular about soil, this lily prefers a stiffish loam containing leaf-mould but the presence or otherwise of lime seems of no account.

Stem roots are not generally produced but the bulbs should be planted 6 ins deep. Sometimes little growth is made during the first year after planting. Once established, the stout stems grow from 3 to 6 ft high, the many dark green leaves being arranged in whorls. According to position, the length of time the bulbs have been established, from 4 to 40 flowers may be produced on each stem during June and July. The colour varies from light purple to purplish-pink, spotted in varying degrees with purple and the colour has frequently been referred to as a muddy purple. It is partly due to its colour that *L. martagon* is often placed away from other species.

A number of forms of *L. martagon* are in cultivation, the colour of the flowers and habit of growth being better in some than in others. This is partly because it is easy to raise it from seed and unless the seedlings are rigidly selected, inferior hybrids may predominate.

Among the best named varieties of *L. martagon* are the following: *L. martagon* 'Album'. This is a beautiful, vigorous-growing pure white unspotted form. Like most albinos, it requires a little more care than the type but if kept top-dressed with rich soil or leaf-mould annually, or removed to a fresh site every 4 to 5 years, it will continue to give good results.

L.m. cattaniae is a fine variety growing 6 to 7 ft high, flowers being a maroon or wine purple colour giving it the name of black martagon.

L.m. 'Dalmaticum' appears to be another name for *L.m.* 'Cattaniae'.

There are a number of hybrids of which *L. martagon* is one of the parents. Most are vigorous growing. One particular group is known as Backhouse hybrids of which the parents are mainly *L. martagon* and *L. hansonii*. Among these are some with flowers flushed pink on a yellow or orange ground such as 'Brocade' and 'Mrs R. O. Backhouse'.

L. michauxii is a native of California, and this lily is sometimes known as the Carolina lily. Although it has been in cultivation for many years, it has never become established in British gardens. It appears to be allied to *L. superbum* but is less hardy than that species. Stem-rooting, it dislikes lime and should be planted 5 ins deep in a peaty, well-drained soil.

Growing 1 to 3 or 4 ft high the small, dark green leaves are sometimes scattered, but on other occasions are arranged in whorls up the stem. From 1 to 5 scented nodding flowers open in July, the shapely reflexed petals being orange-red, shading to yellow-white in the throat. Sometimes flowers are almost pure yellow.

L. monadelphum is a native of the Caucasus where it grows freely among shrubs and other plants of low stature. Known in Britain for nearly 160 years, it is one of the earliest lilies to bloom. The lemon-yellow flowers, tinged with gold are wine coloured at the base of the petals, with small purple spots, and appear from June onwards.

The stems reach a height of 4 to 5 ft and carry between 20 and 30 scented, pendulous recurved blooms, while there are numerous leaves scattered up the stems. The name of this lily comes from its stamens, which are fused together over part of their length. It resents disturbance and is often a year or two before it settles down after being moved while it is not unknown for little top growth to be made first season. It prefers an unexposed position where there is light shade. The bulbs need well cultivated soil and should be planted 5 ins deep. Seed forms a ready means of increasing stock and should be sown in the autumn. This is one of several lilies of which seedlings sometimes go through their first season without showing any top growth.

L. neilgherrense is a comparatively rare species and, as its name indicates, is a native of Southern India. Except in the mildest districts and most favourable situations it can only be grown in the cool greenhouse. As a pot plant it is really superb.

On stems 2 to 4-ft high it produces, in August or September, from 1 to 4 fragrant, very large trumpets, 6 to 9 ins long and sometimes more. These are handsome, being pure white within and having yellow throats with creamy-white exteriors, the petal tips being slightly reflexed. Well-drained sandy loam with a large proportion of leaf-mould suits this lily. When grown in the greenhouse border, the bulbs should be planted at least 6 ins deep since this is a vigorous stem-rooting species.

L. nepalense was first discovered in Nepal early in the nineteenth century, but is still not well known. It cannot be regarded as suitable for general garden cultivation in Britain, but is ideal for the conservatory or cool greenhouse. Under glass, it is not very difficult, although it is best grown in the border, since the stems are inclined to run under ground, making it unsuitable for pots. Plant the bulbs at least 6 ins deep using sandy loam containing a high proportion of leaf-mould. *L. nepalense* usually grows from 2 to 3 ft high, the stems being clothed with broad, dark green, glossy foliage and in the greenhouse the flowers appear from May to July. These rather pendent funnel-shaped blooms are greenish-yellow, blotched and stained claret-purple.

There has, in the past, been some confusion between this species and *L. ochraceum*, but the flowers of the latter are not so trumpet-shaped and the stem does not run under ground.

L. nepalense 'Concolor', was first brought to notice in 1939 and has flowers which are without the purple staining, making it an almost clear yellow variety.

L. nevadense may be described as a smaller edition of *L. pardalinum*, the panther lily, and has sometimes been described as a variety of that species. A native of California, it is more than 60 years ago since it was first recorded. The slender stems well clothed with rather spreading light green leaves, usually reach a height of $2\frac{1}{2}$ to 3 ft although it will grow taller. The fragrant flowers are orange-yellow, the tips of the petals being stained red. There are several forms of this lily, some with less red in the petals and others being different in the way the flowers are carried or in the shape of the petals. Plant the bulbs up to 5 ins deep in good, well-drained soil containing plenty of leaf-mould or other humus matter. A partially shady or fully sunny position will prove suitable.

L. nobilissimum is indeed a noble lily from Japan and is yet another species not often seen in cultivation. An excellent subject for the greenhouse it produces stems up to 2 ft high. These bear dark green, lanceolate leaves and, in July, produce 2 or 3 large, scented, funnel-shaped white flowers, each having prominent dark brown anthers.

The 'Bellingham Hybrid' lilies are among the easiest to grow but prefer damp soils

L. occidentale is a native of Oregon and California, and was first discovered towards the end of the last century. Plant the small bulbs 3 or 4 ins deep in well-drained, lime-free soil containing plenty of peat or leaf-mould. It grows from 2 to 6 ft high, the stems bearing whorls of scattered dark green narrow leaves, and in July they produce up to a dozen or more rather small pendent Turk's cap flowers, of which the colour is orange with maroon spots, the petal tips being crimson.

L. ochraceum, see *L. primulinum*.

L. paradalinum, the leopard or panther lily, is a native of California and Mexico. Hardy and easy to grow, it will usually increase rapidly. It is often referred to as a bog lily but grows well in ordinary garden soil. The thick-scaled bulbs should be planted at least 4 to 5 ins deep but more if the soil is on the light side. It likes a lime-free, moist soil which remains moist, but which is never waterlogged. Sun and shelter from winds are required. The stem reaches a height of 6 to 7 ft and carries long, narrow leaves which are sometimes arranged in whorls

and in July the sharply recurved, orange-red flowers open. The tips of the petals are usually shaded crimson spotted crimson-brown.

There are various forms of *L. pardalinum*, including *L. pardalinum* 'Augustifolia' with red-tipped petals and narrow leaves. *L. pardalinum giganteum* is known as the sunset lily and red giant. It grows 6 to 8 ft high and carries up to 30 crimson and yellow spotted flowers, while *L. pardalinum* 'Luteum' has yellow flowers spotted brownish-purple.

L. parryi, discovered by Dr Parry in southern California, is an attractive lily often referred to as the lemon lily. When established, the plants produce slender stems of 4 to 6 ft although if conditions are not quite to its liking, it may not

Lilium humboltii

grow more than 2 or 3 ft high. The long, rather grassy foliage is usually placed in whorls. The number of blooms produced depends on the height of the stem and varies from 2 to 12 or more. Opening in July, the funnel-shaped, citron flowers have recurved petal tips and orange-brown anthers, and are delicately scented.

Although it does not like swamp conditions, the home of this lily is on the banks of mountain streams. In gardens the aim should be to plant the bulbs 6 ins deep in good, sandy loam, which is lime-free and rich in leaf-mould. Moisture should always be available during the growing season. If the base of the stems can be in the shade so much the better. Sometimes established bulbs fail to produce flower spikes, merely sending up several flowerless stems, and investigations have shown that this is because the bulbs have broken up into separate portions, which are not big enough to flower until the following season.

L. parryi 'Kessleri' has larger flowers and broader stems and appears to be rather later flowering than the type.

L. parryi hybrids are strong in constitution and of good form and habit. In July, the flower stems, growing 4 to 5 ft high, produce up to 20 fragrant, pendent blooms, the colour varying from lemon-yellow to golden-yellow spotted crimson. Plant the bulbs 4 ins deep and give protection against severe frosts.

L. parvum has been grown in Europe since 1872. A charming Californian lily it has been known to reach a height of 5 or 6 ft but is more often only 3 to 4 ft high. One of the smallest-flowering species, the dainty, bell-shaped blooms are variable in colour but are usually bright orange or orange-red with purplish spots. There is a clear yellow from known as *L. p.* 'Luteum' and another with dark spots all flowering in July. The leaves usually form in whorls but are sometimes scattered up the stem. This lily grows well on or near the banks of streams or pools but good drainage is essential and ground with a high humus content is preferred. Plant the bulbs 3 or 4 ins deep, if possible in a partially shaded position. Propagation can be effected from bulb scales as well as from seed which is best sown in the spring.

Lilium philadelphicum and its varieties are found in eatern North America. By no means easy to establish in gardens, this is a showy species and it has several popular names which are indicative of its appearance. These include orange cup lily, flame lily and glade lily. It does well in full sun or light shade and the fringe of woodland or the shrubbery is a suitable site. Of dainty habit, it grows from 1 to 3 ft high, the stems carrying many light green leaves up to 4 ins long and more than $\frac{1}{2}$ in. wide. Sometimes the foliage is scattered up the stem, but it also occurs in whorls. From the end of June onwards, there are usually 2 to 6 upright, cup-shaped, orange-scarlet flowers. The colour is brilliant, well-spotted purple-maroon.

The bulbs should be planted not less than 5 ins deep, preferably in early autumn. A well-drained loam, rich in leaf-mould, suits this lily. It is advisable to give some overhead protection from heavy rains and severe cold during winter. Propagation is from bulblets, scales and seed sown in spring. Among the varieties available are the following: *L.p. andinum*, which is sometimes given specific rank. It is deeper coloured than the type, the large cup shaped blooms on stems up to 2 ft high being from 2 to 3 in. in diameter. *L.p.* 'Brown Berry' has flowers of a brownish gold colour. *L.p.* 'Flavi-florum', of Canadian origin, has clear yellow flowers spotted purple.

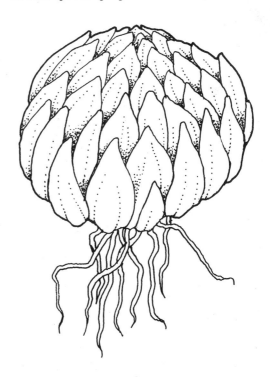

Lilium candidum

99

L. philippinense is named after its place of origin, although it has been known in Britain for nearly 60 years. It grows up to 3 ft high, the stem being furnished with narrow, bright green leaves up to 5 or 6 ins long. The scented flowers appear from July onwards and are pure white on the inside of the trumpet, the exterior being marked red and often showing traces of green. This is a lily with a particularly narrow, elegant trumpet, which has been known to grow as much as 8 or 9 ins long. In the past it has been confused with *L. formosanum* but this is a separate species. A native of the Philippines, this is obviously a lily for the greenhouse. A soil mixture containing loam, leaf-mould and sprinkling of silver sand is suitable. Seed can be sown as soon as ripe in autumn.

L. polyphyllum, which first flowered in Britain in 1873, is a native of the Himalayas. In its native habitat it reaches a height of 6 or 7 ft. In gardens or the cold greenhouse it grows between $1\frac{1}{2}$ and 4 ft. The smooth, green stems bear numerous leaves 4 or 5 ins long. The petals of the fragrant, nodding flowers which appear in July and form a short tube, are yellowish-green on the outside and as the segments spread and recurve they expose the inner surface which is creamy-white, spotted and marked lilac-purple. Not an easy lily to manage, it should be planted 4 or 5 ins deep in well drained lime-free soil, rich in leaf-mould in a sunny sheltered situation where the lower part of the stem is in the shade.

L. pomponium, an old garden lily, is a native of the Maritime Alps. Usually growing 2 to 3 ft high it produces, during June and July, up to 18 nodding dainty sealing-wax red, turkscap blooms with tiny black spots, the stems being clothed with narrow leaves. It does best in good loam which is on the heavy side, but improved with the addition of coarse sand or limestone chips. When the latter are not available, an occasional dressing of lime will help to bring good results. The flowers have quite a strong scent, which, however, is not pleasant.

L. ponticum is a native of north-east Asia Minor. Its strong stems will often grow up to $4\frac{1}{2}$ ft high, but frequently are no more than $2\frac{1}{2}$ to 3 ft. The upper part of the stem is fairly thickly clothed with long, narrow leaves and in July from 1 to 6 pendulous, recurved flowers are produced. These are primrose-yellow well spotted with purple, and they have a rather unpleasant smell. Plant the bulbs 4 or 5 ins deep in semi-shaded situations. This is not a striking lily, but even so deserves to be widely grown.

L. primulinum is a lily which has been subjected to name changes. Long known as *L. ochraceum*, it is now certain that the present name is correct. This lily has also been confused with *L. nepalense*. The latter, however, has funnel-shaped blooms whereas *L. primulinum* is a true martagon with reflexed segments and a definite fragrance.

L. primulinum burmanicum is found in Burma, Yunnan and Thailand. Although hardy in milder districts it is really most suitable for pot culture in the cool greenhouse. The flowers are greenish-yellow with conspicuous purple staining. Growing 4 to 7 ft high the stems carry numerous leaves 5 to 6 ins long. A late-blooming lily, it shows colour from August onwards, often lasting until October or November. The bulbs should be planted 5 ins deep in a compost of loam, leaf-mould and sand.

L. primulinum ochraceum is the name of a smaller-growing form with light coloured bulbs which darken with age. This lily is hardier than the other forms and grows from 4 to 6 ft high and produces 8, but sometimes double that number, pendulous blooms. The yellowish-green colour of the petals contrasts well with the purple blotch in the throat.

L. pumilum, a native of north-east Asia, was first grown in Europe about 1810. It is one of the most dainty species often referred to as *Lilium tenuifolium* in reference to the slender stems and narrow grassy foliage.

The wiry stems rarely grow more than 18 ins high, but in June established plants will often bear up to 18 or even more nodding, bright scarlet or sealing-wax red, martagon-like flowers of fine form, the petals recurving sharply. They are usually unspotted, but occasionally black dots appear and the pollen is scarlet. The 4-in. leaves appear at intervals up the stem but usually form clusters in the middle. This stem-rooting lily is suitable for the rock garden or the front of the border and the bulbs should be planted 3 or 4 ins deep in well-drained loam and leaf-mould in a sunny situation, where there is ground shade. A little lime is not objected to while decayed manure well worked into the soil will be beneficial.

L.p. 'Golden Gleam' is generally considered to be a hybrid between *L. pumilum* and *L. martagon* 'Album', but there is some doubt about this. Vigorous and free flowering, this form has lovely golden-orange blooms.

L.p. 'Red Star', is of unknown origin. Growing 2 ft high it has star-shaped flowers and comes true from seed. *L.p.* 'Yellow Beauty' is a canary-yellow hybrid raised in Canada.

L. pyrenaicum the Turk's cap lily of the Pyrenees is easy to manage and is said to be naturalized in some parts of Britain. A first-class plant of strong growth and simple requirements, it will grow more than 4 ft high, but is often considerably less; the stem is generously clothed with rather spreading leaves as much as 5 ins long. The pendulous, reflexed flowers open from May onwards, the colour being greenish-yellow brightened by deep crimson spots, while the orange pollen makes a striking contrast. These flowers emit a strong and not altogether pleasing perfume. Like *L. martagon*, this plant is best suited for growing in the shrubbery or wild garden. It is hardy, producing stem roots and should be planted 4 ins deep.

L. pyrenaicum 'Rubrum' is a fine form from Spain, and is better than the type, having bright orange-red petals which are spotted in maroon.

L. regale is a trumpet lily which was discovered by Dr E. H. Wilson in 1903. A native of west Swechwan, China, it first flowered in 1905 under the cultivation of Messrs Veitch. It was distributed as *L. myriophyllum* not then being recognized as a new species. This is one of the lilies of which bulbs may often be seen offered in shops in a dried, shrivelled state and bought in such condition they are hardly likely to prove satisfactory to the purchaser. It will succeed in all parts of the country, although early growth is susceptible to damage from late frosts just as the new shoots are pushing up in the spring. Its strong, wiry stems will grow 5 to 6 ft high and they are furnished with numerous, scattered dark green, narrow leaves. In July it produces from 3 to 30 funnel or trumpet-shaped fragrant flowers which are stained rose-purple on the exterior. The mouth of the trumpet is white while the throat is suffused sulphur-yellow.

L. regale is a stem-rooter and should be planted not less than 5 or 6 ins deep. In really light soil 9 or 10 ins is not too much. Almost any soil is suitable as long as it is well drained, while lime does not seem to prevent good results. Leaf-mould or other humus matter is appreciated. Ideally, the bulbs should be planted where the roots are shaded by low-growing shrubs or herbaceous plants, but the top growth should be in the sun. Seed can be sown in the spring although there is bound to be some variation in the seedlings. It usually takes 3 years before blooms are produced.

L. rubellum, a native of Japan, received a first-class certificate from the RHS in 1898, the first year it flowered in Britain. This is one of the earliest outdoor lilies, the flowers showing colour from May onwards. The bulbs are fairly small, seldom more than 2 ins in diameter, being composed of rather loosely arranged white scales. They do best when planted among dwarf growing shrubs or plants. The slender stems, usually flecked brownish-red, rarely grow more than 2 ft high and carry a few bright green fairly broad-veined leaves. From 1 to 6, but occasionally more, fragrant bell-shaped, delicate, shell-pink flowers about 3 ins long are produced on each spike.

L. rubellum is also a stem-rooter and should be planted not less than 4 or 5 in. deep in fairly rich, sharply drained sandy loam and leaf-mould which for preference should be lime free. Home-raised seed seems to be more reliable in that it germinates readily if sown in the early autumn, whereas imported seed may remain dormant for months. This lily can also be increased by scales. *Lilium rubellum* 'Album' is the rarely-seen white form, made more lovely by the prominent golden anthers.

L. rubescens, an American species, known in cultivation since 1873, is not unlike *L. washingtonianum*, to which is it related. The bulbs are not as compact as those of most lilies, being more or less rhizomatous. This lily varies in height from 2 to 5 ft and produces during June and July many loosely-arranged, white-tinged, lilac flowers, finally dotted with purple. As these scented trumpets open, they become suffused pinkish-purple. Plant the bulbs 8 to 10 ins deep in moist, well-drained loam, preferably among low growing shrubs to give some shade to the roots.

L. sargentiae, a species from western China, was discovered in the early part of this century. It is closely allied to *L. regale* but the leaves are broader and the flowers larger. The long, funnel-shaped, sweetly-scented flowers appear during July and August, on stems 4 to 5 ft high. They are white with a golden yellow throat, the outside of the petals being shaded or suffused brownish-pink or rose-purple with traces of green. This lily thrives in a sunny position and does well when planted among low-growing plants or shrubs which shade the bases of the stems. Plant the bulbs 4 ins deep in well-drained, loamy soil, well supplied with leaf-mould. Lime does not appear to have any adverse effects, as long as the soil has a good humus content.

Not as hardy as *L. regale*, *L. sargentiae* is best grown in the cool greenhouse. Unfortunately, it is liable to botrytis disease and should therefore be sprayed with Bordeaux mixture, while in some seasons this lily is attacked by mosaic virus disease. This is why, in order to maintain a really hardy stock, it is advisable to sow seeds which germinate freely in the spring. The bulbils which form at the leaf axils can also be used for propagation but only where the parent plant is perfectly healthy.

L. speciosum is a dependable Japanese lily introduced to Europe in 1830. Most popular for market work and pot culture, it is a first-rate garden plant for an open sunny, but sheltered position. The bulbs are very distinctive, the scales being purplish-brown on the outside and yellowish-brown in between. According to variety, the stems vary in height from 3 to 7 ft and have leathery, green leaves usually more than 5 ins long. The large, slightly nodding flowers are most attractive.

The stem-rooting bulbs should be planted not less than 6 ins deep in well-drained, rather gritty soil, rich in leaf-mould. Propagation is by detaching bulblets, while scales can also be

rooted, and seed is not difficult to germinate.

Among good varieties available are: *L. speciosum* 'Album', with brownish stems and pure white flowers. *L. speciosum* 'Kraetzeri' is particularly good for forcing, the white flowers having a pale green stripe down the centre of each petal and snowy orange-brown pollen.

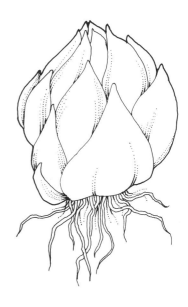

Lilium hollandicum

L. speciosum 'Magnificum' is a most handsome lily, the rose-coloured flowers having a white margin, and being freely spotted crimson.

L. speciosum 'Melpomene' is a hybrid of American origin and a particularly good form. Each petal has a clear white border, the rest being shaded blood-red. The form now generally in cultivation is rather different to the original in that the colour is deep carmine.

L. speciosum 'Roseum' has rose-coloured flowers and green stems. *L. speciosum* 'Rubrum' is carmine with a purplish-brown stem. *L. speciosum* and its forms are all-purpose lilies which rarely, if ever, fail to give satisfactory results.

L. sulphureum is a lily which has been subject to various name changes, and was once known as

L. myriophyllum 'Superbum'. The globose bulbs are a reddish-purple colour and produce stems 4 to 7 ft high. These carry many dark green leaves, which often produce bulbils in their axils. Up to 15 large, fragrant flowers are produced on each stem from August to October and sometimes later. The very long segments recurve slightly. The colour varies, probably because there are several forms which are now grouped under the one name. The typical flower may be described as yellow, shading to creamy-white at the petal tips and being flushed on the outside with pink or greenish pink. A stem-rooting lily; deep planting is necessary, 5 ins being the minimum in a lime-free soil, rich in leaf-mould; is best in a sheltered position outdoors. A good greenhouse plant, it does well in pots.

L. superbum is a native of the eatern United States and has the common names of Turk's cap lily, nodding lily and swamp lily. This handsome plant was introduced into Britain fairly early in the 18th century. The stems reach a height of 4 to 6 ft. The lower leaves are arranged in whorls, and the pendulous flowers vary in colour, but the typical form is orange deepening to red towards the petal tips. There is a conspicuous green star at the centre and some red spots.

From July onwards, 25 to 30 of these showy flowers are produced and look much like those of *L. pardalinum* but are larger. Plant the bulbs in lime-free soil which never dries out, and where there is an abundance of peat or leaf-mould and shade from the brightest sunshine.

Stem-rooting, the bulbs should be placed 5 ins deep, preferably over some stones for sharp drainage. They are rhizomatous and in established specimens new plants may appear some distance from the main bulb. This lily can be raised from seed sown in the autumn and results in flowering plants 3 to 4 years later. This is one of several lilies which rarely show any signs of any top growth in the first year after sowing.

There are now several named forms available, chiefly those found by Mrs J. Norman Henry. Among them are the following: *L.s.* 'Herc Henry' having flowers of butter yellow with scarlet tips. *L.s.* 'Mary Henry Davis' is also yellow but with dark spots and *L.s.* 'Norman Henry', pure yellow except for a green star in the centre of each flower.

L. szovitsianum is a Caucasian lily often regarded as a variety of *L. monadelphum*, but some authorities say there are distinct botanical differences between them. This species has a more southern distribution, and so far no overlapping of growing areas has been recorded. The stem varies in height from 2 to 5 ft, according to situation and season, and carries many scattered, long leaves. From 2 to 18 or more canary-yellow, campanulate, rather pendulous flowers open in June. Occasionally these are marked with black spots. Of easy culture, the bulbs of this lily should be planted not less than 5 ins deep, in good, loamy soil, where there is a little lime. The name of this lily commemorates Nepomuk Szovits, an Hungarian apothecary, who died in 1830 and who is credited with the introduction of the species.

L. taliense, first discovered in 1883, did not flower in Britain until 1935. Coming from Yunnan, in western China, it takes its name from the hills known as the Tali Range. Still a comparatively rare lily, it resembles both *L. wardii* and *L. duchartrei*. It is vigorous growing, but while in its native surroundings it reaches a height of 9 or 10 ft it grows from 3 to 4 ft in Britain. The light-coloured bulbs are speckled in purple which gives them a distinctive appearance. The stems too, are mottled purple and have scattered narrow leaves 4 or 5 ins long.

In August, up to a dozen flowers are produced on each spike, and the sharply recurved, white petals are clearly spotted in purple. Although this lily has not proved easy to grow or keep, which accounts for its rarity, it can be raised from seed which grows freely and it may be that after several more generations have been bred in Britain, *L. taliense* will become more at home in these climatic conditions.

Lilium × testaceum is a stately lily which has been known in England since about 1840, and is believed to have originated in Holland or Germany as the result of a natural cross between *L. candidum* and *L. chalcedonicum*, the former being the male parent. The plant resembles *L. candidum* in growth, having its stems clothed with green foliage, and the leaves appear to have a very thin, silver margin all round. At the top of the 4 to 6-ft purplish stems there appear, from May to July, from 4 to 12 large, fragrant, recurved, flattish flowers of nankeen or maize-yellow with contrasting red anthers.

The bulbs should not be planted deeper than 3 ins and they have no objection to lime. They prefer the sun and do well among low-growing shrubs since these prevent the soil drying out, a condition which this lily does not like. Often known as the Nankeen lily, L. × *testaceum* is unfortunately susceptible to botrytis and sometimes to basal rot so that growth must be watched.

Lilium tsingtenense is an uncommon lily from eastern China and Korea, and although known for more than a century it did not receive its specific name until 1904. The formation and the placement of the flowers has caused it to be confused with some other species, and certainly as far as its bright, orange-red flowers are concerned, it is much like *L. concolor*. From the loosely imbricated bulb there arises the glabrous stem, varying in height according to season, from $1\frac{1}{2}$ to 3 ft. This lily is not difficult to grow, especially if given a lime-free, sandy soil containing leaf-mould or peat which does not dry out in summer. The bulbs should be placed 4 ins deep, and being stem-rooting appreciate some shade on the lower part of the stem.

L. tsingtenense 'Carnea' is a form with unspotted reddish flowers. *L. tsingtenense* 'Flavum' has yellow blooms with dark red spots.

Lilium vollmeri is a species which was long known and catalogued as *L. roezlei* but was given specific rank in 1948. A native of California, it is a lovely plant and although it has been known for many years, it is only since its authoritative naming that its value has become appreciated. This lily forms a creeping rhizome. The stems reach a height of $2\frac{1}{2}$ to 3 ft and usually bear 2 or 3 flowers, although in California it is said to produce up to 24 blooms. The orange segments are spotted purplish black and recurve gracefully. It is not really an easy lily and does not seem likely to become very popular in the garden.

Lilium wallichianum is a small trumpet lilly

ideal for the greenhouse border and it will do reasonably well in pots. Named after a Danish botanist, this lilly was known in cultivation as long ago as 1826. A native of Nepal and Sikkin, it grows 3 to 6 ft high, and from August onwards the stems carry from 1 to 4 fragrant, well-placed, funnel-shaped flowers, each with a slender tube about 4 ins long and an expanded mouth which is remarkably wide considering the narrowness of the tube. The colour is creamy-white with green shading on the outside. Stem-rooting, the bulbs should be planted not less than 5 ins deep in porous, loamy soil containing leaf-mould, while the addition of sand and charcoal will prove beneficial. Propagation can be effected by detaching some of the bulblets which form on the underground stem, for this lily rarely sets seed in Britain.

L. wardii was discovered in Tibet by Captain Kingdon Ward in 1924. It belongs to the martagon group, having sharply reflexed petals. The colour seems to vary, sometimes appearing as quite a pale pink and on other occasions being a rich rosy-pink. The petals are spotted in purple with a purple line down the centre, and the purple anthers shed bright orange pollen. These scented flowers are produced in July and August on 4 to 5-ft stems, on which are numerous but scattered leaves each about 3 ins long. The rather small bulbs have tightly imbricated scales spotted red on a fawn-coloured ground.

Plant the bulbs 4 or 5 ins deep in lime-free soil containing plenty of humus matter. Shade from strong sun is desirable. This lily seeds freely and the seeds can be sown either as soon as they are ripe or in the spring. It is usually about 3 years before seedlings reach flowering size. Since the colour of the flowers is liable to vary, any special variety should be propagated by detaching the bulblets which form on the underground stem or by using scales.

Lilium washingtonianum is a splendid Californian lily but not one of the easiest to manage. It should be grown in a well-drained, deep, loamy soil in which the bulbs should be buried about 6 ins deep. The roots must not dry out during the summer and as it dislikes disturbance, this lily will not usually flower the first season after moving. The stems produce light green leaves, and normally become about 4 ft high but have been known to grow nearly twice as much. In June and July from 3 to 18, scented, shapely blooms of pure white dotted with purple are produced. This lily, which is said to have been named after the wife of President Washington, can be raised from seed which should be sown when quite ripe in the autumn.

Good forms very similar to the type include: *L.w.* 'Album' which is less strong growing and has unspotted blooms. *L.w. minor* has the common name of Shasta lily because of the place where it can be found wild in North California. It is smaller growing than the type. *L.w.* 'Purpurascens' (or 'Purpureum') is the form most common in cultivation. Although of similar appearance, occasionally the petals are tinted purple, passing to a winy shade on opening.

L. wilsoni is a showy lily from north-east Asia which has, at various times, been known under other names. It is now generally accepted that Max Leichtlini named it in honour of G. F. Wilson whose great pleasure it was to cultivate lilies, and whose land eventually became the starting place of the RHS Gardens at Wisley.

The first reference to this lily appears to have been in 1868 when it was described as *L. thumbergianum pardinum*. This was probably due to the panther-like spots on the petals. It has also been thought to be a form of *L. dauricum*, but it is now recognized under the specific name of *L. wilsonii*.

The bulbs should be planted 5 ins deep in sun or partial shade, preferably where there is a good porous loam. In August, the reddish-orange flowers, which are flushed or marked in yellow, are produced on 3-ft stems on which are scattered lanceolate leaves up to 4 ins long.

Pink Perfection Strain, a group of hybrid lilies with flowers in the subtlest shades of pink

In view of the very many choice species and hybrid lilies which have been in cultivation for some years, one might not unreasonably suppose that there was no point in attempting to raise new varieties. If this were so, we should now be without many altogether first-class groups of hybrids including those created by hybridists such as Jan de Graff, Miss Preston and others. In some instances, the hybrids are vastly superior to one or both parents.

'*Aurelian*' *hybrids.* This group of lilies was created through the appearance of a hybrid at the Royal Botanic Gardens at Kew in 1900. The pollen from *Lilium henryi* was used on *L. leucanthum.* Unfortunately, this outstanding seedling was soon lost in cultivation, but the cross was tried again by Monsieur Debras of France, who used the pollen of *L. henryi* on *L. sargentiae.* Similar crosses were made at the Oregon Bulb Farms. By back-crossing, a remarkably wide and choice colour range has been secured, some being even more beautiful than the original hybrids.

The main types were recognized and singled into separate strains. First were those that resembled *Lilium henryi,* but with broader, stiffer, more vigorous stems, and these have been identified as the 'Sunburst' strain, the colours embracing white, ivory, greenish-white, and yellow. Those producing trumpet-shaped flowers in shades of rich yellow were named the 'Golden Clarion' strain, while the lovely, intermediate plants with bowl-shaped flowers are now recognized as the 'Heart's Desire' strain.

After the plants were selected, there still remained a number of hybrids that did not fit into any of the three groups, and these are now known as the Aurelian Hybrids which are hardy, vigorous lilies for general garden planting, and for cutting. The flowers have the main characteristics of *L. henryi,* but have broader petals in various shades of colour which are more trumpet-like in shape.

'*Fiesta*' *hybrids.* This strain is based on the original crosses made by Dr Abel of New York. The lilies used in this strain include *L. amabile, L. luteum* and *L. davidii.* The resulting plants are tall-growing and bear as many as 20 well-spaced, reflexed and nodding flowers in colours that range from pale straw-yellow, through to vivid red, to orange and maroon. All the flowers are lightly sprinkled with small, maroon-black spots. The colours include many pastel shades and rich tones of terra-cotta and burnt sienna. Resistant to virus and other diseases, Fiesta Hybrids have proved to be a wonderful addition to the summer flowering lilies.

'*Green Mountain*' *hybrids.* This is yet another strain which originated in the United States. Among the lilies involved in the production of these hybrids were *L.* 'Crow' hybrids, *L. princeps* 'Shelburne', *L.* 'George C. Creelman' and *L. centifolium.* When the seedlings first flowered, only those showing green and bronze-shaded flowers were selected for further breeding, and from the very finest plants a fine range of late-flowering trumpet lilies has been built up. All of these are predominantly greenish-bronze in appearance. The very finest of these hybrids has been named 'Green Dragon'. This is goblet shaped, the substantial petals being a fine chartreuse colour.

'*Golden Clarion*' *strain.* This is a strain of golden and lemon-yellow trumpet lilies selected from *Lilium henryi* crossed with various trumpet lilies. They are not only suitable for exhibition purposes, as they are sturdy, vigorous garden plants, but also flower over a period from July onwards, reaching a height of 5 to 7 ft. They should be planted 4 or 5 ins deep, in a well drained soil containing plenty of humus matter.

'*Golden Chalice*' *hybrids.* This strain has been built up from crosses between various upright-flowering Chinese species and their garden variants. This is a further evidence of marked improvements in hybrids over parent plants and of hybrids which have been introduced as a strain, rather than separating a few individuals and propagating them for eventual naming and introduction. These hybrids are very resistant to drought and this is why they do so well in warm, dry situations where they flower on $2\frac{1}{2}$ to 4-ft stems during the whole of June.

'*Mid-Century*' *hybrids* are the result of the careful crossing of *L. tigrinum,* forms of *L. hollandicum* and some other lilies. All these are well known for their good qualities for they

Agapanthus orientalis need greenhouse protection in all but the mildest areas

Fritillaria meleagris. There is a subtle charm about the
chequered flowers few other bulbs possess

The 'Mid-Century' lily hybrids are among the easiest for general cultivation

succed under greatly differing conditions, often in gardens and climates that do not seem favourable. Back crossing to both parents has produced an even larger number of good hybrids. Some are of upright growth, others have pendent flowers, while a third group have blooms facing outwards. Both flowers and foliage are good and this means that these hybrids respond to greenhouse culture. Both the named and unnamed hybrids grow 4 to 5 ft high and when established there appear from June onwards 8 to 20 flowers on strong self-supporting stems.

Among the named hybrids are 'Croesus', goblet-shaped golden-yellow flowers spotted black; 'Destiny', soft lemon-yellow, spotted brown; 'Enchantment', bright nasturtium-red upright flowers; 'Fireflame', crimson-red, being specially adaptable for cutting; 'Harmony',

upright, apricot-orange spotted brown; 'Prosperity', lemon-yellow, lightly spotted brown and 'Tangelo', with outward facing star-shaped orange flowers.

'Olympic' hybrids. Another achievement of the American lily hybridist Mr Jan de Graaf has been the production of the 'Olympic' hybrids. Long and intensive work has resulted in the creation of a very fine strain of trumpet lilies. There is a good variation among the individual plants of the strain. All types from the trumpet-shaped flowers to the more unusual forms are represented, including the wide-open, bowl-shaped types and those with twisted and ruffled petals.

G

The colour range is wide, and includes cream, soft pink and icy-green. The outside of each petal is delicately shaded with light greenish-brown or soft wine tints. In some cases they are a pure glistening white. They flower in July, just a little later than *L. regale* and last over a period of 3 or 4 weeks. The bulbs form basal roots and should therefore be planted 5 or 6 ins deep in well-drained soil where they may be left for some years to establish themselves.

An interesting development from these hybrids is the Olympic Pink selections, the colour extending over the inner surface as well as the outside of the petals, and in many cases the colour is a moderately deep pink, although it varies from plant to plant. The depth of colour is greatest when the plants are grown out of full sun.

'*Stookes*' *Hybrids*. This is the group name for a number of Turks' cap lily hybrids of which *L. davidii* has been much used as the main parent. Of the other reliable hybrids 'T. A. Havemeyer' resembles both its parents *L. henryi* and *L. sulphureum*.

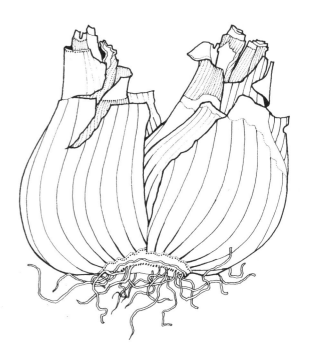

Lycoris radiata

LYCORIS Related to the amaryllis and nerines, and natives of China and Japan, this genus consists of about 8 species all having short, tunicated bulbs. The funnel-shaped flowers appear in the autumn and are very similar to those of nerines, and the plants have the same type of strap-like leaves, and although perhaps most suited for the cold greenhouse, they may be planted very shallowly outdoors in favourable positions in the milder parts of Britain. Whether grown in pots or in the open they should be moved in September or October immediately after flowering and given a sandy, loamy soil. Plenty of water should be available during the growing period but keep them dry when the foliage has died down.

Of the species available *L. incarnata* is rare, the flowers having an unusual colouring of purple and carmine. *L. radiata* produces slender stems 12 to 15 ins in height with bright red flowers. It is best given the protection of straw or bracken during the winter to save it from damage by frost.

L. sanguinea, 12 to 18 ins high, bears umbels

Lycoris squamigera

of bright red flowers in August and September. Again, some protection should be given during winter. *L. squamigera* has flower stems 2 to 3 ft high, each with an umbel of large sweetly-scented, rosy-lilac flowers. Of similar appearance to *Amaryllis belladonna*, the foliage does not usually show until spring. The normal method of propagation is by offsets, since seed rarely sets in Britain.

MONTBRETIA Of South African origin, most of the species and varieties for so long known and offered in catalogues as montbretias have now been transferred to other genera such as *Crocosmia* and *Tritonia*. Even the *M. rosea*, so valuable for cutting, has now been classified as *Tritonia rosea*.

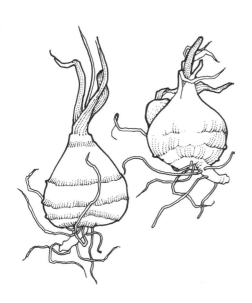

Montebretia aggregate

M. laxiflora provides continuous colour in the garden from June to September. Spikes 1 to 2-ft tall, bearing a host of tubular flowers of a pinkish-orange, copper and red combination are accompanied by deeply-grooved, sword-shaped leaves, emerging from every inexpensive corm of

this half-hardy relative of the popular gladiolus. They increase rapidly, so rapidly in fact, that clumps formed require lifting and dividing about every 3 years.

Montbretias are most useful summer-flowering subjects for they not only enliven mixed borders, add colour between shrubs and thrive beside foundations of the house, but will even flourish along the base of light hedges. They make dainty and long-lasting cut flowers too.

Plant the corms in deep, well-drained soil with plenty of leaf-mould or decomposed manure and ensure they get the sun for at least part of the day. The best depth of planting is 3 to 4 ins, spacing 4 to 6 ins, and time of planting can be from April through May. Corms must be planted upon arrival and, like most gladioli, need plenty of water when growing and flowering. There is no need to lift montbretias in the autumn, merely give them an early spring dressing of bone meal and they will go on year after year. Splendid mixtures of montbretias are obtainable from garden centres and bulb merchants.

MORAEA Often known as the peacock flower or butterfly iris, this native of South Africa and Australia was named after a British botanist. In the past, some species have been listed as irises but there is a botanical difference between the two. The foliage of all species is narrow and rush-like.

Moraeas need some kind of winter protection and a cold or cool greenhouse is advisable. Since it is dampness which encourages mildew and other fungus troubles, just a little heat helps to keep the plants healthy. It is worth trying the corms outdoors in very warm, sheltered places. Well-drained, sandy soil should be provided and, because of their 'running roots', they do better in beds than in pots. While the flowers, which appear from March to July, do not last long, they are freely produced.

M. glaucopis is often catalogued as *Iris pavonia* and widely known as the peacock iris. On 12 to 20-in. stems, this very pale blue flower bears a rich, peacock-blue spot ringed in dark purple.

M. iridioides, 4 ft, has white flowers with gold-blotched, lavender standards.

M. ramosa produces, in June and July, on 12

to 30-in. stems, fluttering yellow flowers.

M. pavonia has large, orange-yellow flowers each with a blue eye, and appears to have several forms with slight colour variations.

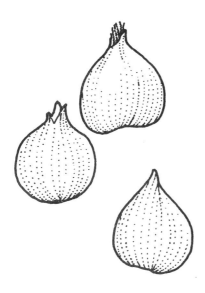

Morea glaucopsis

M. spathulata produces large, bright yellow flowers on 2-ft stems and will succeed outdoors in warm corners.

M. villosa, growing to 18 ins, is velvety-violet marked in mauve and cream shades, each petal having a blotch of peacock blue. Best grown in sandy soil.

Propagation of moraeas is by division or seeds, the latter taking several years to reach flowering size.

MUSCARI Easy to grow, and thrive in almost any well cultivated soil. Many of the species are scented, and the name originates from the Latin *muscus* or 'musk'—a reference to their perfume. In some gardens they increase rapidly, so much so that they are liable to become a nuisance. This applies particularly to the dark blue *M. racemosum*, a widely grown species both in Britain and other European countries. All like plenty of sun.

Only a few of the several dozen species are in general cultivation, but all produce clustered spikes of bells. In many instances the narrow, often channelled leaves begin to grow in autumn and come through ordinary winters unmarked. Planted in generous groups alongside early-flowering red tulips or yellow daffodils, or around some pink flowering shrubs such as ornamental almonds or prunus, they provide an impressive display.

Ideal for flower border edgings and the rock garden, muscari need watching in their situation so that they do not take up too much room, for they increase rapidly by the offsets which form at the base and sides of the bulbs. For this reason established clumps should be lifted and divided every 3rd or 4th years. Some species are suitable for growing in pots or pans in the cold or cool greenhouse but should not be subjected to great heat. All should be planted in September or October, and the bulbs covered with 3 ins of soil.

M. armeniacum is one of the best known species with 8 or 9-in. spikes of rich, azure-blue, scented flowers which appear in April and May. It not only produces many bulblets but seeds freely, often spreading widely. Among its forms are the following: 'Blue Spike', large, double and sweetly-scented, flowering on 6-in. stems; 'Cantab', clear Cambridge-blue; 'Heavenly Blue' a widely grown cultivar with 6 to 8-in. spikes of gentian-blue and excellent for cutting; 'Early Giant' is a slightly earlier-flowering form.

M. azureum is the earliest growing, the tight heads of soft, powder blue flowers showing from late Feburary onwards. *M.a.* 'Album' is a splendid white form.

M. botryoides or the Italian grape hyacinth produces 6-in. spikes of deep blue at the end of March. The form 'Coeruleum' is a lovely china blue, while *M. b.* 'Album' is pure white. Since all of these are shorter-growing than the other species they are most suitable for cultivation in the rock garden as well as in other positions.

M. cosmosum, a common plant in some European countries, grows 15 or more ins high.

The flowers, which appear in June, form loose heads of purplish-blue through which a greenish tinge can be seen. The leaves are broader than those of the other species, while the bulbs show a pinkish tinge on the outside. *M.c.* 'Monstrosum' has mauvish-blue flowers and is often known as the tassel or feather hyacinth. *M.c.* 'Plumosum' is the best known variety. It produces, at the end of April, striking plumes of reddish-purple flowers, the long, branched filaments being like silky, intertwined tufts.

M. latiflorum is an uncommon sort, freely producing upright spikes of dense, hanging bell-shaped flowers, the top bells being sky blue while the lower part is purplish blue, the foliage being wide.

M. moschatum, the musk hyacinth, produce in April 5-in. spikes of sweetly-scented, greyish-purple flowers, which shade to a yellowish brown, and *M.m. flavum*, from Asia Minor, has yellow flowers with purple tips. It does well in a sunny sheltered corner. Growing 6 ins high, its highly scented flowers appear in March and April. Some authorities classify this as *M. macrocarpum*. *M.m.* 'Major' is probably the best musk-scented muscari of all. The purplish flowers, which change to yellow, are freely produced once the bulbs are established in a light well-drained soil.

M. neglectum, an attractive free flowering, dark blue, scented species has bright, yellowish-green foliage which shows up well against the colour of the 9-in. spikes.

M. paradoxum produces 6-in. flower spikes of blackish-blue, each flowerlet being marked green, thus giving a most distinct appearance and showing up well against the brighter varieties.

M. racemosum, the starch hyacinth, has been known in Britain for many years. It has long, chennelled, drooping leaves and 6-in. spikes of plum-scented flowers in May.

The newer *M. tubergenianum*, from Persia, is one of the finest muscari of all, the strong 8-in. flower spikes, which appear in April, being true blue with no darker markings. The turquoise-blue buds open to a deep blue, so that the two distinct shades on the same spike give this variety the name Oxford and Cambridge muscari.

NARCISSUS The vast, expanding narcissus family has been divided into 11 sections, each group being sub-divided according to colour and the length of the petals and corona, cup or trumpet. It is possible to mention only a few of the more reliable varieties in each section. New cultivars are constantly being introduced.

Division I. **Trumpet narcissi.** This division consists of varieties having a corona or trumpet as long or longer than the petal segments and has 4 sub-divisions.

(*A*) Perianth coloured, corona coloured, not paler than the perianth.
'**Clonmore**', large, rich golden-yellow.
'**Dutch Master**', deep golden-yellow, serrated trumpet.
'**Golden Harvest**', brilliant yellow, a fine garden variety.
'**Kingscourt**', a good deep yellow of faultless form.
'**King Alfred**', an old form, but dependable yellow trumpet.

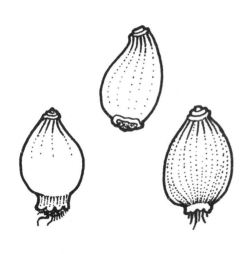

Narcissus triandus

'**Magnificence**', an early all-yellow variety with gracefully waved petals.

'**Unsurpassable**', very large trumpet of deep yellow, the petals being flat and broad.

'**Hunters Moon**', cool lemon-yellow, flanged and serrated trumpet.

'**King's Ransom**', an attractive rich golden-yellow trumpet of fine form.

(*B*) Perianth white, corona coloured. This section is often known as the bicolours.

'**Bonython**', early-flowering with creamy-white trumpet and pale primrose petals.

'**Preamble**', very large, rich yellow trumpet. Excellent for exhibition and garden.

'**Trousseau**', very pretty perianth and well-proportioned, soft-yellow trumpet. One of the best varieties.

'**Spellbinder**', distinct, luminous greenish-yellow, the flanged trumpet passing almost to white making it a reversed bicolour.

(*C*) Perianth white, corona white, but not paler than the perianth.

'**Beersheba**', white flower of good substance.

'**Broughshane**', large, well-shaped flower with trumpet widely flanged.

'**Cantatrice**', graceful and of smooth texture.

'**Mount Hood**', a vigorous variety and one of the best of all white sorts. The large trumpet is slightly flushed in very pale yellow when it first opens.

Division II. Large-cupped narcissi of garden origin.

(*A*) Perianth yellow, corona or cup coloured.

'**Air Marshal**', broad, white, sturdy golden perianth, orange-red cup.

'**Carbineer**', a reliable variety, yellow petals, rich orange cup.

'**Carlton**', yellow petals with graceful, frilled, slightly paler crown.

'**Fortune**', lemon-yellow with coppery-orange cup.

'**Galway**', golden-yellow with large, lemon-yellow corona.

(*B*) Perianth white, corona coloured.

'**Duke of Windsor**', overlapping petals with expanded, apricot-orange crown.

'**Flower Record**', large, expanding orange cup.

'**Mrs R. H. Backhouse**', old variety but still good. The corona is almost a short trumpet of apricot-pink.

'**Sempre Avanti**', creamy-white perianth, bold, orange cup.

'**Green Island**', the shallow bowl-shaped crown passes to greenish-white.

'**Salmon Trout**', one of the best 'pink' varieties, the corona being salmon-pink as it opens fully, the colour not fading.

(*C*) Perianth white, corona white, but not paler than the perianth.

'**Castella**', a well-proportioned flower for exhibition.

'**Ice Follies**', saucer-shaped crown opens pale yellow but turns to white.

'**Silver Lining**', a fine white for exhibition and garden.

(*D*) Any other combination of colours.

'**Binkie**', clear, sulphur-lemon passing to white with a yellowish corona.

Division III. Small-cupped narcissi of garden origin.

(*A*) Perianth yellow, corona coloured.

'**Chunking**', one of the best in this section, the shallow corona being vivid orange.

(*B*) Perianth white, corona coloured.

'**Blarney**', perianth white with a saucer-shaped corona of salmon-orange.

'**La Riante**', apricot, flanged cup.

'**Matapan**', pure white petals, orange-red centre.

(*C*) Perianth white, corona white, not paler than the perianth.

'**Frigid**', a late-flowering variety with small crown, having an emerald eye.

'**Portrush**', pure white petals, white cup with a golden eye.

Division IV. Double narcissi of garden origin.

'**Inglescombe**', a large flower of uniform primrose colour.

'**Irene Copeland**', creamy-white segments interspersed with apricot.

'**Mary Copeland**', white petals with orange-red petalodes.

'**Texas**', yellow, intermixed with orange-scarlet.

'**Cheerfulness**', several sweetly-scented, white-and-cream flowers on each stem.

Among the other older double varieties are *N. albus* 'Plenus Odoraus', white; *N. capax* 'Plenus', often known as Queen Anne's daffodil, lemon-yellow, and *N. telemonus* 'Plenus', which is the old double yellow daffodil.

Division V. **Triandrus narcissi of garden origin.** Mostly in miniatures which are dealt with separately.

Division VI. **Cyclamineus narcissi.** Many of these will be found mentioned among the miniature narcissi, but several larger varieties are worth growing including:
'Beryl', slightly reflexing primrose petals, orange cup.
'Peeping Tom', graceful, narrow, yellow trumpet with sharply reflexed petals.

Division VII. **Jonquilla varieties.** Many of these, too, are classed with the dwarf-growing varieties but slightly larger sorts include:
'Cherie', ivory-white perianth, the small cup flushed shell-pink.
'Sweetness', highly perfumed, golden-yellow.
'Trevithian', soft lemon-yellow.

Division VIII. **Tazetta or Poetaz varieties.** These are bunch-flowered varieties excellent for cutting and for growing indoors. Varieties include:
'Geranium', clusters of pure white with orange-scarlet cup.
'Scarlet Gem', primrose-yellow petals, orange-scarlet cup.
'Silver Chimes', small, nodding, white flowers with creamy-lemon cups.

Division IX. **Poeticus narcissi.** These old-fashioned varieties are greatly prized for cutting and for their perfume.
'Actaea', has white petals, the large yellow eye being margined in red.
'Old Pheasant Eye' or **'Recurvus'**, most dainty, the reflexing white perianth contrasting well with the deep red eye.

Division X. **Miniature narcissi and various species.**

Division XI. This is the miscellaneous section which includes any variety not falling into the divisions already mentioned.
Narcissus bulbocodium. This is the group name of the dwarf narcissi often known as hoop petticoats; they are both quaint and

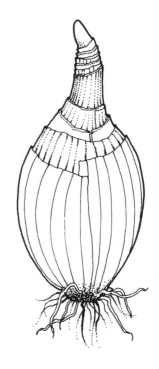

Narcissus jonquilla

attractive. The flowers consist of very narrow petals, the centre, crown or corona being funnel-shaped. There are now many forms probably due to the fact that they seed freely, some of the seedlings showing variation.

There are some reliable named forms well worth growing, among which are the following, all flowering well in April where the soil does not dry out.

N.b. 'Citrinus' is one of the tallest, sometimes growing 6 ins high. The pale yellow flowers have an expanded corona as much as an inch wide.

N.b. 'Conspicuus' is deep yellow and the most widely grown.

N.b. monophyllus is snowy-white with a very slightly frilled corona. While correctly it should be entered under the name of *N. cantabricus monophyllus* it is still usually offered in catalogues as a bulbocodium. Since it is a native of southern France and Spain it likes a warm, sunny situation with a short drying-off period in the summer. There are several good forms of this dainty narcissus.

115

Narcissus cyclamineus is so-named because of the way the petals reflex like a cyclamen

N.b. 'Nivalis' is smaller and shorter growing, with pale yellow flowers.

N.b. romieuxii is one of the most attractive forms. Excellent for pots and pans or the alpine house, it will also grow well in sheltered places in the rock garden showing colour from January onwards. The yellow flowers eventually rise above the foliage. It received an Award of Merit from the RHS in 1938.

N. canaliculatus is a miniature polyanthus narcissus. It produces on 6-in. stems 3 or 4 sweet-scented flowers, each with white petals and a golden cup.

N. cyclamineus is a most elegant early flowering species of distinct form. It produces a bright yellow, long, tube-like corona with petals which recurve or turn back sharply. It likes a position where the soil does not dry out and produces its flowers on 4 to 7-in. stems in February and March. As the result of crosses with the larger trumpet narcissi a number of forms have been produced. Among these are some well-known varieties such as 'February Gold', 12 ins, 'Peeping Tom', and 'Caerhayes',

all fine, yellow hybrids. There are also a number of bicolour hybrids raised by using *N. cyclamineus* as one of the parents.

N. × gracilis is late-flowering and is often to be seen in bloom in late May when the light, silvery, scented blooms are valued.

N. jonquilla is a popular species because of its sweet fragrance. On each 10 to 12-in. stem 3 to 6 short-cupped, yellow flowers appear in April and are particularly useful in pots or pans and groups in the rock garden. The deep green leaves are rush-like. *N.j.* 'Flore-pleno' is the double jonquil.

N. juncifolius is an unusual species doing well in moist places. The leaves are rush-like, the very short trumpets being surrounded by deeper yellow petals. Blooming in April and May it has 3 to 4-in. stems.

N. lobularis is a form of *N. pseudo-narcissus*. It is probably one of the earliest of daffodils to bloom, showing colour from late February. In all respects it is just like the larger single daffodils but has a stem of only 7 to 8 ins.

N. minimus is probably the smallest of all miniature trumpet daffodils, far smaller than *N. nanus* or *N. minor* which are sometimes offered in its place. The small trumpet is delicately fringed. *N. asturiensis* is also a very tiny trumpet daffodil, but because of the weakness of its stem it cannot be recommended for general planting.

N. nanus is another dwarf daffodil, rarely growing more than 6 or 7 ins high and following *N. lobularis* in its time of flowering.

N. odorus 'Rugulosus' produces grass-like foliage and clusters of sweet-scented, yellow flowers. This is often regarded as a form of jonquil. In April and May the flowers open on 9 to 12-in. stems. The vigorous form known as 'Plenus' has double flowers which are often more sweetly scented.

N. pseudo-narcissus is the English wild daffodil, often known as the Lent Lily.

N. rupicola, similar to *N. juncifolius*, produces a single flower on each stem. The colour is rich yellow, the perfume strong. The cup or corona is saucer-shaped and 6-lobed, whilst the foliage is rush-like. First-class for pots and pans, it is also very suitable for garden cultivation.

N. tenuior is an uncommon, elegant slender-

growing jonquil-like plant with creamy petals and sulphur-coloured cup borne on 12-in. stems.

N. triandrus is the name of a group of smaller narcissus species and hybrids which are characterized by their pendulous flowers produced on 6 to 12-in. stems.

N.t. albus is often known as angel's tears and produces, in April and May, 2 or 3 creamy-white flowers on each 6 to 9-in. stem. Excellent for pots and pans it can also be grown in suitable places in the rock garden.

N.t. 'Aurantiacus', deep golden yellow.

N.t. calthinus is thought to be a form of *N.t. loiseleurii.*

N.t. 'Concolor' is pale, golden-yellow, scented, with narrow foliage.

N.t. loiseleurii is very pale cream, somewhat larger than *N.t. albus*, the leaves often curving attractively.

N.t. pulchellus, white or creamy-white. This variety is not easy to find in cultivation.

There are now a number of hybrids of *N. triandrus*, one being known as April tears, which are sometimes to be found listed as jonquils. Other hybrids which are definitely of *N. triandrus* habit include 'Silver Chimes', growing 12 to 15 ins high with 5 or 6 creamy-white flowers on each stem. 'Thalia' is similar but larger. *N. ×johnstonii* is probably a natural hybrid. It is often known as Queen of Spain. It has lemon-yellow flowers with reflexed lemon yellow petals and a narrow trumpet produced on stems of 1 ft.

N. watieri has an exotic pure white, flattish flower produced on 3 to 4-in. stems. First-class for pot culture it never fails to attract attention when seen growing in the rock garden or at the edge of the shrub border. *N.w.* 'P. Milner' is a well-known and reliable hybrid with small, sulphur white trumpets on 9 in. stems. First-class for the rock garden.

There are several unusual almost rare autumn-flowering *Narcissus* species. These are native of Mediterranean areas. In Britain they flower in September or October and all are made more valuable by their sweet scent. They should be planted in sheltered positions and in a place where they ripen off well during the summer. *N. elegans* produces 1 to 3 flowers on each 6 to 8-in. stem, the petals being greenish-white and the corona and cup pale yellow and saucer shaped. The narrow leaves appear before the flowers.

N. serotinus normally has one or two flowers on each 8 to 10-in. stem. The petals are white, the shallow crown being yellow and deeply lobed. The rush-like leaves develop as the flowers begin to fade.

N. viridiflorus is an unusual green daffodil, up to 4 flowers appearing on each 6 to 8-in. stem. Again, the narrow leaves develop as the flowers fade and very often only a single leaf is produced. This is a very ancient variety although

Narcissus 'Cheerfulness', a fascinating multi-flowered double variety

little known and grown.

Wherever dwarf narcissi are planted they will bring colour to the garden often where little else is available and dramatic effects can be secured by planting some of the species with the botanical tulips which flower at the same time.

The dwarf species narcissus, especially *C. cyclamineus* and *C. bulbocodium* and its forms naturalize very freely and rapidly, seedling themselves in unmown grass and making a veritable carpet of colour in spring. They do particularly well in damp areas and naturalize well in acids soils, where snowdrops, for example, prove difficult to establish satisfactorily.

NERINE The family amaryllidaceae includes many beautiful bulbous subjects including the nerines, natives of South Africa, and most ornamental plants. The dainty, more-or-less funnel-shaped flowers, of which the petals are often recurved, are carried in umbels on strong, yet slender stems. With nearly all species and varieties, the long narrow strap-shaped leaves develop after the flowers appear. Except for *Nerine bowdenii*, all require cool greenhouse treatment when grown in Britain.

N. bowdenii, however, may be grown in sheltered positions outdoors in the south west or other favourable districts. When established at the foot of a wall, or similar place where the ground does not become water-logged or very wet during the winter, umbels of large beautiful pink blooms are produced in September.

A form of *N. bowdenii* known as 'Fenwick's Variety', has bigger blooms which are brighter in colour and are carried on thicker stems up to $2\frac{1}{2}$ ft high. This form does not appear to increase as rapidly as the species, which is why it is much less well known. In favourable sites, some form of protection is helpful. Straw or bracken are suitable and these can be removed once the severe weather has passed.

Nerine sarniensis and its many varieties should be potted during August and early September. This should be done by firmly placing one bulb in a 3 or $3\frac{1}{2}$-in. pot, while several bulbs look well in larger receptacles. Well crock the pots to ensure good drainage, and use a compost of good, fibrous loam, silver sand and a little decayed manure, while a sprinkling of bone meal is very suitable. Leave part of the neck of the bulb exposed.

Flower spikes appear soon after potting, and with most of the greenhouse varieties the stems vary in height from 15 to 18 ins, having umbels containing from 6 to 15 flowers. They like plenty of light and air, and when showing flower the pots may be brought into the living room where they provide a very bright decorative display. The spikes can also be cut and last a long time in water.

To prevent danger of overwatering, and subsequent sourness of the soil, stand the pots in shallow water so that the moisture seeps up and moistens the compost evenly. As the foliage follows, the flower's moisture should be available for the roots after the blooms have finished, for the proper development of the foliage largely influences the blooms to be produced the following year. For this reason, keep the pots in a sunny position and give occasional applications of good, liquid manure until the leaves die down in the spring. This helps the bulbs to recover from the efforts of flowering, giving strength for the formation of the next season's blooms.

It is only necessary to repot the bulbs every 3 or 4 years, for they bloom freely when well established. Each summer before growth commences it is a good plan to remove the top inch or two of the soil and replace it with some good rich compost. After the foliage has withered the pots should be stood in a cold frame or sheltered position, gradually lessening the water supplies. Keep them there until the following August.

Apart from *N. sarniensis*, which is bright red and often known as the Guernsey lily, the following are well worth growing. *N.s.* 'Corusca Major', orange-red; *N.s.* (*fothergillii*) 'Major', crimson and *N. flexuosa* with pink, waxy flowers which show at the same time as the foliage. *N. filifolia* has slender stems of 1 ft, bearing rose-pink flowers in Octobr. *N. humilis* bears its deep pink flowers on 1-ft stems. *N. undulata* has large umbels of rose-pink flowers on 15 to 18-in. stems. A number of the *N. sarniensis* hybrids have been named and are gradually coming back again into favour. There is also a particularly good strain known as 'Borde Hill' hybrids which are notable for their strength and colour. All have prominent anthers and petals which seem to be sprinkled with gold dust.

Propagation is by offsets which can be detached when the bulbs have dried off. Seed is not very difficult to secure, and should be sown in heat in the spring. Nerines can be raised from seed, and this has resulted in the availability of many fine forms.

NOMOCHARIS A native of China and Tibet, and similar in many respects to both lilies and fritillarias, this is an interesting subject although not always easy to establish. The flowers of all species are pendulous, mostly facing downwards, although a few develop horizontally. They must have ample moisture at all times, without becoming waterlogged and seem to prefer partial shade. Apart from the species there are a number of hybrids in cultivation all flowering during the summer. Excellent for pots, the bulbs should be covered by at least $2\frac{1}{2}$ ins of soil. They can be propagated by seed which, however, is usually available in mixture only.

N. aperta, growing $2\frac{1}{2}$ to 3 ft high, produces 5 or 6 nodding, pale pink, spotted flowers. *N. farreri* is very strong-growing, the white-stained, pink flowers developing on 3-ft stems. *N. mairei* is one of the most beautiful and best known, having drooping, saucer-shaped white flowers spotted in rose-purple. The petals are fimbriated.

N. pardanthina grows 3 ft high and has pale pink flowers spotted in purplish-crimson. *N. saluenensis* produces, on 3 ft stems, really large bell-shaped flowers more than 2 ins in diameter. Their colour is pale pink, sometimes almost white, and the petals are marked purplish-red.

All *Nomocharis* species look exotic and have orchid-like blooms. Care is needed to prevent slugs from damaging the young growths.

ORNITHOGALUM This genus contains many species suitable for the border, rock garden and cutting. Most are hardy, but a few need greenhouse culture. Any good, well-drained soil will suit the bulbs, which look their best in bold groups. Plant the hardy varieties from

September to November. For some of the choicer kinds, a light top dressing of decayed manure or peat applied in the early part of the year will keep them in good, free-flowering condition.

O. aureum is a form with yellow flowers. *O. balansae* is fairly scarce, but a good plant for the rock garden, having an umbel of white,

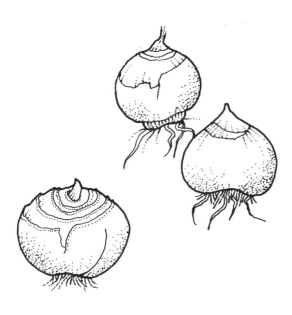

Ornithogalum thyrsoides

star-like flowers borne on short stems. A little later to flower is *O. narbonense*, which grows 9 ins high. Its white flowers, with green central stripes show up well in the rock garden or under trees and shrubs. *O. nutans* produces, in May and June, on 6 to 9-in. stems, umbels of silvery-grey flowers shaded green on the outside. Particularly good for growing in grass or under trees, it increases freely.

O. pyrenaicum is a hardy, European species producing small, greenish-yellow flowers on 2-ft stems in May and June. *O. pyramidale*, known as virgin's spray, is a most accommodating species for the border, producing, in June, long, pointed leaves and spikes of starry, white flowers some-

times tinted green. *O. saundersae* is known in South Africa as the giant summer ornithogalum. Growing 3 ft high, it bears umbels of creamy-white long-lasting flowers.

O. umbellatum is the Star of Bethlehem, which freely produces starry white flowers in May. It is a good subject for brightening up dull corners and, although it is inclined to spread, if the clumps of bulbs are lifted and divided every 3 years, it will prove an effective and attractive subject for the front of a border.

The less hardy species of *Ornithogalum* are best planted in the spring, lifted in the autumn, and stored in slightly moist sand or peat until the following spring. *O. arabicum* is a handsome species, flowering in June and July and bearing clusters of elegant, creamy-white flowers with shining black centres on stems of about 18 ins. Excellent for the conservatory, when grown outdoors this variety should be given a warm, well-drained position and some light protection in the winter.

O. lacteum produces, in June and July, racemes of large white flowers on 2 to 3-ft stems. Needs to be grown in the cool greenhouse.

O. thyrsoides is commonly known as the chincherinchee. This has long, thickish foliage and a closely-clothed flower head of starry white, growing 15 ins high or more. It has become very popular during the last few years, chiefly as a plant for the conservatory. For growing outdoors in warm places, it makes a first-class cut flower, and if cut as the buds are opening, the flowers will last at least 4 to 5 weeks in water. Plant bulbs in the open about 3 ins deep from mid-April onwards, and lift them in the autumn before frosts come.

OXALIS The name of this genus means 'sharp' or 'sour', referring to the bitter taste of some of the leaves. Many, but not all species have tuberous root-stocks. All like congenial conditions and well-drained soil in sunny situations.

O. adenophylla is first class, growing in gritty soil in pots, or in the rockery where its crinkled, silvery-green foliage and rose-pink, semi cup-shaped flowers on 3-in. stems appear in succession from May to July. This is an easy plant for pots in the greenhouse. Plant it

½ in. deep in sandy loam and keep it in a dark place until the leaves are visible. Water sparingly and only after growth is developing.

O. bowienana has 3 to 5 glowing rose flowers with yellow centres on 9-in. stems and was once described as 'most precious'. *O. deppei*, of which the roots are edible, is coppery-red and should be divided in October. It always attracts attention, whether in pots or in the garden. *O. enneaphylla*, whose flowers are white, is hardy and very attractive with fan shaped, much-divided leaves and waxy-white flowers.

O. floribunda (*rosea*), is the most common species with bright pink flowers. It is of invasive habit and must be kept in its place. A less rampant, white form is *O.f.* 'Alba'.

O. hirta, from South Africa, is best grown in the alpine house, although in sheltered places it looks well outdoors, the stems being studded with clear pink flowers. *O. lasiandra* has rosy-carmine flower heads on 9-in. stems and attractive foliage. *O. lobata* has an unusual habit of growth for it produces in May a crop of small, clover-like leaves which seem suddenly to disappear and then reappear in

Ornithogalum umbellatum, the star of Bethlethem, opens its glistening white flowers only in full sun

September when the golden-yellow flowers develop. This habit often leads to the plants being considered dead or destroyed in error.

O. vespertilionis, from South America, is lilac-rose in colour and particularly suitable for the rock garden.

Propagation is by divisions in July, when bulblets can be separated and grown on in the open or in boxes of fine loam, leaf-mould and sand. Bigger specimens can be potted singly and planted in the open as soon as the foliage shows signs of developing.

PANCRATIUM   The members of this small genus of plants have the common names of sea daffodils or Mediterranean lilies, a reference to the fact that, in their native habitat, they grow near the sea shore. The large, roundish bulbs give rise to strap-shaped leaves. The scented flowers are produced in an umbel, the outer petals being narrow and recurved. Pancratiums make good pot plants, but should not be re-potted too frequently. Outdoors, they need a

121

very shelted, sunny, well-drained position. After flowering the bulbs should be gradually dried off. Propagation is done from offsets in autumn or spring.

P. calathinum is now known as *Hymenocallis calathina*. *P. canariense* has white flowers in September and is excellent for the cool greenhouse. *P. illyricum* bears in June an umbel of white flowers marked in green, on 15 to 18-in. stems. It is a useful plant for the cold frame.

P. maritimum carries, from July to September, delightfully scented, white flowers striped in green on 1-ft stems. The foliage of this species is usually persistent.

The other species of this genus are not readily obtainable in Britain.

PARADISEA   A genus of one species, this is a hardy, bulbous plant of easy culture and looks best when planted in groups.

P. liliago, known as St Bernard's lily, is usually listed under its correct name of *Anther'cum liliago*.

P. liliastrum, growing $1\frac{1}{2}$ to 2 ft high, is St Bruno's lily which has wiry stems, bearing in June and July loose spikes of 6 or more pure white, funnel-shaped flowers as much as 2 ins wide at the mouth. Each petal is tipped with a green spot. It has the general appearance of a small *Lilium candidum*.

POLIANTHES TUBEROSA   This is a single-species genus belonging to the family amaryllidaceae. Frequently known as the tuberose, it is a native of Mexico and an excellent bulbous plant easy to culture in the greenhouse. The bulbs, which are really tuberous rootstocks, flourish in sandy loam enriched by leafmould and well-rotted manure, and can be planted singly or several in a large receptacle, their top portion being left exposed.

To obtain a succession of blooms, bulbs can be planted at any time from February to May. Start them under cool conditions to encourage a good root system. When this has been formed they can be given a temperature of from 60 to 70° F. By careful regulation of heat it is possible to secure flowers during the whole of the autumn and early winter when they are particularly valuable. Provided good compost has been used,

no additional feeding will be required, although an occasional application of liquid manure may be given. A weekly syringeing with clear water will keep the foliage in good condition.

In warm sunny gardens, tuberoses may be grown outside. The bulbs which should be planted with their tops at ground level in May or early June, are best lifted after they have flowered in August and September. Secure fresh bulbs annually, for although offsets can usually be obtained they do not ripen well and this naturally affects the following season's blooms.

'The Pearl' is the best-known and most reliable variety, with waxy-white flowers on stems 18 ins or more high. These emit a delightful fragrance and are well offset by the long narrow leaves which usually have brownish-red markings on their undersides.

PUSCHKINIA   Related to both *Chionodoxa* and *Scilla*, this member of the lily family is native to the Caucasus and Asia Minor and was named after the Russian botanist, Count Puschkin. Small drifts of bulbs growing in a partially-shaded position create a pleasing effect in the spring garden. The fluffy, striped bells resemble *Scilla*, each 4 to 6-in. stem bearing a cluster of a dozen or more pale silver-blue blooms each segment lightly marked with a slightly darker blue line. There is only one known species in cultivation, *P. scilloides*, which is listed in bulb catalogues as *P. libanotica*—the Lebanon or striped squill. *P. libanotica* 'Alba' is the pure white form which flowers at the same time. The small, tunicated bulbs should be planted in autumn about 3 ins deep and 3 ins apart, where they can be left undisturbed. They also like sunny spots in the front of the border or where the soil does not dry out. The flowers are excellent for including in small arrangements and posies.

As long as they are not forced, puschkinias can be grown indoors like crocuses. Plant them in rich, light soil in October, about 1 or 2 ins deep and $\frac{1}{2}$ to 1 in. apart, in 5-in. pots. Plunge the pots outdoors in the garden or place in a cool cellar for 6 to 8 weeks before bringing them indoors to a cool living room.

RANUNCULUS   This is a very large genus

taking in fibrous and tuberous-rooted plants. The name is derived from the Latin *rana* meaning a 'frog', apparently because many species grow in damp places such as are inhabited by frogs.

The tuberous-rooted species produce a

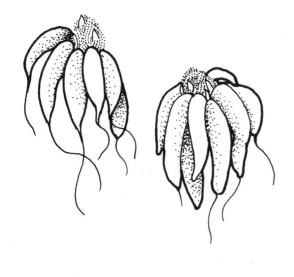

Ranunculus hybrida

gorgeous effect in summer with their large double flowers ranging in colour from white to deepest purple and running through the whole spectrum of yellow, pink, red, scarlet and orange. The plants have deeply scalloped leaves with magnificent flowers up to 4 in. in diameter, according to type and variety.

All cultivated or garden ranunculus are derived from a single species *R. asiaticus*, originating in Asia Minor where it has been grown for centuries. As a result of selection and hybridization, four main types of ranunculus are now available.

'*French*' *ranunculus*. This type was evolved in France about 1875 and later the semi-double flowers were improved by Dutch growers. A vigorous strain, this has large blooms in many

delightful shades, all with a central black blotch. Flowering in May and June on 9 to 12-in. stems, they like sunny, sheltered positions. Best planted in early March, they come in mixed or named varieties.

'*Paeony-flowered*' *ranunculus*. The large double or semi-double flowers of this strain were developed in the early 1900s by an Italian horticulturist, and later a number of Dutch growers raised identical forms. They are free flowering and come in all the colours of the rainbow. Blooming from May into July on 10 to 14 in. stems, they thrive in sunny, well-drained borders. While they can be planted in the south in November and December and given winter protection, it is advisable to wait until March before planting.

'*Persian*' *ranunculus*. This type was brought back from Turkey about 1700. The plants bear single or double, medium or small flowers on stems 10 to 16 ins high. Plant mixed or named varieties from the end of February selecting sunny positions.

'*Turban*' *ranunculus*. Hardiest of the four types and available for planting from December to April, these have large, full, globular or semi-double flowers on 9 to 12-in. stems. When planted in mixture in sunny, sheltered positions they are extremely showy and have a wide range of colours. Natives of Turkey, they were introduced into Europe by the famous botanist Carolus Clusius in 1580.

The soil, preferably gritty and peaty, should be well watered before planting ranunculi, claws down, about 2 ins deep and 6 to 8 ins part. All sites must be well drained. Do not water too much until the plants are fully grown. Ranunculi welcome a layer of peat in April or early May. Tubers can be lifted when the foliage dies down and stored in a cool, frost-free, well-ventilated place until the next planting time, or can be left in the ground if you give them a dressing or organic fertilizer each autumn and protect them carefully from frosts.

They make very effective cut flowers and can also be grown in a cool greenhouse if planted in pots and plunged outdoors until well rooted.

SAUROMATUM A small genus of Central-Asian aroids, these plants are named from the Greek *sauros* meaning a 'lizard' because of the speckled markings of the spathe. The tuberous-rooted plants grow in the greenhouse where they like a rich, sandy soil.

The species *S. guttatum* is familiarly known as monarch of the East. Often regarded as a curiosity in the warm living room, when stood on a saucer or bowl without soil or water, it grows rapidly. Within a few weeks, the arum-like flowers up to 2 ft high appear, oddly speckled and marked with purple, yellow and green. After flowering in late spring the tubers can be potted up or planted outdoors in a warm place, lifted at the end of August, kept in cool conditions, then placed in saucers again in October or November.

A few other species are somtimes available. These are for growing in pots in the usual way and include *S. brevipes*, purplish; S. nervosum, purple and yellow and *S. punctatum*, green and purplish-mauve.

The normal method of propagation is by detaching the offsets in the autumn.

SCHIZOSTYLIS

SCHIZOSTYLIS The name of this genus refers to the divided, thread-like stigma 'stalk''. These plants originated in South Africa. The form of the flower spike is not unlike that of a gladiolus, varying in height from 18 to 24 ins and occasionally more. Perhaps its greatest value is that it blooms from September right up to mid-winter when often there is very little colour in the garden. One of the many plants which are less grown or known than they deserve, this is an attractive, late-flowering subject which flourishes in a fairly rich, moist but well-drained soil.

Occasionally injured by severe frosts, *Schizostylis* is hardier than often supposed, but it does best if given sheltered conditions. Even then a covering of peat or leaf-mould will do nothing but good and may be pricked into the surface soil in the spring to provide humus matter. Straw and bracken will give welcome winter protection too, and are essential in exposed and northern districts if a good display of late blooms is to be obtained. A liberal amount of moisture should be available throughout the summer especially as, when planting, a plentiful supply of silver sand should be added to the soil.

Plant schizostylis outdoors in March and, when necessary, divide clumps of rhizomatous roots. This operation should be carried out in spring. Stock increases by the development of small stolons which in time produce the flowering stems.

S. coccinea, the best-known species, is sometimes known as the Kaffir lily or crimson flag. The flowers, up to 2 ins in diameter, are crimson-scarlet and usually go on showing colour well into December. A form known as *S.c.* 'Mrs Hegarty' has satiny-rose flowers and is particularly successful when grown in pots in the unheated greenhouse. *S.c.* 'Viscountess Byng' produces spikes of flesh-pink blooms of great beauty and not infrequently goes on flowering until January. All make excellent cut flowers.

SCILLA Related to the chionodoxas, this is a large genus of bulbous plants with a wide distribution which covers Europe, Asia and South and North Africa. The tunicated bulbs produce strap-shaped leaves and spikes bearing

Scilla tubergeniana

Eucomis bicolor, the exotic pine-apple flower

Beautiful though this tulip looks, its beauty is in fact caused by a disease

'Enchantment', a modern deep yellow lily hybrid

Crocus sativus 'Album', a rare white autumn-flowering crocus

6-petalled flowers. Practically all are hardy. For most, October is an ideal month to plant. Since the bulbs vary considerably in size, a good guide as to depth of planting is $2\frac{1}{2}$ times the depth of the bulb itself. All can be increased by offsets (although seed is another means) which partly accounts for the fact that some species and varieties multiply when bulbs are left undisturbed for many years.

The following are spring flowering species: *S. amoena* produces deep bluish-mauve flowers on 6-in. stems in April and May.

S. bifolia blooms from February onwards, producing star-like, bright blue flowers on 6 to 8-in. stems. It has a number of named forms including 'Alba', white; 'Praecox', very early and a brighter blue; 'Rosea' is rose pink while the rare 'Taurica' is deeper blue with reddish-pink shading on the stem.

S. bithynica bears, in April, purplish-blue flowers on 10 to 12-in. stems.

S. campanulata, see *Endymion*.

S. hispanica, Spanish bluebell, see *Endymion*.

S. nutans, English bluebell, see *Endymion*.

S. sibirica, the Siberian squill, is the best-known and most popular scilla. It has vivid, Prussian-blue flowers on 4 to 6-in. stems and never fails to attract attention. It is first class in the front of the border, the rock garden, or in pots and pans. Its variety 'Atrocoerulea', better known as 'Spring Beauty', is usually earlier flowering, larger and strong looking.

S. tubergeniana is early flowering, the 4-in. stem producing very pale blue flowers of which the exterior of the petals has a deep blue marking. It is first class for the alpine house.

S. verna can occasionally be found growing wild in Britain. The insignificant, bluish-mauve flowers, borne on short stems, open in March and April.

Among the summer flowering species the following are worthy of note. *S. autumnalis*, a British native plant, produces pinkish-blue flowers on 6 to 8-in. stems. These often appear before the foliage.

S. odorata. In May and June this produces 6 to 8-in. spikes of sweetly-scented, bell-shaped, light blue flowers.

S. peruviana, is known as the Cuban lily, which is a little odd since it is a native of the

Scilla siberica is probably the bluest flowered of all bulbous plants

central Mediterranean area. It likes well-drained soil in a sunny, warm situation. The 8 or 9in. stems carry dense heads of several dozen star-like, lilac-blue flowers during May and June.

There are a number of other easily grown species which, however, are rarely grown or seen outside botanical collections. A few are suitable for the alpine house or other unheated glass structure where they do well in pots. Some are quite small in size, others not entirely hardy.

The better known of these species include: *S. cooperi* with starlike, purple flowers borne on 6-in. stems in spring.

S. natalensis, produces 2 to 3-ft stems from quite large bulbs, which makes it distinct from all other scillas. In late summer or early autumn, the blue flowers are quite attractive.

S. violacea bears greenish flowers in spring on 4 to 5-in. stems. Once established, it increases freely. The leaves are quite ornamental, being blotched green or purplish-green.

SPARAXIS Natives of South Africa, and often known as African harlequin flowers, these are closely related to both freesias and ixias and require similar treatment. Except in warm, sheltered positions they are best grown in the greenhouse, either in pots or in beds on the greenhouse 'floor'. Under glass, the bulbs can be planted from October onwards. Then they will begin to show colour in April. Outdoors, it is not wise to plant until early April. Plant bulbs up to 3 ins deep and be prepared to provide some protection in case of late frosts. If this is done, the narrow leaves will not become discoloured at the tips and edges as they will do if exposed to very low temperatures. Propagation is by offsets or seeds.

There are two species in general cultivation. *S. grandiflora* has wiry stems 15 to 18 ins high. The whitish-purple flowers, which have dark centres, are up to 2 ins in diameter. This

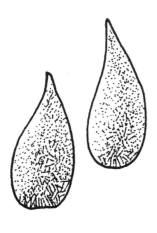

Sparaxis hybrida

is the latest to flower and sometimes does not show any colour until August.

S. tricolor is the better species. The 15-in. stems carry flowers of variable colour taking in orange, yellow, scarlet and pink usually with darker central markings. These are at their best during May and early June. The separate variety *S.t.* 'Scarlet Gem' is particularly fine having brilliant, velvety-scarlet flowers with a yellow and black centre. *S.t.* 'Ariadne' is white, shaded in violet, the yellow centre having a black border. A pure white form is also known.

Sprekelia formossissima

SPREKELIA   A monotypic genus related to *Hippeastrum*, this is a decorative Mexican flower, known as the St James' lily because the segments of the perianth look rather like the red cross embroidered on the cloaks of the Knights of St James. It is also well known as the Jacobean lily. Once regarded solely as a greenhouse plant, it adapts itself easily to garden cultivation provided it is not planted outdoors until the end of April. Bulbs should be planted shallowly in well-drained soil about 12 to 18 ins apart in sunny positions. Lift the bulbs in autumn before the first frosts, and keep them in a dry, temperate storage place during the winter. The bulbs increase by division and the offsets usually take 2 years to flower.

Sprekelias can be grown in pots in the greenhouse or house. Plant them as you would hippeastrums in John Innes potting compast No. 3 or a similar mixture, leaving the top third of the bulb exposed. When planted in pots sprekelias should be allowed a prolonged period of dryness after flowering—when the leaves begin to turn yellow—to ensure flowering again the following year. Whether grown outdoors or indoors, the leaves usually appear at the same time as the flowers, but do not be surprised if the flower sometimes blooms before the foliage appears or vice-versa.

Sprekelia formosissima produces, in July, 6-petalled flowers which are curiously orchid-like in appearance and which have slim and erect, long, upper petals partially enclosing the stems. The large, oval-shaped, long-necked bulbs with black tunics produce solitary stems, each crowned with an imposing, vivid crimson-scarlet flower. They are in full bloom in the garden in June and July and the flowers are extremely long lasting.

STERNBERGIA

STERNBERGIA Named after the Czech botanist, Count von Sternberg, this subject is sometimes known as the autumn daffodil. Like the well-known daffodil, it is a member of the amaryllidaceae family, but this Mediterranean plant looks like a large crocus. Botanically, it is distinguished from the crocus by having 6 stamens instead of 3.

There are 4 species of *Sternbergia*, all with yellow flowers, but by far the best and easiest to grow is *Sternbergia lutea*, which boasts golden-yellow flowers and rich foliage in September and October. Although not common, the larger bulb specialists will be able to supply it to any gardener who wants something unusual and attractive in his garden.

Growing 4 to 6 ins tall, *Sternbergia lutea* is most effective planted in sunny places, on grassy banks and slopes, or in rock gardens and borders. If left undisturbed over a long period—and they need a year to become established—the bulbs form large clumps. The brilliance of the flowers contrasts beautifully with the green of their strap-shaped leaves. Plant the bulbs, which have black tunics, in sunny positions 4 to 6 ins deep in good soil mixed with leaf-mould

Sprekelia formossissima, one of the most exotic-looking of all bulbs, has blood-red flowers

in July. The roots start growing in August and late planting can endanger proper flowering. They may also be grown in the garden frame or in pots or bowls to flower a few weeks after planting.

S. fischeriana is similar in appearance to *S. lutea*, but shows its colour in spring. The large, roundish bulbs produce yellow, funnel-shaped flowers on 4 to 6-in. stems.

Two other little-known species which flower in the autumn produce their flowers well before the foliage appears. They are *S. clusiana* (*macrantha*), a native of Turkey, Palestine and Persia and the rare *S. colchiciflora*, which is also found in the Balkans. This has quite small flowers, the leaves developing in spring.

None of these species compares with *S. lutea* for general cultivation. All flower most freely after a really hot summer.

TECOPHILAEA This small genus of Chilean bulbous plants contains only two known species. Sometimes referred to as the

Chilian blue crocus it is among the most beautiful spring flowering bulbs—and perhaps the most temperamental. The name commemorates the daughter of an Italian botanist. Even in South America, their native home, tecophilaeas are now quite rare.

T. cyanocrocus has a fibrous, tunicated corm from which develops slender foliage. In March and April it bears, on 3 or 4-in. stems, beautiful gentian-blue flowers each with a white centre, the 6 petals making an open funnel shape. A form known as *T.c.* 'Violacea' has darker blue, almost purple flowers, while *T.c.* 'Leichtlinii', has flowers in which the white centre is larger, reaching out into the petals. *T. violiflora* is not nearly as good as *T. cyanocrocus* and it seems doubtful if it is now in cultivation.

The Chilean crocus is ideal for the alpine house. Outdoors it needs sandy soil and a sheltered, very well-drained position. The base of a wall or a similar place would be ideal. If established colonies are lightly top dressed with decayed manure it will not only give winter protection but provide the feeding matter the corms appreciate.

Success seems more assured if the corms can be ripened by being planted where the summer sun reaches the site in which they are grown. Offsets form the best means of propagation. Seed is rarely produced.

TIGRIDIA These natives of Mexico and Peru are interesting bulbous subjects with beautifully spotted and marked flowers. This gives them the name of tiger flowers. The ovid bulbs have loose, brown coats. Admirable pot plants, they should be grown under cool conditions and provided with a good rooting medium containing silver sand and leaf-mould. Though not quite hardy, in favoured positions in the south of England they can easily be brought into flower outdoors.

Select a sunny, well-drained position and plant tigridias in March or April, covering the bulbs with 3 or 4 ins of good, sandy loamy soil to which decayed manure and bone meal have previously been added. An envelope of sharp sand around each bulb will provide the required conditions. From July until September,

tiger flowers present a gorgeous display and although each bloom makes a fleeting appearance a fresh supply is produced daily. The quaint shape and markings of the flowers attract attention wherever they are grown.

When in growth the plants like plenty of moisture, and a mulching of old manure or litter will keep the surface soil from drying out

Tigridia pavonia

in the summer. To induce continued flowering, a few applications of liquid manure from the time the first buds open will not only encourage plenty of blooms but also bring out their real colour tones. Stock can be increased by separating the offsets at lifting time. If the bulbs are lifted annually, as they should be in all but very warm positions, they are best dried off and stored in a frost-proof, airy place throughout the winter in dryish sand or peat fibre. When growing tigridias indoors, plant 5 bulbs in a 6-in. pot which should be placed in the frame or cool house until growth has started, then moved into warmth and given water as required.

There are a number of species and varieties, but for the average gardener the following, growing 15 to 18 ins high, are suitable for both pot or outdoor culture. *T. lutea*, which is uncommon, is an unspotted pure gold; *T. pavonia* 'Conchiflora', yellow heavily spotted scarlet; *T.p.* 'Alba', large white petals, cup spotted ruby; *T.p.* 'Rubra', scarlet petals, cup spotted crimson, yellow ground; *T.p.* 'Ruby Queen', ruby-rose with mauve shading and *T.p.* 'Le Geant', salmon-scarlet with a striking primrose-yellow edge to the 3 larger petals. In addition, it is possible to secure a good mixture. *T. violacea* is pale violet with deeper markings.

Most of the other species and varieties available are for pot work only, but all are worth the attention of bulb enthusiasts.

TRILLIUM These delightful plants, mostly of North American origin, have several common names such as wake robin and wood lily. The plants in this family are distinguished by having their parts, such as leaves and flowers, in three sections. The three outer segments (sepals) are green and the three petals are white, cream, or reddish tones according to variety. The roots are made up of an irregularly shaped tuber. Trilliums thrive in semi-shade and under woodland conditions, although they will grow almost anywhere except in dry soil. Under trees, they form an ideal ground cover where otherwise the site would be bare. Once established, they usually remain in healthy condition, flowering regularly for many years.

There are 2 or 3 dozen known species. Many are similar, and natural hybrids, developed over the years, do not make it any easier to separate them. There are certain botanical features such as the shape of the petals and the presence or otherwise of a flower stalk, which are a guide in naming plants.

T. cernuum, the nodding trillium, has pinkish-white flowers in April. *T. erectum*, 1 ft high, has forms with white, cream, pink and red flowers. *T. grandiflorum* is probably the best for the ordinary garden, the large white flowers being produced on 18 to 24-in. stems.

T. ovatum, growing to 10 ins, has white flowers which change to pink in March or April. *T. sessile* has crimson-purple flowers,

Tigridia pavonia the tiger flower. Each flower lasts only a day but is stunningly beautiful

which 'sit' on the leaves. It is sometimes known as the toad trillium and has several forms. *T. umbellatum* is the painted trillium, with rose-pink flowers, blotched in crimson and with coppery foliage. Propagation is easy by division.

TRITELIA, see *Ipheion*.

TRITONIA This is a genus of South African plants which are related to other well-known bulbous families such as freesias, ixias and *Sparaxis*. Few species are available, although some which were previously classed as tritonias have now been transferred to other genera such as *Crocosmia*.

T. crocata is a particularly attractive plant which, while it can be grown outdoors in sandy loam in warm, sheltered districts, makes a fine show in pots or pans in the cool greenhouse. The cup-shaped flowers are produced on thin, wiry stems and last well both when growing and when cut. They like plenty of water when in growth but will not stand frost. One way of avoiding damage is to plant the bulbs in pots in December and transfer them in spring to the sheltered border.

T. crocata bears cup-shaped, coppery-orange flowers with purple anthers on 12 to 18-in. stems in June. There are several forms, particularly good being 'Prince of Orange', 'Orange Delight' and 'White Beauty'. *T. lineata* has creamy-yellow funnel-shaped flowers. *T. nelsonii* is rare. Growing only 8 or 9 ins high, the flower colour is an intense orange-red.

T. rosea is the species most suited for outdoor cultivation. Given a well-drained, sandy position it grows 18 to 20 ins high. The pink flowers, marked in yellow and crimson, open in August and September.

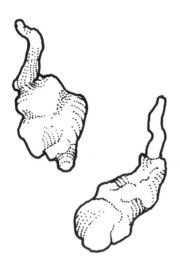

Tropaeolum tuberosum

TROPAEOLUM The name of this genus comes from the Greek *tropaion*, a 'trophy', and is designated because the leaves closely resemble a buckler and the flowers a helmet. The name also covers a number of fibrous-rooted plants including nasturtiums. There are many excellent tropaeolums, mostly of South American origin,

all more-or-less of climbing or rambling habit. Most have deeply lobed leaves and irregularly-shaped flowers with 5 petals.

T. × leichtlinii is a good hardy plant, probably a hybrid between *T. polyphyllum* and *T. edule*. It has deeply cut, grey-green leaves and, in June, orange-yellow, red-spotted flowers, the stems trailing attractively.

T. polyphyllum, from Chile, although not well known, is certainly attractive. It is useful for covering unsightly objects. The trailing stems, 3 or 4 ft long, are well supplied with grey-greenish leaves and freely furnished with bright, orange-yellow flowers from June until August. This *Tropaeolum* species can be propagated by separating the oblong tubers in March. It is not a difficult subject to grow in any good, well-drained soil.

T. tuberosum comes from Peru. A showy twiner, it likes a sunny position and light, sandy soil, apparently preferring a rather drier position than the other species. The stems, which are 4 to 6 ft long, carry well-divided foliage and, during late summer and autumn, produce clusters of showy red and yellow flowers. Again, planting is best performed in the spring and normally a good display of flowers is procured in the same year.

Other lesser-known species from South America include: *T. azureum*, tender species with blue flowers; *T. brachyceras*, yellow; *T. edule*, light red; *T. pentaphyllum*, vermilion; *T. umbellatum* which forms large tubers and red and orange flowers and *T. violaeflorum* which is sky-blue. All these are much more suitable for growing in the frame or greenhouse than outdoors.

TULIPA Many tulips found in today's gardens have been propagated from the species named after Conrad Gesner who made the tulip known by botanical descriptions and drawings. He first saw it in the beginning of April 1559, at Augsburg, in the gardens of Counsellor John Henry Herwart. The seeds had been brought from Constantinople or, according to others, from Cappadocia. These had produced a large, single, beautiful red flower, like a red lily. It had a sweet, soft and subtle scent. The first reference to the tulip in literature is contained

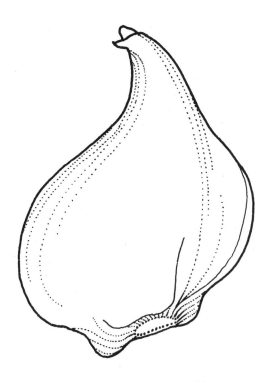

Tulipa kaufmanniana

in a letter written by the Ambassador of the Emperor Ferdinand I at the Court of the Sultan of Turkey, as he was travelling. Journeying near Constantinople an abundance of tulips which the Turks called '*tulipan*' was offered him everywhere he went.

After the tulip became known, Dutch merchants and rich people in Vienna sent to Constantinople for various kinds. According to the Dutch writer Hakluyt, the first bulbs planted in England were sent from Vienna about the end of the sixteenth century.

The beauty of tulips quickly caught the imagination of a wide public, and the craze known as 'tulipomania' swept Holland and much of Europe. People paid thousands of pounds for single bulbs of unique varieties, many of which were simply virus-induced malformations. Today values have changed and beauty of form and colour are most sought after.

Since that time an extremely large number of varieties have been introduced in many sepa-

rate sections, so much so that it would be difficult to determine to which section a variety belongs if some official guidance had not been given. The Royal Horticultural Society of London and the Royal General Bulbgrowers' Society of Holland have now reclassified the thousands of tulips in cultivation, taking into account recent developments in breeding and the introduction of new races and varieties since the beginning of this century. The new Register has reduced the total of divisions to 15, while there are changes in the descriptions of the divisions to give a better idea of particular groups.

Today few varieties of 'Duc van Thol' and 'Breeder' tulips are cultivated, so they have now been included in respectively the 'Single Eearly' tulips and 'Cottage' tulip divisions. Some 'Breeder' tulips, however, which, according to their shape, belonged to the 'Triumph' or 'Darwin' races of tulips, have been placed in the relating division. Equally, because few varieties of 'Rembrandt', 'Bizarre' and 'Bijbloemen' tulips are now cultivated, these 3 divisions have been united in a single division called Rembrandt tulips.

Under the old classification system the different species tulips and their hybrids embraced no less then 8 divisions. In the new list there are only 4. With the exception of the *T. kaufmanniana*, *greigii* and *fosteriana* species and their hybrids which remain as separate divisions, all the other divisions of species have been included in the division of 'Other Species'.

The divisions, including the 4 divisions of species tulips, have been arranged according to flowering time. This has involved moving Darwin Hybrids forward to the mid-season flowering category of garden tulips from the late flowering category. The various changes naturally meant that a number of cultivars or varieties had to be re-classified and the description of some divisions redefined to incorporate the inclusion of transferred varieties. Because many tulip varieties stem from crosses between tulips of different divisions, some have been more accurately classified according to their dominant characteristics—in effect, a tidying-up measure.

Relatively few of the most popular varieties of garden tulips grown by British gardeners have

The hybrid tulip 'Bellona' has rich golden-yellow goblets and quickly forms clumps

part of flower usually rectangular in outline and tulips which have the same habit. VII Lily-flowered tulips. Flowers with pointed reflexed petals. VIII. 'Cottage' tulips (Single Late tulips). Flowers oval, which do not belong to divisions 6 or 7. IX. 'Rembrandt' tulips. Broken tulips, striped or marked brown, bronze, black, red, pink or purple on red, white or yellow background. X. 'Parrot' tulips. Tulips with laciniate flowers, generally late flowering. XI. Double Late tulips (Paeony-flowered tulips).

Species (*Tulipa* and its hybrids). XII. *T. kaufmanniana*, varieties and hybrids. Large, early-flowering, sometimes with mottled foliage. XIII. *T. fosteriana*, varieties and hybrids. Large, early-flowering, some cultivars having mottled or striped foliage. XIV. *T. greigii*, varieties and hybrids. Always with mottled or striped foliage, flowering later than *T. kaufmanniana*. XV. Other species and their varieties and hybrids.

Garden tulips are divided into a number of sections, each different from the other and containing many delightful varieties. The earliest-flowering section is that known as 'Duc van Thol', although they are not much grown nowadays and are difficult to obtain. They grow 6 to 8 ins high and are of value for forcing. Because of their size and when subjected to too much heat, they often look poor little things.

Single Early tulips. The earliest of the garden tulips in general cultivation. Derived from crosses between *T. generiana* and *T. suaveolens*, they are single cupped in form with sturdy stems, 10 to 15 ins tall. They come in striking shades of almost every known colour and are most popular. They begin to flower in early April and are invaluable for massing in beds and borders to produce early splashes of colour in the garden. They finish flowering in time for the ground to be cleared for planting summer bedding subjects. Because of their short stature and sturdy habit, Single Early tulips are excellent for edging and ideal for window boxes and terrace tubs. Most varieties do well in pots and bowls indoors too.

Varieties available for both indoor and outdoor culture include: 'Bellona', golden yellow, scented; 'Brilliant Star', bright scarlet; 'Couleur Cardinal', purplish-crimson; 'De Wet', fiery orange, stippled orange-scarlet; 'Dr Plesman',

been affected by this re-classification. Some 'Mendel' varieties, 'Her Grace' and 'Orange Wonder', for example, are now classified as 'Triumph' tulips. The popular 'Cottage' tulip, 'Mrs Moon', is now classified as a 'Lily-flowered' tulip because of its shape, and the 'Breeder' tulip 'Dillenburg' has been transferred to the 'Cottage' division.

The new classification is as follows:

Early-flowering. I. Single Early tulips; II. Double Early tulips; III. 'Mendel' Tulips, chiefly the result of crosses between the old 'Duc van Thol' and 'Darwin' tulips which generally do not have the habit of 'Triumph' tulips.

Mid-season flowering. IV. 'Triumph' tulips, chiefly the result of crosses between Single Early and Late (May-flowering) tulips, plants of stouter habit than 'Mendel' tulips. V. 'Darwin' hybrid tulips. Chiefly the result of crosses between 'Darwin' tulips with *Tulipa fosteriana* and the result of crosses between other tulips and botanical tulips, which have the same habit and in which the wild plant is not evident.

Late-flowering. VI 'Darwin' tulips. Tall, lower

orange-red; 'Ibis', deep rose; 'Keizerskroon', scarlet, edged in yellow; 'Pink Beauty', pink, shaded white; 'Princess Irene', orange and purple; 'Prince of Austria', orange-red; 'Sunburst', yellow, flushed in red and 'Van der Neer', plum-purple.

Double Early tulips. These flower a little later than Single Early tulips—at about the end of April. About the same height as the Single Early varieties they have large, open double flowers which are long lasting. Double Early tulips are unrivalled for mass plantings in beds and borders and do well in sunny or partially sheltered positions. Their neat, even growth makes them ideal for edging and for window box and terrace tub display. Many can also be grown in pots and bowls indoors.

Varieties available for indoor or outdoor culture include: 'Boule de Neige', pure white; 'Dante', deep red; 'Electra', deep cherry-red; 'Goya', salmon-scarlet and yellow; 'Maréchal Niel', yellow and orange; 'Mr van der Hoef', golden yellow; 'Murillo', white, tinged in rose; 'Orange Nassau', orange-scarlet; 'Paul Crampel', scarlet with yellow centre; 'Peach Blossom', rosy pink; 'Scarlet Cardinal', bright scarlet; 'Triumphator', rosy pink; 'Vuurbaak', bright scarlet; 'Wilhelm Kordes', orange, flamed in yellow, and 'Willemsoord', carmine edged in white.

'Mendel' tulips. These varieties help to fill the gap between the early and late or May-flowering tulips. First introduced in 1909 they are the result of crosses between 'Duc van Thol' and 'Darwin' tulips and produce large, handsome single flowers in a broad range of colours on stems 16 to 24 ins tall. 'Mendel' tulips are superb for forcing in the cool greenhouse, blooming from January onwards. Although they like somewhat sheltered positions in the garden they do extremely well under ordinary conditions, flowering from the last week of April and at least a fortnight before the 'Darwin' varieties. Most are self-coloured or edged with deeper or contrasting hues and look most elegant in clumps in beds and borders or beneath the light shade of trees.

Among varieties available the following are reliable. 'Apricot Beauty', salmon-rose, tinged in red; 'Athleet', pure white; 'Krelage's Triumph',

crimson red; 'Olga', violet-red edged in white; 'Pink Trophy', pink, flushed in rose, and 'Sulphur Triumph', primrose yellow.

'Triumph' tulips. These tulips produce much mid-season colour in the garden, for the blooms come in a wide range of colours and are borne on stiff stems, 16 to 24 ins tall. They are weather resistant to all but the extremes of Britain's late April climate.

Derived from crosses between Single Early tulips and 'Darwin' tulips, 'Triumph' were first introduced in 1933 and have become increasingly popular every year since. They have large, single-cup flowers striped and margined, not to be found in other divisions of tulips. They are particularly valuable for exposed positions in beds, borders and other garden sites. Generally they bloom immediately after the 'Mendel' tulips. 'Triumph' tulips are just as adaptable as 'Mendel' tulips for forcing, but they flower a little later in the cool greenhouse, from mid-February, and, whether grown indoors or in the garden, they make most useful cut flowers.

A tremendous choice of varieties is available today. These include: 'Arabian Mystery', deep purple violet, edged in white; 'Aureola, bright red, edged in golden-yellow; 'Bandoeng', mahogany-red, flushed in orange; 'Denbola', cerise-red, edged in yellow; 'Dreaming Maid', violet, edged in white; 'Edith Eddy', carmine, edged in white; 'Elmus', carmine-red, edged in white; 'First Lady', reddish-violet; 'Garden Party', pure white edged in carmine; 'Kansas', white, yellow base; 'Kees Nelis,' red edged yellow; 'Korneforos', brilliant red; 'Merry Widow', red, edged in white; 'Madame Spoor', mahogany-red, edged in yellow; 'Paris', orange-red, edged in yellow; 'Paul Richter', geranium-red; 'Preludium', rose with white base; 'Prominence', dark red; 'Reforma', sulphur-yellow; 'Rijnland', crimson-red, edged in yellow; 'Telescopium', violet-rose, and 'Topscore', geranium-red, yellow base.

Gardeners can also obtain mixtures of 'Triumph' varieties.

'Darwin' tulips. These made their debut in 1889 after permission had been obtained to name this splendid new type of tulip after the great naturalist Charles Darwin. 'Darwin' tulips are almost as important historically as the first few

Tulipa 'Red Riding Hood', a brilliantly coloured early-flowering dwarf variety

bulbs and seeds brought from Turkey to western Europe some 300 years earlier. Not only have the 'Darwins' shown themselves to be fine tulips, they have also proved to have an exceptional capacity for being hybridized with other classes of tulips. From 'Darwins' have come the twentieth-century classes of 'Mendel', 'Rembrandt', 'Darwin' hybrid and Lily-flowered tulips.

'Darwins' are excellent in beds, borders, kitchen gardens or orchards as they have long, sturdy stems 26 to 32 ins in height, which also make them superior cut flowers. Many can be grown in pots and bowls. The large, cupped flowers are squared off at the bases and tops of petals and come in virtually all colours. Many have a distinctive satiny texture. All are resistant to wind and rain, and can be grouped effectively among shrubs or evergreens or interplanted with roses and other subjects. All varieties flower in May.

Gardeners can choose from dozens of superb varieties now available, and some of the richest coloured include: 'Aristocrat', soft purplish-violet, edged in white; 'Blue Aimable', lilac; 'Campfire', rich crimson; 'Clara Butt', soft salmon-rose; 'Cordell Hull', blood-red on white; 'Demeter', plum-purple; 'Flying Dutchman', vermilion-scarlet; 'La Tulipe Noire', purple-black; 'Mamasa', bright buttercup-yellow; 'Nephetos', soft sulphur-yellow; 'Ossi Oswalda', creamy-white flushed pink; 'Pride of Haarlem', cerise-red; 'Queen of Bartigons', pure salmon-pink; 'Queen of Night', deep velvety-maroon; 'Rose Copeland', pink; 'Sweet Harmony', lemon-yellow, edged in ivory-white; 'The Bishop', violet-purple; 'Utopia', cardinal-red; 'William Pitt', cochineal-red and 'Zwanenburg', pure white.

Mixtures of 'Darwin' varieties blended and made up from named varieties flowering at the same time produce a fine display of brilliant and contrasting colours.

'*Darwin*' *hybrid tulips*. This is the name of a group of mid-season tulips producing flowers of very large size. They were obtained comparatively recently from crosses between 'Darwin' varieties and *T. fosteriana* 'Red Emperor'. They are noted for their brilliance of colour. Of tall stature, with stems ranging from 22 to 28 ins in height, the giant flowers have huge, single cups. Planted at focal points in the garden they are real eye-catchers but all have strong and sturdy stems and are suitable for mass planting. They begin flowering the last week of April and make excellent cut flowers.

Named varieties include: 'Apeldoorn', orange-scarlet; 'Beauty of Apeldoorn', flushed magenta, edged in yellow; 'Dover', poppy-red; 'General Eisenhower', orange-red; 'Gudoshnik', sulphut-yellow; 'Holland's Glory', orange-scarlet; 'Lefeber's Favourite', scarlet; 'London', vermilion, flushed scarlet; 'Oxford', red; 'President Kennedy', yellow flushed rosy-scarlet; 'Red Matador', carmine flushed scarlet and 'Spring Song', bright red, flushed salmon.

'*Breeder*' *tulips*. These are May-flowering tulips. Few are offered under this name but are frequently grouped with the Cottage varieties. The single blooms are rather oval in shape and their size and habit are somewhat similar to the 'Darwins'. First class for cutting, they are not quite so reliable for bedding purposes as most other sections.

Good varieties include: 'Bacchus', purple marked in violet-blue; 'Dillenburg', orange terra-cotta; 'Louis XIV', bluish-violet marked in golden-bronze and 'President Hoover', orange-scarlet. These are old-fashioned varieties but well worth growing.

'Lily-flowered' tulips. These are among the most graceful and elegant of all garden tulips. There is no doubt that they create a beautiful sight when planted in groups in beds, borders or the rock garden, or when featured in terrace tubs or window boxes.

Beautifully reflexed and pointed petals form handsome flowers on tall, wiry stems some 20 to 24 ins tall. All Lily-flowered varieties make excellent cut flowers. The distinctive shape of the blooms, which resemble lilies, is responsible for their placement in a separate division. 'Lily-flowered' tulips were first introduced in 1914 and were derived from a cross between *T.* × *retroflexa* and a 'Cottage' tulip. *T.* × *retroflexa* which was itself introduced in 1863 after crossing *T. acuminate* with a form of *T. gesneriana*.

The colours of 'Lily-flowered' tulips are deep, rich and glowing and groups of different varieties in the garden invariably make a splended display.

'Cottage' tulips. There is greater variation in this section of single-flowered varieties than in any other class. They are also known as Single Late tulips. 'Cottage' tulips, so named because they were originally found in old cottage gardens of Britain and France, often have slender buds with long pointed petals, of distinct habit. They are strikingly effective when planted in groups. When planting, remember that these tulips have long stems, ranging from 20 to 32 ins.

The large egg-shaped flowers come in pastels and pastel blends are in light hues of many colours. They bloom early in May. Within this class, too, come the 'Viridiflora' or green tulips, as well as some multi-flowering varieties, each carrying 3 to 6 flower heads per stem.

The following are some outstanding 'Cottage' varieties. 'Advance', light scarlet, tinted cerise; 'Artist', salmon-rose and green; 'Balalaika', turkey-red; 'Bond Street', yellow and orange; 'Claudette', ivory-white, edged in cerise-rose, multi-flowering; 'Dillenburg', salmon-orange; 'Georgette', yellow, edged in cerise-rose, multi-

flowering; 'Golden Artist', golden-orange, striped in green, viridiflora; 'Greenland', green, edged in rose; 'Henry Ford', carmine, spotted white; 'Maureen', marble-white; 'Mother's Day', lemon-yellow; 'Monsieur Mottet', ivory-white, multi-flowering; 'Mrs John T. Scheepers', clear yellow; 'Princess Margaret Rose', yellow, edged in orange-red; 'Rosy Wings', salmon-pink, merging to cream; 'Smiling Queen', rosy-red, edged in silvery-pink and 'White City', pure white.

Mixtures of 'Cottage' tulips are available for large plantings and for cutting.

'Rembrandt' tulips. These are 'broken' tulips of the 'Darwin' type with single, squarish cups, striped and streaked against a self-coloured ground, usually white. Growing 22 to 26 ins high, they are useful for bedding and cutting. Few varieties are available but include: 'American Flag', dark red, striped on a white ground; 'Cordell Hull', flamed and splashed in cherry red on white and 'Montgomery', pure white edged rosy-red.

'Bizarre' tulips. These are also called 'broken' tulips which, in this case, have a yellow ground with brown, bronze or purple markings. Varieties include: 'Arsalon', 'Insulinde' and 'Golden Hawk'.

'Bijbloemen' tulips. The few varieties in this class are marked or veined in violet-rose or purple on a white ground. 'May Blossom' is one of the varieties most readily obtainable. All of these 'broken' sections look best growing in front of shrubs or herbaceous plants. The markings or breakings of the colours are caused by virus and this is why some gardeners prefer to grow these types of tulips separately from all others. They are very ancient and can sometimes be seen illustrated in old paintings. They are not quite so vigorous-growing as most other tulips but, because of their unusual markings, they always command attention.

'Parrot' tulips. Dating back to 1665 but recently improved, these have huge, heavy flowers with deeply laciniated, curled and twisted petals on good, strong 20 to 26-in. stems. The blooms come in a range of colours tinged with green. The foliage is light green and serves as an excellent contrast against the rich brilliancy of the flowers. May-flowering, they are

excellent for cutting and make good splashes of colour at focal points in the garden.

Many excellent varieties are available including; 'Black Parrot', almost black; 'Blue Parrot', lavender-mauve, often crested in green; 'Fantasy', pink, crested in green; 'Firebird', scarlet; 'Orange Favourite', deep orange; 'Sunshine', golden-yellow and 'Texas Gold', soft yellow edged red and crested green.

Double Late tulips. These tulips resemble paeonies and are often referred to as paeony-flowered tulips. They have large, double flowers on sturdy and erect stems ranging from 16 to 24 ins in height. Breeders have devoted considerable time and skill in producing new colours and the result has been the creation of extremely handsome varieties which are magnificent for bedding, for planting in groups in borders, for tubs and window boxes or for interplanting with evergreens. They are all excellent for floral arrangements and come in many charming shades and two-tones. Plant them in sheltered positions for colour in May.

The following varieties do well under normal culture. 'Bonanza', carmine-red, edged in yellow; 'Eros', old-rose; 'Golden Nizza', golden-yellow, feathered red; 'Livingstone', bright cherry-red; 'May Wonder', clear rose; 'Mount Tacoma', pure white; 'Nizza', yellow with red stripes; 'Orange Triumph', orange-red, edged in yellow and 'Uncle Tom', dark red.

Mixtures of harmonious colours can be purchased for a bold and spectacular display in the garden.

Tulip species. Tulipa acuminata is known as the horned tulip or Turkish tulip. Its origin is unknown and it appears to vary in colour and shape. It blooms in April and May, on stems of 18 ins or more. The thin, spidery petals are waved and curled, sometimes as much as 3 in. long. The colour is yellow stained with red. It makes a most unusual cut flower, while in the garden it looks grand planted in groups of a dozen or more.

T. aitchisonii is somewhat similar to the better-known species *T. clusiana*. Rarely growing more than 4 ins high, it sometimes produces more than one flower on a stem. The colour is white, flushed in crimson, although forms with a yellowish tinge are sometimes produced.

T. aucheriana, from Persia, is a hardy, dwarf species rarely more than 3 ins high. The scented, orange-pink flowers open to a star-shape in late April. It is sometimes offered as a form of *T. humilis.*

T. australis, see *T. silvestris.*

T. batalini, from Turkistan, is an exquisite species varying in height from 6 to 9 ins. First class for the rock garden and alpine house, the creamy-yellow flowers have pointed petals. A number of forms have been produced as the result of hybridization, the colours varying from apricot to shades of pink and white. A bronze variety is also known.

T. biflora comes from the Caucasus and sends up, in March and April, 4 to 6-in. branching stems carrying several small, star-like, creamy-white flowers. The outside of each petal is stained green and sometimes red.

T. chrysantha, see *T. stellata.*

T. clusiana, often known as the lady tulip, is a native of Persia and several Mediterranean areas. It is one of the most graceful of all tulips. Easy to grow, it makes a superb cut flower, while outdoors it always commands attention. The narrow, pointed leaves add to the attraction of the cherry-red and white petals each of which has a violet base, and which appear on 9 to 14-in. stems in April. Sometimes referred to as the peppermint stick tulip, it is marvellous for cutting. They make a bright splash of colour in the rock garden and border. Plant the bulbs in warm, sheltered, well-drained positions. Stock increases freely by underground stolons.

T. cretica, see *T. saxatilis.*

T. dasystemon, see *T. tarda.*

T. didieri. The origin of this species is a little uncertain although it is known to be a native of France and Switzerland. The flowers appear in April on 12-in. stems, the colouring varying from a brownish geranium-red to a yellowish-red.

T. eichleri. A native of Asia Minor, this has proved an excellent tulip for beds and borders where the position is not exposed. On stout stems of 14 to 16 ins, the brilliant-coloured scarlet flowers appear in April. When fully open they are more than 4 ins in diameter. The shapely petals show a waist when young but eventually open widely with reflexing tips. The foliage is broad and glaucous.

Tulipa fosteriana from Central Asia, and growing 12 to 16 ins high, is one of the finest of *Tulipa* species. The flowers, which appear in April, are as much as 9 or 10 ins in diameter

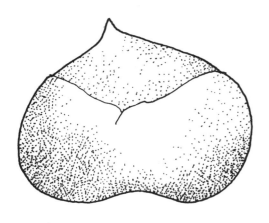

Tulipa gesneriana

when fully expanded. The petals are vermilion-scarlet on the exterior, the insides being slightly darker with a silky sheen. The darker, central blotch is surrounded by yellow markings. The bulbs, which are large for a tulip, are best lifted and dried annually. Replant them in October or early November.

Several of the wild species including *T. fosteriana* have been crossed, while the Single Early and the 'Darwins' have also been used so that we now have a fabulous group of 'Fosteriana' hybrids. The fresh green foliage of the *T. fosteriana* species, as well as glowing colours, have been transmitted to this new range, noted for its massive blooms and sturdy stems ranging from 8 to 18 ins in height.

These named hybrids can be used for dramatic effects in the garden. Plant them in focal spots in the rock garden, border, at the base of light trees, in terrace tubs or urns, or employ them to emphasize the colour of drifts of muscari or early-flowering daffodils. All of the dozen or more named hybrids now available can be planted from October to mid-December, about 4 to 5 ins deep and 6 ins apart, preferably in clusters of 6 to 12 or more. They all produce their neon-like, glowing flowers in early April.

Among the best are: 'Cantata', vermilion-red; 'Easter Parade', pure yellow flushed red; 'Galata', orange-red; 'Golden Eagle', deep yellow, blazed in flame-red; 'Golden Emperor', pure golden-yellow; 'Princeps', orange-scarlet; 'Red Emperor' ('Mme Lefeber'), vermilion-scarlet.

Tulipa gesneriana is an ancient species from which many of the garden tulips have probably arisen. The large, cup-shaped flowers are orange-scarlet with a dark basal blotch. It is said that this species can still be found wild in Asia Minor, but even there there is some variation in growth, colour and shape.

Tulipa greigii is another Central Asian species. It is noteworthy for its glaucous-green, attractive leaves marked and mottled darker shades. Vigorous-growing, it is best lifted annually after the foliage has discoloured. It grows 18 to 24 ins high, the colour of the petals being a brilliant, vermilion-scarlet usually with darker red markings on the outside of petals.

The *T. greigii* hybrids now available to gardeners have huge, long-lasting, brilliant oriental-coloured blooms and beautifully marked and mottled leaves. The mottling of the leaves in wild species discovered in the Chirchick Valley of Turkistan has changed in some of the hybrids into broad, well-defined stripings so that the leaves have marvellous decorative value. In addition, they cover the soil in a way no other tulips do.

The showy hybrids are the result of crossing *T. greigii* with *T. kaufmanniana* as well as with traditional garden tulips. Many of these hybrids have the darker leaf markings showing the influence of *T. greigii* in their parentage. These hybrids grow 14-18 ins tall, and have large cup-shaped flowers, some 5 ins in diameter or more. The shorter-stemmed varieties should be planted 4 to 5 ins deep and the taller-stemmed kinds up to 6 ins deep, as for garden tulips.

Tulips are ideal for bedding in tubs. After flowering they can be lifted and the tub replanted

Space them a good 5 to 6 ins apart and in groups. From mid-April these tulips will add gay colour to beds and borders, to the rock garden, to the base of walls or trees, and the shorter varieties are superb for terrace containers. All have stout stems.

Good varieties include: 'Bokhara', purple-red, orange-scarlet interior; 'Cape Cod', apricot, bronze-yellow interior; 'Golden Day', yellow and red; 'Margaret Herbst', vermilion; 'Odessa', vermilion; 'Oriental Beauty', carmine-red, vermilion-red interior; 'Oriental Beauty', carmine-red, vermilion-red interior; carmine-red, vermilion-red interior; 'Oriental Splendour', red, edged in yellow; 'Red Riding Hood', carmine-red with scarlet interior and 'Yellow Dawn', old rose edged yellow.

A mixture of hybrids gives a very bright display in the spring.

T. hageri, see *T. ophanidea*.

T. hoogiana is characterized by a thick, woolly coat under the outer skin of the bulb. In the past, it has been considered by some specialists to be the same as *T. lanata*, but it is later flowering and has more leaves than that species. There now seems little doubt that it is a distinct species. *T. hoogiana* grows about 15 ins high and the flowers are a brilliant scarlet with black anthers. The centre of each flower is greenish-black, margined in yellow. The leaves are glaucous-grey and the bulb large and roundish. It does best in warm, well-drained positions.

T. humilis, from Persia and Turkey, is dwarf growing. The flowers show from later February onwards, according to situation and weather. The colour ranges from pink to almost magenta, although there appear to be several forms in which the shade varies from almost white to a pale violet shade. A few of these forms have been given separate names. The leaves are often late in appearing and may not show fully until the flowers are well developed.

T. ingens comes from Bokhara and other central-Asian districts. The huge, handsome, almost egg-shaped flowers are crimson-scarlet with a dark basal blotch. Excellent for the alpine house or cold frame, the flowers appear in April on 1½ to 2-ft stems.

T. kaufmanniana, a native of Turkistan, is often known as the water-lily Tulip. The good-sized flowers have rather narrow petals which reflex widely in the sun, thus giving rise to their common name. On stems varying from 6 to 14 ins, the whitish-yellow flowers, marked in crimson, show from March onwards. The broad leaves are glaucous-green. Easy to grow it is best, where possible, to lift the bulbs in summer and replant in October.

T. kaufmanniana hybrids have been secured by crossing *T. kaufmanniana* with *T. greigii* as well as with some garden tulips. The influence of *T. kaufmanniana* has been to introduce new and subtle colour combinations, to give early flowering and transmit the unique shape of bloom. The mottled, striped, and spotted foliage has been inherited from *T. greigii*. The flowers are usually bicoloured, the outside segments being deeper than the inside. The hybrids establish themselves easily, coming up freely year after year. They are useful for the rock garden, the border, between shrubs, beneath trees, on walls or steps and in window boxes, tubs or urns. Choice named hybrids are now available, the following being specially good:

'Alfred Cortot', 8 ins, deep scarlet with strong pointed petals and coal-black centre in the shape of a rounded 6-pointed star.

'Berlioz', 5 ins, bears, in April, lovely, neat flowers with pointed petals of clear yellow opening to citrus-gold, the outer petals flushed Turkish-red.

'César Franck', 8 ins, golden-yellow petals and exterior of carmine-red is very striking, with grey-green foliage. It flowers in March. 'Fair Lady', 7 ins has, in April, an elegant, ivory flower with a large, crimson blotch on the outside. The interior is ivory with a deep red and gold base.

'Fritz Kreisler', 10 ins, is a lovely shade of deep pink with a deep yellow base and carmine-red blotches. The exterior is mauve, edged sulphur-yellow. It blooms in March.

'Gaiety', 4 ins flowers in March and April, is very like a water-lily. Creamy-white inside with an orange-yellow base, the outer petals are marked in pinkish-red.

'Goudstuk', 8 ins, is sometimes catalogued as 'Goldcoin'. A charming variety, producing in April large flowers with broad petals of golden-yellow with crimson rings inside.

'Heart's Delight', 9 ins, with flowers of carmine-red, edged in rosy-white and flowering in March and April. Its leaves are dark and heavily mottled.

'Johann Strauss', 8 ins, bears, in March and April, dainty white flowers, each with a cream centre. The exterior is flushed with red. The foliage is deep green striped brown.

'Scarlet Elegance', 8 ins, is one of the first *T. kaufmanniana* hybrids to flower in March and is a bright dazzling scarlet.

Shakespeare, 7 ins, is a beautiful blend of salmon, apricot and orange, the interior shaded red. It is April-flowering.

Parrot tulip 'Orange Favourite', an almost shockingly bright orange with fimbriated petals

'Stresa', 9 ins, bears in April golden-yellow flowers each with an orange-red band on the outside.

'The First', 6 ins, is one of the earliest to flower. The ivory-white flowers, carmine-red on the exterior, are edged in white.

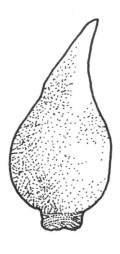

Tulipa perroquet

A mixture of these hybrids is usually available under the appropriate titles of 'Peacock' hybrids or 'Rainbow' mixture.

T. kolpakowskiana is another elegant species from Turkistan. The slender, 10 to 12-ins. stems carry, in March and April, flowers blotched a vivid cherry-red, the inside of each petal being yellow. The greyish-brown leaves have wavy edges and are inclined to be flat.

T. lanata is a splendid species from Persia. The large flowers, borne on 18 to 20-in. stems, are brilliant scarlet and show from April onwards.

T. linifolia, from Asia Minor, is a dwarf species with open cups of brilliant scarlet on 9 to 12-in stems. The narrow, undulating leaves with reddish margins rest on the soil.

T. marjolettii grows 15 to 18 ins tall. The flowers are a primrose colour and splashed in rosy-red on the outside. First class as a cut flower, there is some doubt as to its origin. Some specialists believe it to be a hybrid.

T. maximowiczii is similar to *T. linifolia*, but the brilliant scarlet flowers are produced a little earlier while the foliage and stems are green and upright.

T. orphanidea comes from Greece. It adds distinction to the rock garden and alpine house while it looks well planted towards the front of a border. The colour of the flowers, borne on stems of 12 to 15 ins, is hard to define but is an orange-bronze shade flushed green with traces of pink. When fully open, from the end of March onwards, the blooms have a star-like shape.

T. ostrowskiana has, in May, elegant orange scarlet flowers heading 8-in. stems. The outer petals have a slight purplish sheen.

T. persica. There is some doubt about the correct naming of this species, but the one grown and offered commercially produces, in May on 5 or 6 in. stems, charming, sweet-scented, orange-yellow and bronze flowers, usually several on each stem. The foliage is attractively twisted and stained brownish-red.

T. praecox comes from the Mediterranean regions. On stems of 15 ins or more, it produces, from the end of April, dull-scarlet flowers. These, when fully open, have a diameter of 12 ins or more, creating a most striking effect. It produces stolons which means that it spreads fairly freely and the stoloniferous bulbs are the usual method of propagation since seed is rarely, if ever, available.

T. praestans, growing 8 to 12 ins tall, from Central Asia, blooms in March and April with 2 to 4 pure orange-scarlet, cup-shaped flowers per stem. The leaves are apple-green with a dark red edge. It is a suitable subject for the rock garden and the alpine house. An exceptionally beautiful form is *T. praestans* 'Fusilier' with 4 to 6 flaming-scarlet flowers on each 6 to 8-in. stem rising out of dark green leaves. Planted in clusters of a dozen or more, it creates fine patches of colour in the garden.

T. primulina, growing to 1 ft, comes from North Africa. It produces creamy-yellow

Hepatica sylvatica, one of the glories of woodland gardens

Crinum x *powellii* 'Album' can produce a bulb nearly a foot in diamete

Clivia miniata, one of the most tolerant bulbs for room conditions

A blaze of colour from clumps of mixed bulbs in spring

flowers, often with greenish-pink markings on the exterior. The leaves are long and narrow. Hardy and easy to grow, it will often naturalize itself freely.

T. pulchella, 5 ins, is excellent for the rock garden. This species is sometimes offered as a form of *T. humilis*. It comes from Persia and shows colour from February onwards. Very early to flower, it has several large star-like purplish-violet blooms to each stem. The form known as *T.p. violacea* is sometimes known as 'Violet Queen' and has the common name of crocus tulip. It should be planted in sheltered positions.

T. saxatilis is a most showy species and is a native of Crete and nearby areas. It usually produces 2 cup-shaded, lilac flowers on each 12-in. stem from May onwards. The colour varies a little, often showing greenish markings, the centre of each flower being a rich yellow. The leaves frequently develop in late autumn and usually come through the winter unmarked. Although quite hardy, this species requires a warm well-drained position for regular flowering. It does not set seed and is increased by means of its freely produced underground stolons. Deep planting is advisable.

T. silvestris is found in many parts of southern Europe and also in North Africa and Persia. Variable in size and colour, the nodding buds eventually turn upwards to allow the greenish-yellow scented flowers to open in April. The reflexed tips are often stained in red. It increases by means of its spreading stolons rather than making offsets as do most tulips. This species has, in the past, been known as *T. florentina odorata*. *T. silvestris* 'Tabriz' produces choice, yellow, scented flowers. Some of its other forms have at various times been listed under specific names.

T. sprengeri is one of the latest of the tulip species to bloom. On 15-in. stems the scarlet flowers with yellow anthers usually show from mid-May onwards.

T. stapfii is a little-known species from Asia Minor. The scarlet flowers appear in April on strong, 7 or 8-in. stems, the leaves being glaucous-green.

T. stellata, 10 ins tall and native of Afghanistan, is of similar appearance to *T. clusiana*;

the pointed petals are flushed or striped red, and open to a star shape in April.

T. tarda comes from Turkistan. The species is also known, incorrectly, as *T. dasystemon*. Growing 4 to 6 ins high, the flowers appear in April and May. The petals are white, strongly tinged in yellowish-green, each with a green mid-rib and yellow base, the inside being yellow with white tips. The long, green leaves are almost prostrate. Easy to grow, this tulip is good for the rock garden or border edges, especially when the star-shaped flowers can be seen fully open in the sun.

T. tubergeniana is a striking scarlet-flowered species from Central Asia. Tall growing, it often reaches 18 ins. The leaves are an attractive glaucous-green. Somewhat similar to *T. fosteriana*, the two need to be grown together to determine the differences. A multi-flowering hybrid has been raised in Holland and named *T. tubergniana* 'Keukenhof'.

T. turkestanica, 9 to 10 ins tall, obviously originates from Turkistan. It is multi-flowering, 5 to 8 flowers appearing on every stem. The colour is creamy-white, tinged green with a bronze flush. It is closely related to *T. biflora*. The flowers, which appear from the end of February, are long lasting.

T. uriemiensis from Persia is botanically close to *T. tarda*. Ideal for the rock garden, it is very hardy. Although it may grow 8 to 9 ins tall it often produces, in April, 3 or 4 star-like flowers on stems of no more than 4 ins. Seen against the rosette of slightly glaucous-green foliage, the buttercup-yellow slightly flushed dull red flowers are a pleasing sight.

T. whittallii, see *T. orphanidea*.

T. wilsoniana provides a superb display when, in May, the cherry-red cups are produced on 7-in. stems. Not easy to obtain it is well worth searching for and may sometimes be found offered as *T. montana*.

VALLOTA is often known as the Scarborough lily, because bulbs were washed up on the coast of that town from a wrecked ship. There is only one known species in this genus which is of South African origin. The name was given in honour of P. Vallot a French botanist. This is an excellent cool greenhouse subject, and has

J

long been greatly favoured for growing in windows where it will remain evergreen, although it can be grown out-of-doors during the summer months.

V. speciosa will on occasion produce scapes or growing stems up to 3 ft high which are surmounted with 6 to 9 funnel-shaped, brilliant scarlet flowers. A variety known as 'Elata' is lower-growing with brighter, almost cherry-red flowers. More often, however, the plants are grown in 5-in. diameter pots and produce 3 or 4 flowers on 12 to 15-in. stems.

It is neither necessary nor desirable to dry off the bulbs. In fact, part of the plant's value lies in its evergreen strap-shaped leaves, which are often 18 to 24 ins long. To keep the plants healthy, the bulbs must be liberally supplied with water during their growing period and the soil kept just moist when the plants are at rest.

When obtaining or potting up fresh stock, offsets can be detached or new bulbs purchased from June until September. A simple potting compost should be used, such as 3 parts good loam and 1 part well-decayed manure, plus a little silver sand, while sharp drainage should be provided. If the bulbs are potted up during the summer they may be stood in a shaded place outdoors, then brought inside in September.

VELTHEIMIA This small genus was named in the eighteenth century in honour of a German count. The common name is the unicorn plant and the flowers are produced in spikes not unlike miniature red-hot-pokers. All the species can be grown with little artificial heat. They flower in the winter months and should be allowed to dry off after the leaves begin to wither. They are then restarted into growth in the autumn. Pot the bulbs in August or September using a compost of loam, peat or leaf-mould and silver sand, with well-rotted manure. Start the bulbs in a low temperature and when growth begins increase the heat. Veltheimias flower most freely when established in large pots, where they may be left for some years. From April onwards, the pots are best stood out-of-doors in a frame or sheltered place to ripen off for the next season's flowering.

V. capensis is often listed as *V. viridiflora* and grows 15 to 18 ins high. The flowers are a pinkish-red with greenish mottlings; the bright green leaves have wavy edges. *V. deasii* is not quite as tall. Its pink flowers are marked in yellowish-green towards the tips. *V. glauca* is first class with strap-shaped, glaucous green, wavy-edged leaves. The mottled stems carry pendulous flowers of whitish-pink spotted red and yellow.

Stock is increased by division or by sowing seeds in spring. It is also possible to insert well-ripened leaves with clean-cut bases, in heat, in pots of very sandy soil where they will form small bulbs which may subsequently be potted separately and which will produce blooms in 3 or 4 years.

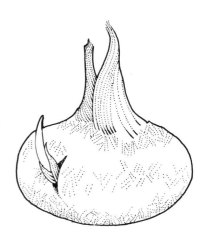

Watsonia pyramidata

WATSONIA Named in honour of William Watson, a London botanist and chemist, and often known as bugle lily, this subject is closely related to the gladiolus with similar corms and sword-shaped leaves. Producing spikes of tubular flowers, which sometimes give the appearance of crocuses on a stem, it is of South African origin. It is possible to grow watsonias outdoors with success in favourable districts in southern England, provided they can be given a sheltered spot which is warm and sunny, but it is really safest to plant them in the cold greenhouse or frame where the frost can be excluded.

Use a compost made up of 2 parts loam, 1 part each leaf-mould or peat, and decayed manure, with a little silver sand to render the whole mixture porous. November is an ideal month to plant. Place 3 to 5 corms in each 5 or 6-in. pot. Cover them with about 1 in. of the mixture and after watering plunge the pots in peat or ashes where they can remain until about 1 in. or so of top growth appears. They should then be brought into the greenhouse and kept watered as necessary.

Watsonias like plenty of moisture when in growth, and applications of liquid manure at 10-day intervals from the time the flower spikes show in summer will ensure good blooms. After the foliage has died down in summer they should be dried off until the next planting time. Similar conditions should be given to the corms when grown outdoors, though planting should be delayed until late March.

There are a number of good species. Among the best is *W. angustifolia*, which bears graceful, delicate rose-coloured flowers on 4-ft stems. Growing to the same height is the handsome *W. meriana*, with terracotta-salmon flowers in May and June, while *W. ardernei*, which is white, produces spikes of flowers on 3-ft stems. *W. alstroides* has shining, deep-pink flowers on 1 to 2-ft stems. *W. rosea* is also known as *W. pyramidata*. Its pinkish-mauve flowers appear on 4 to 5-ft stems.

Plenty of light and air will help to produce strong, free-flowering specimens.

ZANTEDESCHIA This small genus of South African plants is best known as the arum lily, other names being *Calla* or *Richardia*. Widely used as cut flowers, the white species lasts well and is much in demand for church decoration at Easter time. Not reliably hardy, Zantedeschias grow best under glass protection, although some strains can be grown outdoors in damp, unexposed positions. They flourish in

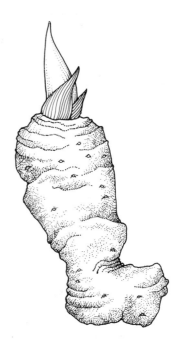

Zantedeschia aethiopica

rich soil and when grown in 5 or 6-in. pots of peaty loam can be placed in the open. The thick, fleshy roots produce large sagittate leaves and a 'flower' consisting of an erect club-like spadix partly enclosed by a large funnel-shaped spathe.

Z. aethiopica is the white arum, or lily of the Nile. It grows 2 to 3 ft high and has rich-green leaves. Flowering time is spring or summer but depends on planting time and on the amount of heat available. It is this species which is sometimes grown in warm places outdoors. This applies particularly to the forms known as 'Crowborough' and 'Little Gem' which will grow in unexposed positions in the garden border. After flowering, *Z. aethiopica* can be allowed to keep in growth continuously but most gardeners allow them a short resting period in summer.

Z. pentlandii (*augustifolia*) is deep, golden-yellow with 'clean'-looking green foliage. When given cool greenhouse culture the 2 to $2\frac{1}{2}$-ft stems develop in June and July. Excellent for cutting.

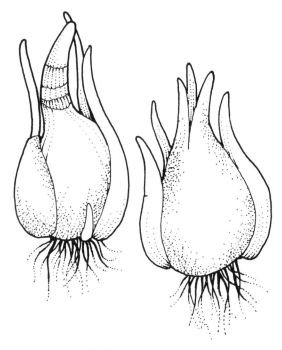

Zephyranthes candida

Z. *elliottiana* is another similar yellow-flowering arum. The deep green leaves are mottled in silvery-white.

Z. *rehmannii* rarely grows more than 1½ ft high. The spathe varies in colour from pale pink to a purplish-pink.

ZEPHYRANTHES Native to the West Indies and parts of America, this genus contains many first-class species. The bulbs grow well in sandy, well-drained loam in a sunny position, where they poduce narrow, strap-shaped leaves and erect funnel-shaped, crocus-like flowers. They have the three common names of zephyr flower, swamp lily and west wind flower.

Z. *aurea*, from Peru, has rich yellow funnel-shaped flowers borne on 6 to 8-in. stems in June. Now rather rare, it needs cool greenhouse treatment.

Z. *candida*, the most widely grown species, has crocus-like flowers appearing in September and October. It will flourish outdoors in warm, sheltered positions.

Z. *citrina* has yellow flowers produced on 4 to 6-in. stems. The medium-large bulbs produce narrow, rush-like foliage.

Z. *grandiflora* (*carinata*) is one of the finest of all, its bright rose-pink flowers appearing in summer and early autumn. Excellent for the cool greenhouse, it will thrive outdoors in sheltered positions, especially if given protection in rough weather.

Z. *rosea* is pale pink with deeper pink veinings, while Z. *tubispatha* is white, with pink flushings. The flowers, on 6 to 8-in. stems, open in July and August. Z. *robusta* produces, during July and August, delicate pink flowers. The leaves develop as the blooms begin to fade.

Z. *verecunda*, from Mexico, produces small white flowers which become flushed in pink as they mature.

Most species produce offsets. These can be detached and grown on separately.

Chapter 8

BULBS FOR SPECIAL PURPOSES

The size, layout and aspect of the garden should always be considered so that bulbs are selected to suit local conditions.

A great many genera contain species, or varieties of varying size and habit. Some may be as suitable for the flower bed as for the rock garden, the terrace tub or the border, and others will flourish in garden, in greenhouse or living room.

Many bulbs that thrive in sun or partial shade will also do so under and between shrubs, evergreens and trees, as well as in open beds and borders. Taking this into consideration, the following are guide lists for the principal decorative uses of various bulbs although these should not be interpreted too rigidly.

FOR FLOWER BEDS AND BORDERS

Acidanthera	Fritillaria	Lilium
Allium	Galanthus	Muscari
Anemone	Galtonia	Narcissus
Camassia	Gladiolus	Ornithogalum
Chionodoxa	Hyacinth	Ranunculus
Colchicum	Iris	Scilla
Crocus	Ixia	Tigridia
Freesia	Ixiolirion	Tulipa species

FOR THE ROCK GARDEN

Allium	Erythronium	Ornithogalum
Anemone	Fritillaria	Oxalis
Babiana	Galanthus	Puschkinia
Brodiaea	Iris (dwarf)	Ranunculus
Chionodoxa	Ixia	Scilla
Crocus	Leucojum	Sparaxis
Cyclamen	Muscari	Tritelia
Eranthis	Narcissus (dwarf)	Tulipa species

FOR NATURALIZING

Anemone	Eranthis	Muscari
Camassia	Erythronium	Narcissus
Chionodoxa	Fritillaria	Ornithogalum
Colchicum	Galanthus	Puschkinia
Crocus	Leucojum	Scilla

FOR CUTTING

Anemone
Dahlia
Freesia
Gladiolus
Iris

Ixia
Lilium
Lily of the Valley
Muscari
Narcissus

Ornithogalum
Ranunculus
Scilla
Tritonia
Tulipa

FOR POTS AND BOWLS

Chionodoxa sardensis
Crocus
Erythronium
Freesia

Fritillaria
Hyacinth
Hippeastrum
Iris

Lachenalia
Narcissus (some)
Scilla
Tulipa (some)

FOR THE COLD GREENHOUSE

Amaryllis belladonna
Babiana
Calochortus
Fritillaria

Gladiolus colvillei
    varieties
Habranthus pratensis
Iris (dwarf)

Ixias
Puschkinia scillioides
Schizostylis
Tigridia

FOR THE COOL GREENHOUSE

Freesia
Hippeastrum
Hyacinth
Ixia

Lachenalia
Lilium (some)
Narcissus (some)
Ranunculus

Sparaxis
Sprekelia
Tritonia
Tulipa (some)

FOR THE WARM GREENHOUSE

Achimenes
Begonias
Caladiums
Eucharis

Gesneria
Gloriosa
Haemanthus
Hippeastrum

Hymenocallis
Lilium longiflorum
Pancratium
Polianthes (tuberose)

FOR FORCING

Achimenes
Convallaria
Crocus susianus
Eucharis

Hyacinth, prepared
Iris reticulata
Lachenalia
Lilium longiflorum

Narcissus
Pancratium
Polianthes tuberosa
Tulips (early-flowering)

FOR SEMI-SHADY POSITIONS

Anemone apennina
Anemone nemorosa
Convallaria

Erythronium
Fritillaria meleagris
Galanthus

Hyacinthus candicans
Narcissus bulbocodium
Ornithogalum
    umbellatum

COMMON NAMES AND THEIR LATIN EQUIVALENTS

African lily
Baboon-root
Belladonna lily
Blood flower
Bluebell

Agapanthus
Babiana
Amaryllis
Haemanthus
Scilla nutans (*Endymion non-scriptus*)

Bugle lily	*Watsonia*
Butterfly tulip	*Calochortus*
Californian fire cracker	*Broadiaea*
Calla lily	*Zantedeschia*
Cape cowslip	*Lachenalia*
Chincherinchee	*Ornithogalum*
Corn lily	*Ixia*
Crimson satin flower	*Brodiaea*
Crown Imperial	*Fritillaria imperialis*
Daffodil	*Narcissus*
Dog's-tooth violet	*Erythronium*
Dragon's mouth	*Arum*
Feather hyacinth	*Muscari plumosum*
Floral fire cracker	*Brodiaea*
Garland flower	*Hedychium*
Glory of the snow	*Chionodoxa*
Golden garlic	*Allium moly*
Guernsey lily	*Nerine sarniensis*
Guinea-hen flower	*Fritillaria*
Harlequin flower	*Sparaxis*
Jacobean lily	*Sprekelia*
Kaffir lily	*Schizostylis*
Love flower	*Agapanthus*
Meadow saffron	*Colchium*
Monarch of the East	*Sauromatum*
Naked ladies	*Colchicum*
Pineapple flower	*Eucomis*
Quamash	*Camassia*
St Bernard's lily	*Anthericum*
Sea daffodil	*Pancratium*
Snake's head Fritillary	*Fritillaria*
Snowdrop	*Galanthus*
Snowflake	*Leucojum*
Squill	*Scilla*
Star of Bethlehem	*Ornithogalum*
Summer hyacinth	*Galtonia*
Swamp lily	*Zephyranthes*
Sword lily	*Gladiolus*
Tiger flower	*Tigridia*
Tuberose	*Polianthes*
West wind flower	*Zephyranthes*
Wind flower	*Anemone*
Winter aconite	*Eranthis*
Wood anemone	*Anemone nemorosa*
Wood lily	*Trillium*

STATISTICS OF PLANTING AND GROWTH

Name	Depth	Distance apart	Height of growth
Acidanthera	3 ins	6 ins	24–36 ins
Anemone	2 ins	6–8 ins	12–18 ins
Brodiaea	3–4 ins	4 ins	6–24 ins
Camassia	3–4 ins	4–8 ins	18–36 ins
Chionodoxa	3 ins	1–2 ins	3–4 ins
Crocus	4 ins	4 ins	5 ins

Name	Depth	Distance apart	Height of growth
Daffodil	6 ins	6 ins	18–20 ins
Eranthis	3 ins	3 ins	4 ins
Erythronium dens-canis	3 ins	3–4 ins	6 ins
Freesia	2 ins	2–3 ins	10–15 ins
Galanthus	3 ins	3 ins	4 ins
Galtonia	5–6 ins	12 ins	36–48 ins
Gladioli	5–6 ins	8 ins	24–60 ins
Hyacinth	6 ins	6 ins	10 ins
Iris danfordiae	4 ins	4 ins	3 ins
Iris reticulata	4 ins	4 ins	4–6 ins
Iris, Dutch	5 ins	4 ins	18–24 ins
Ismene	5–6 ins	8–12 ins	18 ins
Ixia	3 ins	3–4 ins	12–18 ins
Ixiolirion	3 ins	3–4 ins	15–18 ins
Leucojum	3–4 ins	4 ins	8–14 ins
Lilium	5–6 ins	24 ins	24–60 ins
Montbretia	3–4 ins	4–5 ins	12–36 ins
Muscari	3 ins	3 ins	5–8 ins
Narcissus, medium cup	6 ins	6 ins	16 ins
Narcissus, short cup	6 ins	5 ins	14 ins
Narcissus dwarf	2–4 ins	3–4 ins	4–10 ins
Ornithogalum thyrsoides	2–3 ins	4–6 ins	18–25 ins
Puschkinia libanotica	3 ins	3 ins	4 ins
Ranunculus	$1\frac{1}{2}$ ins	6–8 ins	12 ins
Scilla sibirica	3 ins	3 ins	4–6 ins
Sparaxis	2–3 ins	2–3 ins	6–9 ins
Sprekelia	3 ins	12–18 ins	18–24 ins
Trigidia	2–3 ins	6–8 ins	12–24 ins
Tritelia	2 ins	2–3 ins	4–6 ins
Tulip, early	4–5 ins	5 ins	14 ins
Tulip, double late	5–6 ins	6 ins	18–20 ins
Tulip, Darwin	5–6 ins	6 ins	26–32 ins
Tulip, Parrot	5–6 ins	6 ins	20–24 ins
Tulipa	4 ins	5 ins	5–15 ins

INDEX

INDEX

154

INDEX

INDEX

S